AMERICAN MODERN

AMERICAN MODERN

The Path Not Taken

Aesthetics, Metaphysics, and Intellectual History in Classic American Philosophy

VICTORINO TEJERA

ROWMAN & LITTLEFIELD PUBLISHERS, INC.
Lanham • Boulder • New York • London

ROWMAN & LITTLEFIELD PUBLISHERS, INC.

Published in the United States of America
by Rowman & Littlefield Publishers, Inc.
4720 Boston Way, Lanham, Maryland 20706

3 Henrietta Street
London WC2E 8LU, England

British Cataloging in Publication Information Available

Library of Congress Cataloging-in-Publication Data

Tejera, V. (Victorino)
    American modern : the path not taken : aesthetics, metaphysics, and intellectual
history in classic American philosophy / Victorino Tejera.
        p. cm.
    Includes bibliographical references and index.
    ISBN 0–8476–8309–5 (alk. paper). — ISBN 0–8476–8310–9 (pbk.: alk. paper)
    1. Philosophy, American—20th century. 2. Philosophy, American—19th century. 3.
Peirce, C. H. (Charles Henry), 1814–1855. 4. Dewey, John, 1859–1952. 5. Santayana,
George, 1863–1952. 6. Buchler, Justus, 1914–   . I. Title.
B935.T45   1996
191—dc20   96–9045
                                                                                        CIP

ISBN 0–8476–8309–5 (cloth : alk. paper)
ISBN 0–8476–8310–9 (pbk. : alk. paper)

Printed in the United States of America

 ^{TM}The paper used in this publication meets the minimum requirements of American
National Standard for Information Sciences—Permanence of Paper for Printed Library
Materials, ANSI Z39.48–1984.

To Thelma Z. Lavine

Contents

A Word to the Reader

Briefly stated, this book has sought to highlight what is most valuable in four great American thinkers for purposes of non-reductive, non-philistine philosophizing today. With 'philistine' (Matthew Arnold's term) I mean to point to the neglect in philosophic reflection of inputs from the arts and the humanities. As Dewey says, "the history of science in its . . . emergence . . . is a record of a differentiation of arts, not . . . of separation from art." Implicit in my title is the theme that too much English-language philosophizing has fallen into sterile, monological, non-corrigible ways by failing to explore the fruitful—nay, the liberating—approaches to be found in the tradition of classic American philosophizing.

The liberational quality of classic American thought arises within its keen consciousness of our philosophic past, and the unrecognized potential of this past for inhibiting the present when that present neglects the operation of its intellectual antecedents in the habitual, unexamined distinctions by which it lives. The reader will find examples enough of these in the text which follows. My last chapter indeed is concerned to show how integrally the practice of historiography is built into the classic American mode of philosophic analysis.

The reader will notice that associated with the historical consciousness of this mode of analysis is the working hypothesis that one necessary task of philosophy is to uncover and criticize the most basic assumptions of our culture, and of groups and individuals within it. Too many analysts who claim that the main function of philosophy is to clear up the muddles of past thinkers by close attention to the misuse of language that generates the muddle, forget that a more convincing method of clearing up confused distinctions is the historical analysis of the non-viable or inconsistent assumptions which gave rise to them. The genetic or historical analysis achieves what the merely linguistic analysis cannot, namely, it both clears the way to making the needed distinctions under a wider knowledge of the facts they must cover, and more surely prevents the old embedded distinctions from recurring in a different guise.

Because it is non-reductive, the classic American mode of philosophic analysis is also contextualist, and not only historically contextualist. Consequently, both its categorizing style and its way of focusing on subject-matter, are consciously *coordinative* as well as analytic.

To use Peirce's terms, its analyses are not only 'stoicheotic' or grammatical; they achieve—with the practice of 'Critic' and 'methodeutic' (or 'speculative rhetoric')—formal rigor as well as contextualization. Peirce restored 'logic-as-analysis' to non-reductive, non-imperialist comprehensiveness by reconceiving it as *semeiotic*, or semiotics. To the branch of semiotics which he calls *Critic*—the formal examination of the kinds of inference—he added stoicheotic or speculative grammar, and methodeutic. That he also calls the latter 'transuasional logic,' shows that methodeutic is still 'logical' analysis as well as rhetorical and methodological.

Also operative in this book, as well as rehearsed by it, will be the distinctions by means of which Justus Buchler has re-opened philosophy to the input of both the creative arts and the wider range of all human practices *other than assertion*, namely, in addition to the practices and theorizations of the special sciences.[1] These distinctions are those which divide the modes of human judgment into the *exhibitive* and the *active* modes, on top of the already recognized *assertive* mode of judgment found in the special sciences. Judgments in the active mode are those which bring determinacies into existence by means of action or conduct, while judgments in the exhibitive mode are those produced by means of perceptible contrivances or constructions.

In other less accurate words, the differences in the modes of judgment correspond roughly to those between saying, doing, and making. But it needs to be understood that 'doings' and 'makings' are judgments every bit as much as 'sayings' are. For, a judgment is whatever institutes new determinacies in our reality or environment.

In reporting on the philosophies of John Dewey and George Santayana, this book has also sought to make operative the useful distinctions and re-awaken the humanly informed spirit which they brought to the classic American tradition of philosophizing. In sum, this is a book about the classic American tradition written from within that tradition.

CHAPTER I

Peirce's Semiotic Philosophy: A Methodeutic of Art and Science

1
(i) The Theory of Signs: the Matrix of Philosophizing

Charles Peirce both thought of philosophy, and practiced it, as a semiotic activity. Semiotics, "another name for . . . logic in its general sense" (2.227), is the theory of signs. For Peirce, the theory of sign-activity provides the elementary, *stoicheotic* and coordinative foundations of the search for knowledge, as well as the contextualizing rhetoric and methodology of it (*methodeutic*). Where John Dewey gave us an operational definition of logic as the theory of inquiry (LTI 1938), with the purpose of getting the formalist view into perspective, Peirce's strategy was to identify logic with semeiotic broadly and inclusively understood. Peirce didn't deny Dewey's view that "for certain logical problems the entire development of cognition and along with it that of its object become pertinent, and therefore should be taken into account" (8.244). But he was very emphatic in his communication to Dewey that the latter's enthusiasm for the

1

genetic method of analysis[1] should not be taken to preclude research into the normative and formal aspects of the theory of inference. So much so that he was moved to invoke his "first rule of reason" (1.135) and repeat the "maxim" which we must "never infringe:" "*Never permanently bar the road of any true inquiry*" (8.243). Peirce's non-genetic analyses were operational in the sense that they were conducted in full view of actual scientific memoirs and other records of scientific inquiry, in which they lead to denials of conclusions to which bad logic has led their authors (8.243).[2]

Peirce partially describes semiotics at 8.343 as "the *cenoscopic* science of signs." By cenoscopic he means, based on an abstractive observation of the everyday facts of sign-functioning, leading to fallible statements as to what must be the characters of all signs used by a "scientific" intelligence, that is to say, by an intelligence capable of learning by experience (2.227).[3]

It isn't only semiotic theorizing that is cenoscopic but the practice itself of philosophy that is inevitably so: "metaphysics, even bad metaphysics, really rests on observations . . . and the only reason this is not universally recognized is that it rests upon the kinds of phenomena with which every man's experience is so saturated that he usually pays no particular attention to them" (6.2). More specifically, "Metaphysics is the proper designation for the third, and completing department of coenoscopy, which . . . welds itself into idioscopy, or special science. Its business is to study the most general features of reality and real objects" (6.6).

Now, just as the theory of signs, or logic-as-semeiotic begins—as above—by accepting corrigibility and fallibility, it also emphasizes *continuity* explicitly as a methodeutic presupposition of query. If the process of investigation is not to be blocked, the search should be directed to the uncovering of continuities in nature, not of discrete ultimates beyond which query may not go. Accordingly, Peirce practiced metaphysics as a coordinative and categoreal analysis of what there is, and as the pursuit of indefinite open-ended explicability, even while his theorizing about logic and the practice of it was a fallibilist enterprise. Continua, for Peirce are both natural forms and forms of explicability: they are of the nature of *general* ideas (7.535n., 6.143, 4.157).

But in saying that metaphysics, as cenoscopic, is something like a special science (an idioscopy) Peirce does not here distinguish it from philosophic analysis in general. The reason for this momentary ambiguity is, of course, his unwavering attachment to the scientific method of interrogating nature. But when we look at what Peirce has to say about the discourse of the special sciences in relation to "the totality of things" as it comes under philosophic observation, we find the needed clarification.

Peirce calls his emphasis on continuity *synechism*. So, since synechism . . ."[is] the tendency to regard everything as continuous" (7. 565), it must not overlook the less easily observed relatednesses or "substrates" of phenomena—which atomistic, terministic thinking takes to be "nothing." Since synechism does "not admit a sharp sundering of phenomena from their substrates," Peirce can also assert: "That which underlies a phenomenon and determines it, thereby is, itself, in a measure a phenomenon."[4] This reminds us that Peirce's is a phenomenological metaphysics: a phaneroscopic, abstractive observation of whatever appears. But there is a difficulty to be absolved here. To the statement that "synechism declar[es] that being is a matter of more or less," Peirce adds after the comma, "so as to merge insensibly into nothing" (7.569). But since Peirce does not believe that "to be" is "to be perceived" (6.339), his use of "insensibly" to mean "little by little" is loose. It becomes clear, however, that by "insensibly" he meant "asymptotically."

(ii) *The Subject Matter of Metaphysics*

At 7.579 Peirce says, "philosophy is the attempt. . .to form a general informed conception of the *All*."[5] In this note, it is clear that by "the All" he meant the subject-matter of metaphysics; and, in context, this means phaneroscopic nature *as a whole* with no specification whether this "All" (as the whole of nature) creates problems in need of further analyses such as are found in Parmenides or uncovered by Buchler.[6] The problem with the unexamined concept of nature is that it leaves undecided whether nature is one or plural, whether it is all-inclusive or not, and whether it is *an* order or many orders.

The context of Peirce's assumption about nature as a continuum is twofold: that of a denial that the mental and the physical are absolutely distinct (6.268), and that of a discussion of the *affectivity* of protoplasmic *matter* (6.246-264). The assumption also responds to Peirce's view of what kinds of categorization serve indefinite explicability best, and can best keep open the road of query. Peirce must be thinking here of observable nature, not about the All of Parmenides' Goddess or Buchler's 'the world,' as distinct from cosmographic 'nature.' It is *this* nature that is a continuum for Peirce. To appreciate Peirce's conception of philosophy, we will have to clarify the unexamined concept of 'nature.'

The contrast is that, for Peirce it is describable nature or the cosmos that is a continuum, whereas it is the entirety of what-there-is-was-and-will-be, conceptualized as the All that is a continuum for Parmenides. —So, if we ask, would Peirce be agreeable to an extrapolation from the *unanalyzed* idea of nature to the All (in Parmenides' sense), the answer is twofold. First, Peirce would want it to be subject to observation and experimentation. But the All as such is never completely observable, and it can only be the subject of conceptual experiment, since we cannot stand outside it. Secondly, in conceptualizing the All, Peirce does not have to rescind either the principle of continuity or that of keeping open the road of query, whether by "query" we mean scientific inquiry or poetic interrogation. It would seem to follow, that the All has to be reflected upon in modes of query other than the scientific, i.e. on other than special-science principles. Room has to be left for query into nature or the All in the exhibitive or active modes—as in lyric poetry, or Parmenides' hexameters, or as in active or serendipitous explorations.

The All, then, is a conceptual or reflectively constructed object for both Parmenides and Peirce. For the former it is a construction that admits continuity as a result of logical consistency only. But

Peirce's "all"—if it means all of observable *nature*—would have to be a complex but limited (and ever incomplete) set of scientific objects whose continuity is assumed from the beginning, not as a matter of observation, but purely as *methodeutic*. But if it means "the totality of things thinkable" (7.563), the reference must be to a speculative object, like Parmenides' All and Buchler's 'the world,' which is queried or articulated in active or exhibitive, as well as the assertive, modes of judgment.

Now Peirce's conception of nature is also *semeiotic*. For him nature and thought, as processes, are continuous and not different in kind; for, like protoplasm the "chemical compound" which "feel[s]" (6.264), thought is the ability to take on habits (6. 24).[7] But Peirce also demonstrates that man, as thinker, is himself of the nature of a sign (5.238, 313-315; 7. 584-591). The consequence of this is that the lived environment is an ongoing semeiosis.[8] Natural processes are not only like the processes of thought, but mind is treated as a form in nature. At 2.713, Peirce speaks of nature's laws as her major premises; and this allows instantiations of nature's laws to be seen as inferences of nature's mind. But we also note that, while he self-reflectively calls this attitude "our natural and anthropomorphic metaphysics," he has at the same time—as part of the attitude to nature evinced above—been speaking of nature in a nomothetic-deductive, or special-science, way.

Nonetheless, from Peirce's suggestion, at 2.713, that to think is to anthropomorphize it would follow that to think scientifically is to anthropomorphize scientifically. So, we digress to indicate where a mitigating development of this recognition that science is anthropomorphic can be found. In what Randall calls Santayana's "transcendental deduction of nature" (**AFSL** 93), Santayana says (**RM** 9ff.):

> We may therefore confidently attribute the forward tension proper to our life to all the rest of nature, down to its primary elements, without attributing to those elements or to that total, any specifically human quality.

What justifies this faith for Santayana is that "th[is] forward tension in us is precisely what we share with all matter, and renders matter our great companion." "We may *therefore*," he concludes,

> appeal to our experience of action on the human scale to suggest to us the nature of action even in the heart of matter, which a . . . diminution of mathematical scale or use of the microscope may never reach" (RM 91).

Santayana's natural history makes explicit, in other words than Peirce's, the same principle of continuity which Peirce's research had compelled him to assume, and almost made it sound like a matter of cenoscopic observation.—Humanist and scientist, both, are convinced that mind and matter are continuous.

Let us note, next, that Peirce's demonstration that man, as thinker, is himself of the nature of a sign (5.238, 313-315; 7. 584-591) has, as its consequence not only that the lived environment is an ongoing semeiosis, but that nature (like everything else in pragmaticism) is also a *significate object*. As such, nature is like man: of the nature of a sign. Since the natural cosmos is accessed, in Parmenides, through non-strict discourse while the All is reached through strictly consistent discourse, Parmenides can be said, in so far, to have been pragmaticist, since both Being and Becoming are, for his Goddess, significate objects.[9]

Given Peirce's consensualist view of truth as an *ideal* limit, true accounts of the All would have to be corrigibly consistent, ever fallible. And more consistent, here, would have to mean consistent in a wider context as created by the most recent new facts and formulations. On Parmenides' side, the implication of the Goddess's various discourses—both her strict (or metaphysical) discourse about the All and her sample cosmography, as well as what she says about the careless discourse of mortals—is that while the cosmographies are corrigible, her account of the All is not. The Goddess is not fallibilist, except in the sense that poetry does **not** work in the **assertive** mode.

If, however, we take the terms of the Goddess's account of the All in a Peircean way, they are not ultimates in the sense of inexplicables. They are, rather, terms of *utmost* generality. And this, in the Peircean view which equates explicability with generality, means that they are terms of maximum explanatory power. It follows that any reformulation or reconceptualization of the Goddess's account could admit only *more* general terms than those she has used already: that is to say, it follows for a Peircean critique of the Goddess's findings in the poem of Parmenides. By "more general" I naturally mean, consistent in a wider context which has uncovered new relations. Such a critique could only show that the Goddess's account of the All, at any stage of nature-inquiry, was not general enough rather than inconsistent. We say this both because it gives a Peircean operational content to the account of Being as corrigible, and because we will find below that *continuity* as a category must give way to the more general idea of *relatedness*, if we are to make Peircean sense out of the discontinuities and continuities between the All and nature—or out of the continuities and discontinuities among the special sciences and metaphysics. As a species of relatedness, the continuity of any two things supposes a minimum of mediating complexes between them. To say that two things are discontinuous is to say that they are only contextually related or so highly mediated as not to be describable in the terms of the same special science. Buchler's term "relatedness" is more apt, because, as generic, it includes *both* continuity and discontinuity as species of the genus.

But what the Goddess has established about nature-inquiry is that it asserts contraries, much as we today can say that the special sciences assert contraries as unavoidable working hypotheses, namely: "all is social," in sociology or "all is physical," in physics. These assumptions cannot both be true, though they might both be false. The Goddess's point, as it applies to the specialized inquiries of science, is that the language of the special sciences is inconsistent because it is about what is less than the All and not a unity. Nature-inquiry, then, is— in the memorable words of the Goddess—backward-turning (*palintropos*) and two-headed (*dikranoi*). Quite consonant with the

Goddess's critique of the discourse of nature-inquiry is Peirce's note, at 4.544, "[material] Universes cannot be described."

(iii) *Peirce and the Discourse of Metaphysics*

We conclude from the above that Peirce's "scientific metaphysics" cannot be a collection of scientific propositions in the special-science sense, when its subject-matter is All of what there is, "the totality of things thinkable" (7.563). Peirce himself classifies metaphysics as the third order of the subdivisions of philosophy (1.279-282) and, therefore, as normative—like aesthetics, ethics, logic (Order II), and phenomenology as the Doctrine of the Categories (Order I). In Peircean terms, what metaphysics says about the All may *signify*, but it does not *denote* as the special sciences do (6.328). Peirce's metaphysics confines itself (like Aristotle's) to those "peculiar parts . . . unlike the rest" of physics and psychology "as can be established without special means of observation" (1.282). As he says at 5.124, "Metaphysics . . . treats of phenomena in their Thirdness," namely, in their representative or mediatory character. Normative science treats phenomena as existences in their secondness, it "treats of the laws of the relation of phenomena to ends" (5.123), while phenomenology "treats of the universal Qualities of Phenomena in their immediate phenomenal character," namely, in their firstness (5.121).[10]

But Reality—what-there-is in its connectedness—he says at 5.12, "is an affair of Thirdness as Thirdness, i.e., in its mediation between Secondness and Thirdness." Since existence for Peirce is the irrational brute presence which forces itself upon us by its persistence, he distinguishes it from reality which "consists in regularity," adding that "metaphysics is the science of reality" (5.121). Lastly, given that "regularity is active law" and "active law is efficient reasonableness," Peirce equates Thirdness as Thirdness with true reasonableness. So the discourse and subject-matter of metaphysics turns out to be, for Peirce, what we would call the rationality of what there is in general. And this does not seem to be any different from the description Parmenides' Goddess gives of the conditions which discourse about the All must meet, if it is to be consistent or rational. Peirce's metaphysics turns out to be, then, a methodic discourse about the discourse of the special sciences which seeks to maximize the intelligibility, in human terms, of whatever is, as it can be analyzed and coordinated by reason—by "agapistic" or loving reason, we should have to say to be completely accurate about his stated philosophic enterprise. For, in Peirce's philosophy there is a strategic identification of nature-in-evolution with processes that advance the growth of concrete reasonableness in the world.

(iv) *Peirce's Dialogism*

Now, Peirce says at 4.551: "it is not merely a fact of human psychology, but a necessity of logic, that every logical evolution of thought should be dialogic."[11] This not only resonates with, and is reinforced by what M. Bakhtin has found in the field of literary studies, it is also in felicitous agreement with what G.H. Mead, M. Buber, and J. Buchler have had to say about it.[12]

Peirce had concluded, in "Some Consequences of Four Incapacities" (5.313), that "the reality of mind . . . the content of consciousness, the entire phenomenal manifestation of mind, is a sign resulting from inference . . . [so that] we must [also] conclude that the mind is a sign developing according to the laws of inference."[13] That two or more sets of signs can have one and the same interpretant, and so "must be determinations of one sign" (i.e., connected within a quasi-mind, namely, be *at one* or *of one mind*) shows, for Peirce, that a mind signing ("the quasi-utterer") is necessarily in dialogue with the interpretant mind(s), ("the quasi-interpreter"). The two (or more) sign-processors, or semiosic respondents, remain distinct, Peirce adds, even though "in the Sign they are, so to say, welded" (4.551). And understanding this, as D. Savan implied (ibid. p.46), makes us realize that Peirce thought of the interpretant not just as a sign-determined idea in someone's mind, but rather that he thought of mind itself as an interpretant or system of interpretants. For, from this conception, given "that there is no [such thing as an] isolated sign," it easily follows that the connection among signs (their non-isolation) is dialogic. Signs respond to one another: "every logical evolution of thought," as already stated, is "dialogic." That, for example, the conclusion of a syllogism literally *answers*, or *responds*, *to* the premises, as Peirce was wont to say, is made clear by the fact that "a conclusion is necessarily an interpretant" (4.540).

In the less technical language of the essay "What Pragmatism Is" (5.411-435), Peirce says that "a person is not absolutely an individual. His thoughts are what he is 'saying to himself,' that is, is saying to that other self that is just coming into life in the flow of time. When one reasons, it is that critical self that one is trying to persuade. . . . The second thing to remember is that the man's circle of society . . . is a sort of loosely compacted person, in some respects of higher rank than the person of the individual organism" (5.421).

In any case, the fruitfulness of Peirce's approach to semiosis is such that when applied to fields such as reading- or reception-theory taken as sign-activities, its implicitly dialogical or triadic nature facilitates the unimpeded extension of poetics into an aesthetics of reader-participation as crucial to the enterprise of literature.[14] This extension (as we shall see in the relevant chapter) is made easier by Buchler's generalized theory of the human product, or utterance. It will thus be no accident, when we go on to apply Peirce's semiotic thinking to interpretation-theory, that it clarifies the problem—crucial to intellectual, philosophic, and literary historians—of the criteria for deciding upon the greater or lesser validity of competing readings in apt operational terms. Historians of philosophy will, in any case become aware, as they read Peirce and Buchler, of the continuities and affinities between them and Aristotle, the functionalist, naturalist, and lover of poetic drama.[15] This is worth noting because it is of a piece with the way Peirce's philosophy avoids the trap in which an insufficient, inherited understanding of the hard sciences prevents them from categorizing distinctively human (or social) phenomena adequately, non-reductively. Peirce's theory of signs, in other words, makes possible and makes coherent the inquiry into mankind as human, more than as a special-science phenomenon.[16]

It is worth noting that the effectiveness of Peirce's and Buchler's technical terms (whether taken hypoiconically or literally) comes from the fact that they dramatize the phenomenon whereby interpretive alternatives are *living interactions* between a human product, the individual, and another human product, the work. That readers' interpretations are in dialogue with the text's subjectivity, is shown by the fact that the more it is interrogated the more it answers, or does not answer, to interpretations that respectively are or are not valid. As a set of *existential* relations, then, they are *subject to subject*, not subject to object, relations. It follows that there are possibilities of good and evil in these relations. This, in turn, confirms that the terms which their theorizing employs *do* safeguard, as such and from the outset, against the dehumanization of human or social subject-matters—as the terms which are borrowed from the hard sciences *do not*, on a positivist understanding of the sciences.

To put it in another way, Peircean and Buchlerian aesthetics can honor the subjectivity of the work or text under consideration because they are able to verbalize the level at which the work addresses the human condition and the quality of its perspective upon that condition. They give us *non-reductive* terms in which to discuss both the human process and the individual, and, therefore, terms in which to judge the acoustic, verbal or visual construction which is the work-of-art. Between them, these two thinkers give to aesthetics and criticism categories with which to legitimate conceptually (i) the relevance of context to text as a source of collateral input into the *interpretant* of the work, and (ii) the radically distinct nature of the kinds of judgment effectuated by work in the active or performative mode, by work in the exhibitive mode, and by work in the assertive mode. Endogenic interpretants are the signs and cues, internal to the work, which constrain interpretations—within permissible but elastic limits—to be *of* the work, both in its perceptible design and in its unpredictable pregnancy.

(v) *Aesthetics, Ethics, and Logic as Semeiotic*

Since Peirce's philosophic thinking was a practice of semiotic analysis which takes **purpose** to be the distinctive trait of intelligence, we need to understand both his theory of signs and the way in which it depends on ethics and aesthetics. As he says, in his papers on pragmatism and pragmaticism, "The elements of every concept enter into logical thought at the gate of perception and make their exit at the gate of *purposive* action; and whatever cannot show its passports at both those two gates is to be arrested as unauthorized by reason" (5.212).[17]

Now philosophy, besides trying to make synoptically intelligible the way things are, has, as its other main responsibility, the task of "find[ing] out with accuracy what are the essential ingredients of reasoning in general and of its principal kinds" (8.316). To this end, Peirce says, "my work in philosophy has consisted mainly in an accurate analysis of concepts, showing what is and what is not essential to the subject of analysis. . . . my motive . . . has been the desire to find out with accuracy what are the essential ingredients of reasoning. . ." (ibid.). Peirce's practice of conceptual analysis, then, is simultaneously oriented to the anchoring of 'logical thoughts' in experience or perception (5.212), and to the final or *teleological* interpretants of the concept. This behavioral interpretant he calls the *logical* interpretant—as if for antinomiasic emphasis on its praxical nature.

Peirce conceptualized "logic" as "a study of the means of attaining the end of thought" (1.573). But, "it is Ethics which defines th[e] end [of life]" (2.198). "The fundamental problem of ethics," for Peirce, is not the essentialist question, "What is right?" but rather, the functionalist question, "What am I prepared deliberately to accept as the statement of what I want to do, what am I to aim at, what am I after? To what is the force of my will to be directed?" From this he concludes: "It is, therefore, impossible to be thoroughly and rationally logical except upon an ethical basis" (2.198). Peirce is saying that the categories of right and wrong *cannot be* established *prior* to a teleological reflection upon the life of practice.

So, when he says that "logic is a study of the means of attaining the end of thought," Peirce has implied that students of logic cannot exempt themselves from becoming clear about the ends of life, as well as of thought, if they are to be secure and clear about the discipline of logic itself. Peirce then reminds us that "thinking is . . . an active operation" (1.573):

> the control of thinking with a view to its conformity to a standard . . . is a special case of the control of action to make it conform to a standard . . . the theory of the former must be a special determination of the theory of the latter.

The matter of the control of action, Peirce—with his aptness for and love of categorization—called *practics* or *antethics*, the "mid-normative" science between the other two normative sciences of aesthetics and logic. Practics is "the theory of the conformity of action to an ideal." But it is ancillary, and only on the way, to ethics— ethics being the discipline which "involves the theory of the ideal itself, the nature of the *summum bonum*."

Peirce pauses to note that so far as "ethics" has [only] studied the conformity of conduct to an ideal, it has always been limited to a particular ideal which . . . is in fact nothing but a sort of composite photograph of the conscience of the members of the community. . . . it is nothing but a traditional standard accepted . . . wisely without radical criticism, but with a silly pretense of critical examination" (1.573). Peirce calls *this* study "*antethics*," and as the study of "morality, virtuous conduct, right living" as understood by the community, it cannot be a discovering or *heuretic* science. Moreover it does not distinguish between motives and ideals, as ethics should and as Peirce wishes to. He therefore says,

> If conduct is to be thoroughly deliberate, the ideal must be a habit of feeling which has grown up under the influence of a course of self-criticism and hetero-criticisms; and the theory of the deliberate formation of such habits of feeling is what ought to be meant by esthetics (1.574).

In saying that ethics concerns itself with the discovery of ideals and the appeal to them, however, Peirce has not forgotten that "the only solid foundation for ethics lies in those facts of everyday life which no skeptical philosopher ever yet really called in question" (8.158). On logic as the control of thinking, he says,

> The phenomena of reasoning are, in their general features, parallel to those of moral conduct. For reasoning is essentially thought that is under self-control, just as moral conduct is conduct under self-control. Indeed reasoning *is* a species of controlled conduct and as such necessarily partakes of the essential features of controlled conduct. (1.606)

Peirce, in fact, "regard[ed] logic as the Ethics of the Intellect," and (in a letter to Victoria Welby) called his argument in 1.573 a "proof [n.b.] that logic must be founded upon ethics, of which it is a higher development."[18] As just stated, he had no doubt that "logic must be founded on ethics" (8.158, 255), and adds that he went on "to see that ethics rests in the same manner on a foundation of esthetics" (8.255). So, in showing that "logic . . . must appeal to ethics for its principles," or that "logic rests on ethics" (8.158), Peirce also came to see that "ethics . . . must appeal to esthetics for aid in determining the *summum bonum*. . . ." (1.191).

Peirce indeed says at 5.130 that, while approval itself may not always be a voluntary act, "the act of [an] inference, which we approve," **is** "voluntary." That is, "if we did not approve, we should not infer." So, since "the approval of a voluntary act is a moral approval," and *"Ethics is the study of what ends of action we are deliberately prepared to adopt,"* it follows that logic (here *critic*) is a part of ethics. That the logical reasoner "exercises great self-control in his intellectual operations," shows that "the logically good is simply a particular species of the morally good" (5.130). Peirce characterizes ethics as "the normative science *par excellence*, because an *end* . . . is germane to a voluntary act in a primary way in which it is germane to nothing else" (5.130).

Given the state of opinion about aesthetics in his time (the Brown and Mauve decades),[19] and that *deliberation* is not the *initiating* phase of the perception of the beautiful, Peirce has to have "some lingering doubt" about "there being any true normative science of the beautiful." However, he retracts the doubt by saying that, since an "end of action *deliberately* adopted . . . must be a state of things that reasonably recommends itself in itself," then it must also be "an *admirable ideal*, having the only kind of goodness that such an ideal *can* have; namely, esthetic goodness." He concludes, "from this point of view the morally good appears as a particular species of the esthetically good." Peirce, as J. Esposito points out, had never taken 'aesthetic judgment' to mean simply judgments about 'beauty,' but judgments of *any* of the forms of 'perfection'.[20] Finally, while all signs or representamens must possess some degree of esthetic goodness or expressiveness (5.140), only propositions (seconds) and arguments (thirds) may possess moral goodness or veracity: an "inference must possess some degree of veracity" (5.141).

Peirce's note 5.132 qualifies and limits his notion of "the esthetically good":

In the light of the doctrine of categories . . . an object, to be esthetically good, must have a multitude of parts so related to one another as to impart a positive simple immediate quality to their totality; and whatever does this is, in so far, esthetically good, no matter what the particular quality of the total may be.

We need to explain that in speaking of positive qualities as *simple* Peirce intends the *achieved* unity of qualities in works-of-art. Compositional unity is only simple in the respect that it is a *felt* unity, but is in every other respect complex. In art, achieved qualities may be highly *mediated* qualities, but they are *felt with immediacy.* Peirce goes on to point out that it follows that,

there is no such thing as positive esthetic badness; and since by goodness we chiefly . . . mean merely the absence of badness, or faultlessness, there will be no such thing as esthetic goodness. All there will be will be various esthetic qualities. . . . I am seriously inclined to doubt there being any distinction of pure esthetic betterness and worseness. My notion would be that there are innumerable varieties of esthetic quality, but no purely esthetic grade of excellence.

This sounds very post-Modern; but for it not to lead to the paradox that no work-of-art can be greater (as art) than another, we have to understand Peirce to be speaking of the purely *responsive* dimension of aesthetic stimuli or works, not of their compositional virtuosity or integrity. Qualities are various, but all present themselves with the immediacy and felt unity that is precisely what makes them qualitative. A first presents itself as a first whether as a sheer possibility such as a nearly contextless color, or the first of a third, such as the sheen on a fasionable code-word.

This, then, is how Peirce makes intelligible and justifies the statements (at 1.191) that "ethics . . . must appeal to esthetics for aid in determining the *summum bonum*. . . ." and that "logic . . . must appeal to ethics for its principles." We can now proceed to unfold this theory of signs or semeiotic as a whole.

2
(vi) Peirce's Theory of Signs, and the Practice of Philosophy

About the categories that he is uncovering Peirce's says (with fallibilist modesty), that "each category has to justify itself by an inductive examination which will result in assigning to it only a limited . . . validity" (1.301). Peirce's long essay "A Guess at the Riddle" (1.354-416), applies and confirms the usefulness of his categories both in philosophy and the special sciences. The categories turn out to also be characterizations of modes of being. *Firstness* is the mode of being of that which is such as it is, positively and without reference to anything else. *Secondness* is the mode of being of that which is such as it is, with respect to a second but regardless of any third. *Thirdness* is the mode of being of that which is such as it is, in bringing a second and third into relation to each other (8.328).

Besides clarifying the nature of sign-relations, the first, the second, and the third are distinguishable factors in human responsiveness. But it should be noted that as *thought*, as dianoetic, they "are all three of the nature of thirds" (1.537). Firsts are "mere possibilities" for ideation. Seconds are thoughts as events, and "of the general nature of experience or information." The third is thought "governing secondness. It brings information . . . or determines the idea and gives it body. It is . . . cognition. . . . G]enuine thirdness . . .[is]. . .the operation of a sign" (1.537).

Complexity as well as some degree of indistinctness can be seen to belong by nature to signs in all the domains in which they operate. This leads Greenlee, in his study of Peirce's concept of sign, to point out that a sign might, therefore, also be defined as "anything which determines an interpretant" (PCS 45). And Buchler, noting that many things that are not "directly manipulatable" or "qualitative configurations" are signs, makes the consequential point that,

> The purview of a sign may be restricted and precisely defined, especially where the sign is introduced by convention or resolution, as in a devised . . . calculus. But it may also be indefinite and undelimited: the sign may be of protracted character" (TGT 35).

Such, to take a historical example, was the French Revolution in its original protraction over time, and so may its many meanings among historians be determined by different limiting conceptualizations of its extension in space and time. And, since signs are potentialities for determination, they must also, when they are firsts or seconds, really be first or seconds of thirds. In other words, even the positing of mere possibilities is interpretive—in the course of queries where direct or material manipulation of the sign is not possible—because these are firsts of thirds.

To remember this is not only helpful in matters philological and aesthetic, but also in the study of the objects of cultural anthropolgy, religion, and sociology. So it is not only of philologists and archaeologists that aesthetic sensibility and a developed literary competence are demanded; "to read the sign at all," Peirce says (1.181),

> and distinguish one sign from another, what is requisite is delicate perceptions and acquaintance with . . . the usual concomitants of such appearances . . . and . . . the conventions of the system of signs. . . .

This is no less true, finally, for the study of the unstated, most basic *presuppositions* of *any* inquiry or undertaking, and the study of such essentially controverted subject matters as ethics and political philosophy.

(vii) *The Continuity between 'Art' and 'Science;' Speculative Alternatives to Dualism & Positivism*

We see, then, as Buchler already noted, that:

> Semiotic . . . . is broader and more thoroughgoing in conception than what is today called the theory of inquiry, since its analysis would penetrate not only to the standards, presuppositions, and forms of the problem-solving situation, but to those implicit in the . . . types of *all* communication (PP xiii, my emphasis).

Since (i) its analyses (as already mentioned) reach into all domains in which signs operate, namely, all areas and occasions from which we derive *cognitive gain*, and (ii) its analyses are, from the beginning, self-reflective, it follows that semiotics is the discipline of best resort in philosophic thinking. Logic as semiotic becomes continuous with rhetoric and poetics—the other disciplines in Aristotle's *organon*; and we have shown its continuity with and dependence upon aesthetics and ethics. As Critic, it is applied to the philosophy of mathematics, whether consciously or not, and avoids the positivist confusion of natural science with mathematics.

In philosophy of science it gets at both the formal dimension and the *heuretic* aspects of hard science, and can make the transition to philosophizing about the social-or-human sciences with increased understanding of the similarities and differences in the kinds of creativity which they, respectively, involve. This, in turn, makes it possible for semiotics to help reconstruct and rationalize the terminology of the social sciences so that they are non-reductive of their subject-matter, and so that this subject-matter in its distinctiveness is not denatured by the time it comes to making value-judgments on the basis of it. In all of this it modulates and replaces both Cartesian and Pyrrhonic skepticisms with methodic *fallibilism* and an open-ended (*corrigibilist*) search for ongoing explicability. We cannot help noticing about Peirce's semiotics, finally, that more than a practice of apt distinction-making it is a practice of apt categorization and recategorization of discriminable phenomena of whatever magnitude or reconditeness. In Peirce, the categorization is sometimes the very means which facilitates the perception of the phenomenon or its substrate.

The inclusiveness of Peirce's semiotic understanding of cognition and methodic query, i.e., his theory of search, can be seen to parallel the breadth of Aristotle's original conception of the arts-and-sciences: of science (*epistêmê*) as an art (*technê*) and the arts (*technai*) as knowledges. This granted, we need not be too concerned that Peirce (as I have read him so far) makes no *explicit* distinction between the special science of cosmology and the cenoscopic study, as he himself calls it, of metaphysics. For, he does in practice take them to be different, as we saw above (in sections ii and iii). And the distinction should not be blurred by his insistence that more than cenoscopic, metaphysics can be "scientific."

For, what the stock phrase "the scientific method" connotes for Peirce is both much more and much less than what it means in either popular or narrow positivism. Most generally, Peirce intends by 'scientific,' respect for the compulsion of evidence: it isn't evidence if it's not subject to universal inspection, and it's good evidence only if it ultimately compels unanimity in the community of investigators. So secondly, he intends by 'scientific,' explicit acknowledgement of the public or communitarian—the competitive or cooperative—nature of the pursuit of knowledge. The scientific method, thirdly, takes its results to be always revisible or corrigible. And this understanding is broad enough to accommodate the demands of the arts upon philosophy for recognition: for legitimation as providing both *cognitive gain*, renewal of or increase in *perceptivity*, and therapeutic or spiritual *solace*. This is the sense in which a method is scientific, for Peirce, if it leads to knowledge. It is more than what is called a "rigorous" attachment to deductivity or to a crude view of verification that fails to recognise other kinds of validation—verification being but a sub-species of validation.[21] Most generally, for Peirce, the human mind in its searching, whether in cenoscopic query, poetic exploration, or nomothetic-deductive inquiry, achieves its representation of the world in the teeth of the resistance to error, of what there is and of the way things are.

Deductivity, after all, is only a matter of observing the transformation-rules which Critic or formal logic monitors. And Peirce's realistic understanding of induction, like Aristotle's, enriches it by granting that particulars come steeped in associations, namely, they already and as such participate in generality. Peirce also brings the notion of hypothesis under the concept of *abduction*, thus expanding it to recognize and include the heuristic or serendipitous nature of knowledgeable non-deductive inference. As we saw in passing, Peirce seems to have a special feeling for the arts and sciences of *discovery*, those which he calls *heuretic*.

Scîo is Latin for "I know"; so that *scientia*, from which we get our "science," means "knowledge." And knowledge comes in many forms that positivism never dreamed of—if, that is, it ever allows itself to dream. Knowledge, as Aristotle knew and told us, comes from *practice* and *production*, it comes from making connections only some of which are deductive, it comes from guessing (abductive hypothesizing) and by accident. Chance (*tychê*) and art (*technê*), he had noted, are closely allied. So that for Peirce, as for Aristotle, any 'knowledgeable' activity is 'scientific,' and ought, therefore, to be allowed by us to be 'scientific' or *artful*. Peirce's thinking, then, is *tychistic* (as he called it) for methodological as well as systematic reasons.

Because he believed that chance is effectively operative in the universe, Peirce gave the name *tychism* to his way of thinking. Because he found that continuity *must* be assumed to prevail both in nature and in inquiry, he also called his philosophy *synechism*. Of course, insofar as all his searches were methodic, Peirce's discourse is not itself tychistic. The substance of his philosophy on the other hand, in being synechistic, is of a piece with the assumptive discourse that conveys it. As also a first-order hypothesis about the way things are, however, it is not the conclusion of a special-science inquiry, although none of the special sciences disconfirm it in their results. It is rather part of his cenoscopic grasp, the synoptic result, of his cumulative inquiries, his "general informed conception of the All" (7.579). As such it is a generative ingredient of his metaphysics, and so must be labeled (true as it might be) speculative. Peirce's synechism, in other words, is not an assertion in cosmology, but a transuasive or contextualizing device compatible with the special knowledges which it complements and with which it appears to be continuous.

In a historical view, Peirce's development of synechism was a response to the prevailing mechanism of such popular philosophers as Herbert Spencer or Karl Pearson. Not only did this mechanism deny the continuity between mind and matter that Peirce reasserts, it was not adequate to either Darwin's new evolutionary findings or to the rationale which Peirce thought the special sciences, as he knew them, demanded. As Morris Cohen points out (**CLL** xii), Peirce was in this at one with such scientific thinkers as Boltzmann who, says Cohen,

> suggested that the process of the whole physical universe is like that of a continuous shaking up of a haphazard or chance mixture of things, which . . . gradually results in a progressively more uniform distribution. . . . Scotus [knew] that every real entity has its individual character . . . which cannot be deduced from [w]hat . . .'is uniform. . . . Such original or underived individuality and diversity is what Peirce means by chance: from this point of view chance is prior to law. All that is necessary to visualize this is to suppose that there is an infinitesimal tendency in things to acquire habits, a tendency which is itself an accidental variation grown habitual. We shall then be on the road to explain the evolution of the existence of the limited uniformities actually prevailing in the physical world.

Mechanistically understood, the laws of physics do not, by themselves, explain for Peirce the development and variety of a natural world in which there is *both* order *and* novelty. Real chance is required, not just chance defined as what we don't know or can't explain.

In Peirce's speculative analysis, the absence of all determination or determinacy is what defines "nothingness," the state of "completely undetermined and dimensionless potentiality" (**6**.193, 200). By chance there develops a world of pure firsts or qualities, mere but real possibilities. Since nothing is actual yet, this state could be called *chaos*. Secondness emerges as the potentialities in chaos are actualized;

this is the world of events, or facts, produced by the interaction of actualized qualities. Regularities or laws, thirdness, have yet to supervene upon it. But there is a habit-taking tendency in the world, due to the occurrence in single random events of particular variations the iteration of which gives rise to trends leading to larger-scale uniformities. This habit-taking, or generalizing, tendency is what explains for Peirce the developed and developing regularities in nature which we call its laws. Peirce goes on to speculate that this overcoming of chance by habit and law should be seen as "a growth toward concrete reasonableness." His reason is that once you have granted continuity among things, you must also grant that there is growth in them (1.175).

Now the whole point of Peirce's realism is its recognition of the existence of generality in nature, and its emphasis on mind as a form in nature. As regularities, then, human habits can be brought under general ideas; so Peirce says, "the consciousness of a habit involves a general idea" (6.269). And he defines "a general idea" as "a certain modification of consciousness which accompanies any regularity or general relation between chance and actions" (*ibid.*).[22] Moreover, "every general idea has the unified living feeling of a person" (6.270). The consciousness of a general idea, therefore, is for Peirce "quite analogous to a person"; and since "a person is . . . a symbol involving a general idea" (5.313-314), "every general idea has the unified living feeling of a person" (6.270).[23]

When we see the connection between Peirce's synechism-tychism, his realism, and what he calls his objective idealism, it becomes clear that the latter as a speculative or transuasional proposal is neither a categorical assertion of the ideal nature of all things nor a denial of matter, but a recognition of the reality of thirdness. It is not an assertion in the special-science sense, as we have seen, but an assumption that query, *when unobstructed*, finds itself inevitably making. This is what's *methodeutic* about Peirce's metaphysics, namely, that while it is assumptive not assertive, it is developed as an expansion upon working hypotheses that proved to be successful in advancing the intelligibility of whatever subject-matters were being inquired into by a special science, dealt with, manipulated or produced by a knowledgeable art or practice.[24]

Unlike special science assumptions that block the road of inquiry in other fields than their own, or metaphors that obscure their subjects, a good philosophic or methodeutic assumption is such that it does not impede inquiry into, or denature, any subject-matter but rather turns out to facilitate interrogation of that subject matter without impairment to its distinctiveness. This, no doubt, was why Peirce thought of his pragmaticism as a method more than 'a philosophy.' As the semiotic approach which it is to both the pursuit itself of knowledge and the products of knowledge-seeking activity, we can see that it has, more than anything else, been a far-reaching, consequential, and coherently synoptic scrutiny of the whole range of the phenomena of representation.

Notes

1. As expressed in the cooperative volume edited by J. Dewey *Studies in Logical Theory* (Chicago U.P. 1909). But Peirce himself did not leave conventionalist formalism uncriticized. Cf. e.g., **4.373, 3.619**; and Buchler's chapter on "Fact and Formalism in Logic," in *Charles Peirce's Empiricism* (N.Y. Harcourt 1939).

2. That Dewey was responsive to Peirce's early criticism can be seen on pp. 12-14, 156, and 468-470 of his later *Logic: The Theory of Inquiry* (N.Y. Holt 1938); *Later Works*, Vol.12 (S. Illinois U.P. 1986).

3. Here are Peirce's words, *in toto*, about the fallibility of logic: "Logic, in its general sense is . . . only another name for semeiotic (**sêmeiôtikê**), the 'quasi-necessary,' or formal doctrine of signs. By describing the doctrine as 'quasi-necessary,' or formal, I mean that we observe the characters of such signs as we know, and from such observation, by a process of . . . Abstraction we are led to statements, eminently fallible, and therefore in one sense by no means necessary, as to what *must be* the characters of all signs used by a 'scientific' intelligence, that is to say, by an intelligence capable of learning by experience" (2.227).

4. "By the *phenomenon*," Peirce means, "whatever is before our minds in any sense" (8.265).

5. In what seem to be his notes for the Lowell Institute lectures of 1866-67.

6. See below; and PIN 161-162f, reprinted in J. Buchler *The Metaphysics of Natural Complexes* 2d ed., Wallace, Marsoobian, & Corrington (S.U.N.Y. Press 1991).

7. Do we come full circle here, given also that matter for Peirce is just mind which has become almost totally habit-ridden, namely, almost totally mechanical?

8. As in Emerson, when he announces that "we are symbols and we inhabit symbols" (ECW 3, 20). We may recollect here that Peirce makes a distinction between consciousness and mind, according to which consciousness is a special accompaniment of mind (7.363).

9. The similarity between Peirce and Parmenides' Goddess is that just as for her *only the conceptualized* All, not cosmographic nature, can be consistently and completely understood, so it remains a question for Peirce whether the understanding of nature achieved by the language of the individual special sciences is ever complete. That Peirce anticipates or hopes that a heuristic or *metaphysical* grasp of the whole-of-what-there-is is possible to objective idealism, does not mean that he is asserting the latter as a system of nature; for, that would make it a special-science assertion in cosmology, not a metaphysical insight. If the scientific description of nature is always corrigible for Peirce, then *a fortiori* it would seem that any consistent account of the All is also corrigible, because it is *heuretic* and hypothetical— particularly because, as never fully verifiable, it must be speculative.

10. See further, N. Bosco "Peirce & Metaphysics," *Studies in the Philosophy of C.S. Peirce* (Amherst: U. of Mass. 1964).

11. Logic, as semeiotic, for Peirce, of course includes speculative grammar and speculative rhetoric or methodeutic, as well as "critic" or logic in the modern formalist sense—and is itself subsumable under ethics and aesthetics, as we shall see.

12. In, respectively, *Mind, Self and Society* (Chicago U.P. 1934), *Das Dialogische Prinzip* (Heidelberg: Schneider, ed. of 1962), and *Toward a General Theory of Human Judgment* (N.Y. Dover, 2 ed. 1979) and *Nature and Judgment* (Columbia U.P.1955). And: M. Bakhtin *The Dialogic Imagination* 1975 (Texas U.P. 1982), *Problems of Dostoyevsky's Poetics* 1929 (Minnesota U.P. 1984), *The Formal Method in Literary Scholarship* 1929 (Harvard U.P. 1985), *Speech Genres & Other Late Essays* 1979 (Texas U.P. 1986).

13. Helpful to the reader here is Savan's reminder, in *An Introduction to C.S. Peirce's Full System of Semeiotic* (Toronto Semiotic Circle 1988), that Peirce never forgot that inference is not only fallible, but is mostly non-demonstrative, i.e. is inductive or abductive. "Throughout his life, when Peirce wrote of inference, reasoning, or logic, he meant to include the two forms of non-demonstrative inference—induction and abduction (hypothesis)—as well as deduction" (p.1-2).

14. As I show, at book length, in *Literature, Criticism, and the Theory of Signs*. The claim should turn out to be equally valid in connection with the problems of viewer- and auditor-participation in the fields of visual art and music.

15. Buchler, in particular, has shown, from the first of his contributions to the theory of judgment, a ready understanding of the *dialogical*, or exhibitive, nature of Plato's works.

16. Both J. Brent and Houser-Kloesel have emphasized this in their recent volumes, *Charles Peirce: A Life* and *The Essential Peirce*, respectively: (Indiana U.P. 1993), p.6, and (Indiana U.P. 1992), p.xxxi.

17. Aptly invoked by N. Houser in *The Essential Peirce* ed. Houser & Kloesel (Indiana U.P. 1992); xxxv, my emphasis.

18. See I. Lieb C.S.P.' *Letters to Lady Welby* (New Haven: Whitlock 1953), p.36; and C.S. Hardwick *Semiotics and Significs* The Correspondence Between C.S.P. and Lady Welby (Indiana U.P. 1977).

19. 'Mauve' equates with *aestheticism*, while 'Brown' was the color of the grim, post-Civil War mood. Paragraph 2.199 justifies Peirce's rejection of aesthetics as the mere theory of beauty. It concludes with the remark that aesthetics, in its proper and comprehensive meaning, "appears to be possibly the first indispensable propaedeutic to logic, and the logic of esthetics to be a distinct part of the science of logic [as semeiotic] that ought not to be omitted. This is a point concerning which it is not desirable to be in haste to come to an opinion."

20. "On the Origins and Foundations of Peirce's Semiotic," *Peirce Studies* (Lubbock: Inst. for Studies in Pragmaticism 1979), 19-24.

21. For a full development of this point, see Buchler **TGT**, Chapter VI "Validation."

22. Insofar as consciousness is sensation it is also "a part of the material quality of the man-sign"; as emotion it is that "which accompanies the reflection that we have animal life" (5.313). Again "consciousness is sometimes used to signify the *I think*, or unity in thought; but the unity is nothing but consistency or the recognition of it." By "man-sign" Peirce therefore means "man"; for, since consistency belongs to every sign as a sign, and signs signify their own consistency, what Peirce calls the man-sign (and the man signing or signifying) is the man.

23. The literary question which this suggests is worth asking, namely: is this why people in books, *ideal* constructions that they are, come over to the reader as *real* or actual persons—not just as successfully actual(ized) in the order of literary discourse, but as actual in the order of our everyday

lives such that, for example, it is apt to say that we can or do live with them, love or hate them, and dialogue with them.

24. If we distinguish, in the body of Peirce's variegated researches, first-order inquiries from his second-order investigations, we find that in the case of the former he pursued, with greater brilliance than most, the methods of the special sciences as he understood and advanced them; in the case of the latter he is perforce metadiscursive or speculative (transuasional).

References & Bibliography

K.A.Apel   *Charles S Peirce From Pragmatism to Pragmaticism* Tr. M.Krois Amherst: U. of Massachusetts Press 1981)

J.Brent   *Charles Peirce* A Life (Indiana U.P. 1993)

J.Buchler   *Charles Peirce's Empiricism* (N.Y. Harcourt 1939)
The Philosophy of Peirce Selected Writings, 1940 (N.Y. Harcourt 1956)
The Metaphysics of Natural Complexes 1966, 2 ed. Marsoobian, Wallace, & Corrigan (Albany: SUNY Press 1991)

M.R.Cohen   *Chance, Love, and Logic* Philosophical Essays by C.S. Peirce, 1923. Ed. with Intro. by M.R. Cohen, & Supplementary Essay by John Dewey (Repr. Peter Smith 1949)

V.Colapietro   *Peirce's Approach to the Self* (SUNY Press 1989)

G.Deledalle   *Charles S.Peirce An Intellectual Biography* (Philadelphia Benjamins 1990)

J. Dewey   *Studies in Logical Theory*, ed.J. Dewey (Chicago U.P. 1909)
Essays in Experimental Logic (Chicago U.P. 1915); *The Middle Works.* Vol.X, (1980)
Logic: The Theory of Inquiry (N.Y. Holt 1938); *Later Works* XII, (1986)
"Peirce's Theory of Linguistic Signs, Thought, and Meaning," *Journal of Philosophy* XLIII (1946); 85-95. *Later Works* XV (S.Illinois U.P. 1989).

C.Eisele   *Studies in the Scientific & Mathematical Philosophy of Charles S. Peirce.* Ed. T. Martin (The Hague: Mouton 1979)

R.W.Emerson   *Collected Works* 12 Volumes (Boston: Houghton 1904) **ECW**

J.Esposito   "On the Origins & Foundations of Peirce's Semeiotic," *Peirce Studies.* (Lubbock: Inst. for the Study of Pragmaticism 1979)
Evolutionary Metaphysics (Ohio University Press 1980)

M.Fisch   *Peirce, Semeiotic, and Pragmatism* Ed. by K. Ketner & C. Kloesel. (Indiana U.P. 1986)

D.Greenlee   *Peirce's Concept of the Sign* (The Hague: Mouton 1973)

C.Hookway   *Peirce* The Arguments of the Philosophers (London: RKP 1985)

T.Z. Lavine   "Peirce, Pragmatism, and Interpretation Theory,"*C.S.Peirce Sesquicentennial*, September 1989, Harvard University

I.Lieb   *Charles S. Peirce's Letters to Lady Welby* (New Haven: Whitlock 1953) **LLW**

H.Parret   *Peirce and Value Theory.* On Peircean Ethics & Aesthetics (Philadelphia: J.Benjamins 1993) **PVT**

C.S. Peirce   *Collected Papers* 8 vol. Ed. Weiss, Hartshorne, & Burks (Harvard U.P. 1931-58)
Writings of C.S.Peirce Chronological Edition Ed. M.Fisch (Indiana U.P. 1982 to date, 4 vols. so far)
The New Elements of Mathematics 4 Vol.in 5, Ed. Carolyn Eisele (Humanities Press 1976)
Semiotic and Significs The Correspondence between C.S.Peirce & V. Welby, ed. C.Hardwick (Indiana U.P. 1977)
Contributions to the Nation 4 Vol. Ed. K. Ketner (Texas Tech U.P. 1987)
The Essential Peirce Selected Philosophical Writings, Ed. by N. Houser & C. Kloesel (Indiana U.P. 1992)
Reasoning and the Logic of Things The Cambridge Conferences of 1898 Ed. K. Ketner & H. Putnam (Harvard U.P.1992)

R.Robin   *Annotated Catalogue of the Papers of Charles S.Peirce* (U. of Massachusetts Press 1967)

D.Savan   *An Introduction to C.S.Peirce's Full System of Semeiotic*
             (Toronto Semiotic Circle 1988)

V.Tejera   *Art and Human Intelligence* (N.Y. Appleton-Century 1965)
             Plato's Dialogues One By One (New York: Irvington 1984)
             History as a Human Science The Conception of History in
                 Some Classic American Philosophers (Lanham: U.P.A.
                 1984)
             Semiotics From Peirce To Barthes (Leiden: Brill 1988)
             History & Anti-History in Philosophy (Dordrecht: Kluwer
                 1989)
             Literature, Criticism, and the Theory of Signs (Amsterdam:
                 Benjamins 1995)
             "Eco, Peirce, & Interpretationism," *The Amer.Journ.of
                 Semiotics*, 8, 2-3 (1991): Review-Essay of Eco's *The Limits
                 of Interpretation*.
             "Peirce's Semeiotic, and the Aesthetics of Literature," *Trans.
                 of the C.S. Peirce Society* XXIX, (1993)
             Review of G. Deledalle *Charles S.Peirce: an Intellectual
                 Biography, Journal of Speculative Philosophy* VI.2 (1992),
                 166-169.
             "The Primacy of the Aesthetic in Peirce, & Classic
                 American Philosophy," in H. Parret PVT.
             "Classic American Starting Points for Interpretation
                 Theory: Peirce and Buchler," *Soc. Adv. of American
                 Philosophy*, Nashville 1993.
             Understanding Parmenides: The Poem, the Dialogue, the All
                 (in press)

H.S.Thayer   *Meaning and Action* A Critical History of Pragmatism (N.Y.
                 Bobb-Merrill 1968)

P.Wiener   *Values in a Universe of Chance* Selected Writings of C.S.
                 Peirce (Stanford U.P. 1958

Abbreviatons

PP	=	The Philosophy of Peirce
CLL	=	Chance, Love, and Logic
ECW	=	Emerson: Collected Works (1904)
PVT	=	Pierce on Value Theory
CP	=	Peirce The Collected Papers (8 volumes)
WP	=	Writings of C.S. Peirce (Chronological Edition)
SS	=	Semiotics and Significs
PFSS	=	Introduction to Peirce's Full System of Semiotics
PVT	=	Peirce on Value Theory

CHAPTER II

Dewey's Philosophy of Culture

(i) *The Conception of 'Experience' as Culture*

The style of problem-solving—namely, the pattern of action which seeks to transform, resolve or stabilize situations calling for change—that John Dewey took it upon himself to analyze and raise to the theoretical level of formulation, can be seen to have been, before he wrote about it, a characteristic way of acting in American culture as it developed from colony to democratic nation in-the-making.[1]

Dewey's approach to methodic human activity as problem-solving is thus not only distinctively American, but more broadly based than the later Popperian appropriation of the approach based on the activities of the natural sciences in Popper's day, in Popper's understanding of science. To be settling or settled in a country that was creating itself, to be surviving the Civil War in the absence of the bread-winning parent, to be getting an education with an eye toward the professions were, as it happened, cultural conditions of Dewey's childhood. Vermont was not the western frontier, but neither had pioneer habits been forgotten by the New England individualists among whom he grew up. There is little doubt that the future social theorist Dewey, practice-oriented as he was, is speaking *out of* personal experience, as well as *with* whatever intellectual equipment was

31

available, when he takes up the themes of nature, experience, culture, society and historical existence as subject-matters of philosophy.

Now, readers of classic American philosophy have all been eager to accept the equating which Dewey desiderated, and made explicit in mid-career, of 'experience' with 'culture' in the reading, rewriting and still-to-be written work of the philosopher. 'Experience' when it occurred was, and is, to be *everywhere* replaced by 'culture' for the better and fuller understanding of Dewey's meaning. But can this in fact be done, with the hoped-for improvement always resulting from the substitution? We will have to see. A recent comment by R.B. Westbrook takes us quickly (if a bit wobbily) to the nub of the matter. In theory, he notes, 'experience' was the term Dewey originally needed "because of its double-barreled meaning," but the term in its history

> which had begun life as part of an effort to liberate philosophy from "dessicated abstractions," had itself become a dessicated abstraction designating a private, mental, psychic way of experiencing (JDAD 345).

Readers, Dewey found, did *not* take 'experience' to "also designate *what* is experienced," as he had meant it to.

The terminological switch would, I believe (contrary to Westbrook), have addressed the contention that Dewey's metaphysics is anthropocentric because (i) the prereflective connotations of 'culture' are so much more public and objective, and because (ii) Dewey's metaphysics is a metaphysics of *existence*, *not* a metaphysics of experience, as Westbrook (following R. Bernstein[2] and others) seems to think. And if (iii) the reference of 'culture' is taken to be as much to the social *background* of human activity (as Dewey took it) as to the "intersubjective" relations supervening upon this activity (as Westbrook takes it), then we see that the cultural objects Dewey discusses are "events-with-meaning" and objective conditions presupposed by inquiry, rather than occupants of the foreground of experience in the subjective epistemological sense of experience. 'Culture,' as Dewey says in *Experience and Nature*,

> possesses . . . just that body of substantial references which 'experience' as a name has lost. It names artifacts which rank as "material" and

operations upon and with material things. The facts named by 'culture' also include the whole body of beliefs, attitudes, dispositions which are scientific and 'moral' and which . . . decide the specific uses to which the 'material' constituents of culture are put and which accordingly deserve, philosophically speaking, the name 'ideal' (even the name 'spiritual,' if intelligibly used) (LW1, 362).

If we can appreciate how circumstantial Dewey's critical recapitulations of intellectual history are, it should not be so difficult to appreciate how *circumstantial* his metaphysics *also* is with regard to objective aspects of the conditions under which inquiry and humanizing action or response are possible. We should not forget that Dewey practiced philosophy within the feeling and under the idea that "both philosophy and science were conceived and begotten by the arts." Dewey is ever aware of, and inspired by, the situation in which "science and philosophy had not parted ways because neither of them was cut loose from the arts. One word designated both science and art: *techne*."[3]

Dewey is ever reverting to reflections not only on how art is possible but how the *reflective* practice of the special arts and sciences emerges from the matrix of survival needs, cultural development, and social interactions. And an ever-present subtext, or agenda item, of his discourse is the rejection of Matthew Arnold's notion of culture as high art or transcendent superstructure, and the subsumption of that dimension of it into his anthropological view of culture.

Dewey's apt term for the Arnoldian dimension of society is "retrospective culture."[4] Yet he is no philistine about it; for, he also says, "the only test and justification of any form of political and economic society is its contribution to art and science—to what may roundly be called culture" (**ib.** 198). Yes, "to [have] settle[d] a continent" came first, but "to settle a continent is to put it in order, and this is a work which comes after, not before, great intelligence and great art." This work, Dewey continues, means nothing less than discovering and applying a method of subduing nature in the interests of democracy, of forming "a community of directed thought and emotion in spite of being masses." This has not yet been effected; but "it has never been attempted before." "Hence," he concludes, "the puny irrelevance that measures our strivings with yardsticks handed down from class[-divided] cultures of the past" (**ibid.**).

And since culture in the inclusive sense "can neither [be] beg[ged] or borrow[ed] without betraying both it and ourselves, nothing remains save to produce one." We must "subdue the industrial machinery to human ends until the nation is endowed with soul. . . . [O]ur culture," to be inclusive, "must be consonant with realistic science and with machine industry. . . . and bring to consciousness . . . the potential significance of the. . . . unspiritualized agencies of today as means of effecting the perception of human meaning yet to be realized" (**ib. 199ff.**). Dewey believed that by wigging out the reflectiveness or reflective quality of variant tendencies that look purely material or mechanical only because they are new, we could have a culture in which 'culture' in the high Arnoldian sense is continuous with, and an expression of, 'culture' in the socio-anthropological and infrastructural or productive sense.

Where Dewey in fact says " 'experience' is a word used to designate, in a summary fashion, the complex of all which is distinctively human" (**EN** Apdx. **LW1** 331), would it not have been more accurate (and in tune with his own philosophy) to say that *culture* is "the complex of all which is distinctively human?" Dewey does say, "the history of human experience is a history of the development of the arts" (**EN** 388), meaning that the history of human experience is the history of the development of the special sciences and special arts out of the matrix of human artfulness and practice made reflective. He still thinks, in the Appendix to **EN** just cited and contrary to English usage, that 'experience' "is a fitting name for the special way in which man . . . in the Western world, has shaped his participation in and dealings with nature" (p. 331).

But, with more accuracy, he does next claim for 'experience' that "its peculiarly distinctive application lies within the cultures that have followed from, and mark the break with, the medieval period." The ellipsis here is that by 'experience' Dewey means 'human experience,' namely *acculturated* experience. The need to substitute 'culture' for 'experience' is reinforced by Dewey's stated conclusion that "the [out]standing problem of Western philosophy throughout its entire history has been the connection-and-distinction of what . . . is regarded as *human* and . . . what is regarded as natural" **(ibid.)**. If, as he admits, Dewey found that it was the indefiniteness of 'experience' that made it fit his need, then is not 'culture' blessed with a less confusing sort of indefiniteness in the amplitude, but non-subjectivity, of its references?

"Ways of experiencing" in even the subjectivist sense of "experiencing," after all, are cultural processes or phenomena. And Dewey understands 'culture' to include "the material and the ideal in their reciprocal interrelationships and . . . [to] designate, also in their reciprocal interrelationships, that immense diversity of human affairs, interests, concerns, values which compartmentalists pigeonhole under 'religion,' 'morals,' 'aesthetics,' 'politics,' 'economics,' etc."

> 'culture' holds [these interests] together in their human and humanistic unity—a service which 'experience' has ceased to render. What 'experience' . . . fails to do and 'culture' can successfully do for philosophy is of utmost importance if philosophy is to be comprehensive without becoming stagnant (**LW1** 363).

What makes a philosophy of culture or civilization necessary for Dewey, or a Deweyan thinker, is the "intimate connection of philosophic systems with culture," and the fact that "the formation of sentiments and . . . values is always based on the cultural apparatus in a society," the sentiments and values defining man's attitudes "toward the realities of his . . . *Weltanschauung*" (p.363f.).[5] And as the culture varies so will the philosophizing that arises within it. Too much philosophy, Dewey had noted, still hasn't learned the lesson taught by the nineteenth century, that every human enterprise, including especially thought-systems in the West, has a history (**LW1** 332).

(ii) *The U.S. Constitution and Dewey's Philosophy of Social Process*

"Is it possible," asks T.Z. Lavine in the essay quoted at the beginning of this chapter, "from the organicist-historicist, relativizing intellectual style to legitimate the Founders' principles or any other normative philosophic principles for the direction of the 'problems of men'?" Can a reconstruction be effected, she asks, of American philosophy, "which would integrate the normative strengths of the American Founding . . . with the richly concretizing, temporalizing and situating intellectual style which Dewey Americanized from Hegelian and Darwinian conceptions of change." The doubt arises from Lavine's critique of Dewey's theory of the problematic. The critique finds that the potentialities for usefulness (in intellectual history, literary theory, sociopolitical studies, etc.) of the notion of problematic inquiry have been eroded or dissolved by Dewey's restrictive formulations of the conception.

Not all fixities, she points out, "have the pathological meaning which Dewey tried to give to the retention of principles, ideals, or institutions." Dewey did not have the conception of *nodal* or *axial* points in the continual process of gross historical change, so he does not recognize them. These are moments when "long-continuing and deeply rooted ideals come to actualization." Also contrary to Dewey's conception of gross socialization, "there is now the conception of identity-formation of individual persons and . . . social groups." The adequacy of the principles, norms and theoretical constructs that serve both kinds of actualization

> extends beyond a unique and passing situation to the wider horizons of a civilization and within it, to the dynamics of impulses and ideals and their consequences for civilizational and personal identity formation.[6]

If we grant that the founding of the independent United States was a world-historical event and a "*nodal, axial point in Western civilization in which realization of the historically long-sought principles guaranteeing the freedom of the human individual coincided with the formation of the American national identity,*" this reasserts and confirms the durability and adaptability if not the fixity of the principles behind the constitutional apparatus constructed by the Founders, against Dewey's remanding of all fixed principles to the dust heap of historical eventuality.

Under the influence of the Darwinian conception of change as genetic and evolutionary, and of the historicist view that all human contrivances are historical products involved in temporal change, Dewey's dilemmatic style of solving problems in the socio-cultural realm had to become *relativist* in addition to being contextualist. Such relativism of course conflicts with the Enlightenment style of problem-solving, with its fixed bases in alienable human rights, self-evident truths of natural law, and the truths of science.

Meantime, great changes in American existential reality, industrialization, immigration, urbanization, bureaucratization, and the imperialism of the war with Spain, were to give birth (as in the Hegelian notion of dialectical change) to the Progressive movement. Accelerated industrialization, and the stresses of the post-Civil War era, political corruption in tandem with economic monopoly, justified the protests of the Progressive Movement, of which Dewey is an important representative.

It was also within this nearly-forgotten but well-attested spiritual and cultural crisis,[7] that what we now call classic American philosophy took its rise. But the Enlightenment Modernist style of thought was already under critical attack in Europe, and in confrontation with the Romantic Modernist way of perceiving things. It is here that Lavine's thesis comes in about the wide cultural significance of American pragmatism. She sees it as

> the attempt on the part of American philosophers, within a nation whose national identity is established upon Enlightenment Modernist rationalistic principles of natural rights, democracy and science, to appropriate and integrate the dialectically opposite cognitive structure of Romantic Modernism (*op.cit.* 7).

Lavine points out, morevoer, that American intellectuality and philosophy did not arise in a mere "revolt against formalism," but "in a burst of creativity" which sought to apply to American life "the provocative doctrines and cognitive structures of Romantic modernism." Yes, we have to add, Dewey was in "revolt against formalism" but not in the way Morton White describes the revolt.[8] White quite side-steps the obsessive formalism of the American logicians who took the neopositivist European route rather than that of Peirce's **non-reductive** formalization of logic in the context of meaning-theory and semiotics, or that of Dewey's interest in the objective conditions of inquiry.

Characteristic of classic American philosophy, Lavine notes, is its inclusiveness, "its attempt to hold together the Enlightenment *instrumentalism* of science and technology and the Romantic *expressiveness* of personal and group life,"

> with Royce expressing philosophically . . . the politics of cultural despair, and Dewey expressing the Whitmanesque America of the open road, the continuous experiment, in secularized form the myth of America the Millenial nation. . . . What pragmatism holds together has everywhere else in secular philosophy fallen apart, into positivism, phenomenology, linguistic philosophies, existentialism, critical theory, action theory, hermeneutics, ethnomethodology.

Pragmatism in its inclusiveness, indeed, is like metaphysics—as practiced or conceptualized by Peirce, Santayana, and Buchler—in being *post-scientific*. It works itself out in Dewey by reference not only to the cognitive enterprise of the special sciences, but also in the light of the complexities of politics, art and social history. And it has dealt with the latter in the thought-modes of Romantic modernism rather than of the eighteenth-century Enlightenment from which British aesthetics and Cartesian epistemologies, for example, have yet to free themselves.[9] We must not forget that, as a diagnostician of the deficits of established institutions, Dewey was not just an advocate of the 'scientific method,' but an advocate of it *for purposes of the reconstruction of society.*

This strength of Dewey's, however, is said by Lavine (and some constitutionalists) to have a weak side in that, if truths may only be advanced hypothetically, then no claim is self-evident or unqualifiable, namely, absolute or unconditional. In his zeal for reform or change Dewey also, as Lavine points out, does not seem to have realized that "in a democracy a source of authority should be out of reach of the contending parties," or that the rights of minorities might be endangered by his undermining of the Constitution. So he inveighs, with Jefferson, against "set[ting] undue store by established mechanisms" and against "the idolatry of the Constitution as it stands" (**FC** 158, **LW**13). If the "American Creed" in politics, as Samuel Huntington has said, is "constitutionalism, liberalism, democracy, egalitarianism, individualism," *as these are given meaning* by the Enlightenment Modernist frame of the Founders, then, in Dewey's Progressivist view, rigid support of the natural rights doctrine of the Declaration, and the legal, moral authority of the Constitution or Supreme Court is a form of objectionable fundamentalism.

Dewey did believe he was advancing the work of his predecessors in the liberal tradition in pursuit of individual freedom of thought and expression (**LSA, MW**11 31f.).[10] He believed that "our political institutions are unusually inflexible," and "tend to favor in substance a privileged plutocracy" (**LSA** 60), namely, that they needed revising. But Dewey nowhere speaks of what would replace our constitutional inheritance as the criterion of reform, other than the method of intelligence enlarged into the methods of *social intelligence*. And for this method the criterion is the "experimental" criterion of democratic success in the business "of [the] further development [and] constructive social application" of our democratic political institutions" (**ibid.**).

From Enlightenment Modernism, then, Dewey did take science and democracy for granted as both the premises and the goals of his philosophy; so he *sacralizes* them. As a post-Lockeian American he likewise takes over and expands upon the scientific method as the only reliable method of inquiry and, along with it, he believed in the power of scientific technology and democratic discussion to reconstruct the world. He also believed in modernization, and claimed that the individualism of American political and economic thought was a hindrance to it. He does not criticize the rationalization and bureaucratization of industry and government; but he does perpetuate the Enlightenment and Puritan concept of the dignity and meritoriousness of work.

On the other hand, while rejecting the primacy given to subjectivity by Romantic Modernism, he does rediscover, in response to the rise of totalitarianism between the two World Wars, the importance of the individual. He strives to bring the human subject back into continuous and sympathetic relation with nature and society. He will have no part of Romantic disdain for the bourgeoisie or the masses, and is in fact an apostle of mass education. And he has little patience with self-named 'lost generations' or alienated intellectuals, save as phenomena in the social process of cultural lag. But he is Romantic, and meliorist, in launching his expressivist challenge to Enlightenment Modernism without benefit of any religious or a priori framework.

In this, I would add, Dewey is like Shakespeare and Machiavelli: he avoids using or invoking on his own behalf the Christian framework of his culture, because his ulterior appeal is to nature and to human practice. He differs from the two great writers in that he is an *explicit* naturalist, where they are tacit, undeclared naturalists.[11] But he is most Romantic of all where he is most implicitly humanist, namely, in speaking of the reconstruction of American society without benefit (as Lavine reminds us) "of American constitutionalism [or] traditional political principles,"—without benefit, I would say, of any criteria other than those which he must have thought were internal to democratic practice and human social nature. The attentive reader, indeed, will find implicit in Dewey's political writing the *non-utopian* hope, anticipation or claim, that political and economic democracy are but stages in a development toward cultural and moral democracy. And this means that, for Dewey, it is the ethical and investigative ideals or standards of a democratic society which keep it viable as a democracy.

(iii) *Dewey's Naturalistic Metaphysics*

In guarding Dewey from whatever anthropomorphic implications there might be in saying that "a situation" is "problematic," Sidney Hook claimed that "nature" (like the situation) "has no problems although the fact that *we* have problems tells us something about nature."[12] But this is simply to make a claim about something which we cannot know, namely, nature **unperceived**. It is also not to take nature as an object of knowledge; for, in Dewey, if nature is not problematic then it is not an object of inquiry. That Hook does not see that the object of knowledge is a *product* of inquiry, appears in the following words: "The object of knowledge, the solution to the problem of inquiry, the objective, if one calls it that, cannot be changed in the course of inquiry without stultification" (p.xix). To this he adds, "but when we are trying to find out or test a hypothesis about *something* doubtful, the situation at some point must be reconstructed to give us a warranted conclusion."

Notice that while this appears to grant that the situation must be reconstructed, the focus or target for Hook is something *in* the situation (e.g. the moon), something about which we have a doubt but which does not otherwise change, save that our doubts about it are removed by reconstructing the situation, namely, by things which the observers do, such as making changes in "the positions of the observers and the experimental apparatus" (p.xx). Here is the positivist gap again, the *dualism* and *discontinuity* between the observer and the observed, between the knowing and the known.

"The assumption," Dewey noted, "of a ready-made mind over against a physical world as an object has no empirical support" (**PJD** 17f.). The object of knowledge is a *product* of inquiry *as* knowledge, not as an existence; otherwise knowledge would be *only* subjective, a matter of consciousness alone, and Dewey would be holding, like the positivists, a correspondence theory of truth. In Peirce's pragmaticist terms, to deny that nature is problematic is to deny that nature is a *significate object*; so, this is a respect in which Hook cannot claim to be either Deweyan or pragmaticist.[13] Hook is also out of step with the classic American traditon of philosophy in denying the possibility of, or need for, a naturalistic metaphysics. Dewey—contrary to Hook's gratuitous call on him to reconceive the role of metaphysics—has a view of philosophy as the criticism of criticism, and of "metaphysics" as providing "a ground map of the province of criticism" (**EN** 413). About it he says, "it has no call to . . . delve into secrets of Being. . . . It has no stock of information or body of knowledge peculiarly its own" (**EN** 407). The "reconceiving" to be done here is Hook's, not Dewey's.

Metaphysics as practiced by Dewey is, as in Peirce, Santayana, Randall, and Buchler, *post-scientific* and culturally *synoptic*. It has the function of bringing out and testing the coherence of the competing, converging, and conflicting components of the culture, *their* pre-suppositions as well as those of the culture as such, in its relations with nature and other cultures.

The archaic and classical Greek conception of man's continuity with nature—of man as, by nature, desiring to know and of nature as knowable—gave way, as Randall reminds us in his essay on "The Nature of Naturalism" (**NHS**, 367-374) to the *denaturalization*, in the Hellenistic and earlier middle ages, of human experience and human nature. But in his synthesis of Christian and Aristotelian thought, St. Thomas reintroduced the Greek idea of a continuity between man and nature in which experience becomes once more a relation between a responsive, rationally selective organism and the world.

Into this "unstable Greek view" however, Randall continues, the scientific revolution of the seventeenth century introduced a new set of ideas which again denaturalized human experience. Nature was transformed into a purely mechanical system of elementary corpuscles following the laws of dynamics. "But it left man. . . . living in a world stripped of all intelligible and valuable structure. Between man, his 'mind' and experience on the one hand, and Nature on the other, there yawned a chasm. Man's only relation with such a world must be exclusively mechanical. . . . Thus human experience was removed from nature and made 'subjective'; its locus was in man, in a separate substance, 'mind,' not in Nature at all." Worse still,

> [t]he varieties of human experience, religious artistic, moral . . . intellectual, became quite literally supernatural—they were in no sense natural processes. . . . The teleological, functional, and logical concepts appropriate to human experience were now wholly irrelevant to the purely mechanical concepts appropriate to Nature. Conversely . . . human life and 'mind' [became] unintelligible in terms of . . . mechanistic science . . . man's experience of science . . . itself became an enigma.

If Kant's is the best attempt to solve the enigma, to bridge the gulf, by locating inside man himself the source of the order we find in our perception of the world, then, says Randall, "his thought remains the classic modern expression of a thoroughgoing dualism and supernaturalism" not to mention that it is a solution that legitimates and confirms the original *egocentrism* of Cartesian epistemologies, as well as the inordinate, imperial importance granted to *the subject* by Modernist Idealism.

For the nineteenth-century idealists, however, concerned as they were with the range of *human* activities rather than the realm of physical nature, "man's experience—religious, moral, artistic, intellectual—[became] once more the clue to the nature of the universe." The systematic omission of which they, in their turn, were guilty was that of the natural sciences. But there was a strand of idealism, typified by Lotze which became increasingly scientific and experimental in its methods of analysis, and which was especially interested in the social sciences. The combination of the idealist "emphasis on continuity . . . against dualisms of every sort with the methods and concepts of biology and anthropology led directly to the contemporary type of anti-reductive naturalism" of which Dewey is representative.

At the same time, the flourishing of biological thought under the stimulus of evolutionary theories, the new experimental psychology and the developing social sciences including especially anthropology, all led to the extension of natural science into the study of human activities and to the bringing back of man into nature. The study of human experience as a subject-matter became possible again, because it was now seen as an interaction of natural processes. Human experience was taken, in biological terms, as an interaction between organism and environment, an affair of stimulus and response; while, in sociological terms, it was conceived as "the complex interactions between the individual and his cultural setting, an affair of education and social and cultural reconstruction in the broadest sense."

Thus from their side the scientists were arriving at the same general view of the status of man in the world that the more scientifically minded idealists were reaching from theirs. And . . . Dewey beautifully illustrates this strand of intellectual development.

Dewey's conception of metaphysics, then, is post-scientific in the sense that it is a speculative,[14] existential history of human institutions—contrivances, assertions, actions—in their reflectiveness. And it is synoptic in the sense that it seeks to identify the generic traits of the existential conditions of human intelligence in its functioning and productivity. Thus he says in "The Subject-Matter of Metaphysical Inquiry," that we may mark off "metaphysical subject-mater by reference to certain irreducible traits found in any and every subject of scientific inquiry" (**MW**8 p.4). In connection with evolutionary biology, for instance, metaphysics does not ask the questions which science goes after, namely, what the causes of evolutionary change are or how they operate; but it does "raise the question of the sort of world which *has* such an evolution." The question about the sort of world which *causes* evolution "break[s] up into just the questions which constitute scientific inquiry."

In actual practice Dewey's *Experience and Nature* takes most cognizance of those traits of *existence* that relate to intelligent human responsiveness and productivity. Existence, to his observation, is a mixture of the precarious and the stable. And even though modern man's science and technology focus on verifiable regularities of nature in order to get some control over it, he finds that "when all is said and done, the fundamentally hazardous character of the world is not seriously modified, much less eliminated" (**EN** 44). Because all existences are eventful (**EN** 71) and everything is processual, things and patterns are never completely stable. It is those for which the rate of change is slow or rhythmic, in contrast to those subject to rapid or irregular changes, that we call stable. There are no changeless entities or patterns in Dewey's metaphysics: "every existence . . . every idea and human act [is] an experiment in fact, even though not in design" (p.70). Every existence is a conjunction of problematic and determinate characters.

The *world* is precarious and perilous (p.42). Fear is a function of the environment; man exists in a fearful, awful world. Herbert Spencer captured "a persistent trait of every object in experience" when he said that every fact has a near or visible side and a remote or invisible side; namely, "the tangible rests precariously upon the untouched, the ungrasped" (ib.44). Of course, we now have better ways of dealing with this contrast than the superstitious ways of our fearful ancestors, but not technology, not religion, and not amusement can eliminate "the fundamentally hazardous character of the world." Dewey then submits that it is the inescapable predicament that this contingency of the world puts us in, which has given rise to philosophy and which can account both for the contrariness between diverse philosophies and the characteristic emphases common to many of them, even in their differences.

> If . . . philosophy says so much about unity and so little about unreconciled diversity, so much about the eternal and permanent and so little about change . . . so much about necessity and so little about contingency, so much about the comprehending universal and so little about the recalcitrant particular, it may . . . be because the ambiguousness and ambivalence of reality are actually so pervasive.

Variant philosophies then appear as "different . . . recipes for denying to the universe the character of contingency" (ib. 46).

Popular, unsophisticated philosophies on the other hand, notes Dewey, do much better in recognizing the world as a mixture of sufficiencies, completeness, order, recurrences (that make control possible) and singularities, ambiguities, uncertain possibilities, indeterminacies, and vital randomness. But he, Dewey, thinks that "such facts . . . have rarely been . . . recognized as fundamentally significant for the formation of naturalistic metaphysics" (**EN** 48). The problem with platonized Aristotelianism is that "a classified and hierarchically ordered set of pluralities, of variants, has none of the sting of the miscellaneous and uncoordinated plurals of our actual world." Worse, the traditional classification was given a diremptive import by Kant. He "assigns all that is manifold and chaotic to one realm, that of sense, and all that is uniform and regular to that of reason"; and this replaces "the concrete problems that arise from the mixed and varied union in existence of the variable and the constant" with a dialectical problem of the relation between sense and intellect.

Yes, says Dewey, the effort to make "stability of meaning" prevail over the "instability of events" is a main task of intelligence. But when the task is taken out of human hands, dropped from the province of art and treated as a property of given things . . . [then unfortunately] effort is rendered useless, and a premium is put upon the accidental good fortune of a class that [is] furnished by the toil of another class with products that give to life its dignity and leisurely stability (**EN** 50).

The romanticism about change of the philosophies of flux, of Hegel, Spencer and Bergson, also sidesteps "the painful, toilsome labor of understanding and of control which change sets us, by glorifying it for its own sake." As "cognizance of the generic traits of existence" (p.51), good metaphysics will accord the same footing to incompleteness and precariousnes as it does to the finished and the fixed. And wisdom as to ends will "depend upon acquaintance with conditions and means"; for, if the acquaintance is inadequate and unfair, and relegates "the uncertain and unfinished to an invidious state of unreal being," it becomes philosophical folly and self-deception.

While the mixture of the hazardous and the stable is an existential condition of our predicaments and problems, it is also and as truly "the condition of all experienced satisfaction (**EN** 62). If there were no deviations or resistances, fulfillment would come at once, and would not be fulfilled but merely be. So, "imagination . . . is the appropriate phase of indeterminate events moving toward eventualities that are now but possibilities." And precariousness is "an indispensable condition of ideality, becoming a sufficient condition when conjoined with the regular and the assured." And what gives meaning to the longing for perfection is the events that create the longing; "apart from them a 'perfect' world would mean just an unchanging brute existential thing" (**EN** 63).

Dewey wants us to understand that "need and desire are exponents of natural being. They are . . . actualizations of its contingencies and incompletenesses; as such nature itself is wistful and pathetic, turbulent and passionate." If it were not so, the existence of wants would be miraculous; for, a world where everything is complete would be wanting nothing. If human experience, or culture, is to reflect or express this world, it must be marked by needs; "in becoming aware of the needful and needed quality of things it must project satisfactions or completions" (ib.64). Note that this is not anthropomorphism, but Dewey's *transactionism:* "satisfaction is not subjective, private or personal; it is conditioned by objective partialities and defections and made real by objective situations and completions." The reflectiveness of the operations leading to satisfaction, or to the creation of determinacy out of problematic indeterminacy, is a natural event occurring within nature because of the traits of the latter (**EN** 64, 68).

Dewey's metaphysics is *contextualist* because thinking is *situational:* "the actually problematic" is the starting point of reflection; and "the problematic phase resides in some actual and specifiable situation. And "thinking is no different in kind from the use of natural materials and energies . . . to refine, re-order, and shape other natural materials" because it uses, or brings to the problem, other materials and agencies (already established ideas or available terms or tools) to construct determinacy out of the indeterminate or dilemmatic.

Thinking, then, is a process of re-organization, a natural function resulting in coherent unification. However, when ontologizers convert this natural function into *an antecedent causal reality,* what you get is an ontology, a metaphysics of reality as a completely rational system. If, in thinking things through, you retain the connection, says Dewey, between *the goal* of thinking (namely, the new determinacies you have instated) and the thinking by which you reached it and, next, identify the goal "with true reality in contrast with the merely phenomenal," you will have grasped in outline the logical procedure of the rational, objective idealisms. For, in these, "thought, like Being, has two forms, one real; the other phenomenal." In seeking reflective form, thought is involved in doubt and hypothesis *because,* here, it starts out from what is mostly sensory. "But the conclusion of reflection affords us a pattern and guarantee of thought which is *constitutive;* one with the system of objective reality" (**EN** 66f.).

But thinking for Dewey is an existential activity, so the traits of thinking have "the same existential character as do the objects of valid knowledge" (ib.69). For naturalistic metaphysics the world has to be such that ignorance and inquiry, doubt, hypotheses and provisional conclusions, arise within it: "the latter being such that they develop out of existences which while wholly 'real' are not as satisfactory, as good, or as significant, as those into which they are eventually re-organized."

> The ultimate evidence of genuine hazard, contingency, irregularity and indeterminateness in nature is thus found in the occurrence of thinking.

When idealism and materialism grant ontological priority to structure over process, they are treating a relational and functional distinction as something fixed and absolute because of their preference for the stable over the precarious. But anything defined as structure is *a character of events*. Structure

> is an arrangement of changing events such that properties which change slowly, limit and direct a series of quick changes and gives them an order which they would not otherwise possess. Structure is constancy of means . . . used for consequences, not of things . . . by themselves or absolutely.

Similarly the structuring "spirit" of idealism is conceived of as something fixed, rigid and external to change, to which all events must accomodate themselves, when actually it is a phase or property of the activities it is supposed to explain. And matter is "that character of natural events which is so related with [perceptible] changes that are sufficiently rapid . . . as to give the latter a characteristic rhythmic order, the causal sequence" (**EN** 73). Matter "designates a character in operation, not an entity." The notion of matter in popular materialism has nothing in common with "the matter of science [which] is a character of natural events and [natural] changes. In popular materialism it is still a rigid structure to which is added "a second rigid structure which [it] calls mind."

In Dewey's metaphysics, matter expresses the sequential order of natural events, while mind expresses the order of their meanings and connectedness. Mind and matter are adjectival or adverbial not entititative; they are phases of the complex of events that constitute nature in process. Here we see, among other things, that the empiricism which characterizes Dewey's thought is an experiential or existential empiricism, and not anything like the dualistic sensationism and atomism that goes by the name of British empiricism.[15]

The problems and issues of life and philosophy, for Dewey, "concern the rate and mode of the conjunction of the precarious and the assured, the incomplete and the finished, the repetitious and the varying, the safe and sane and the hazardous" (**EN** 75). Wisdom is to trust the traits of experienced things as evidence, and to get a sense of the modes of interaction among the fundamental features of natural existence. Wisdom is not to assume an attitude of condescension toward existence; reflection exists to guide choice and effort. Love of wisdom must not be "an unlaborious transformation of existence by dialectic," but instead "an opening and enlarging of the ways of nature in man." Thoughtful observation and experiment are the method of dealing with the unfinished processes of existence so as to give substance to goods that are frail, scope to those that are secure, and actuality to those that are promises.

(iv) *The Nature of Communication in Dewey's Philosophy*

Without neglecting the social context, Dewey stresses more obviously than Mead the *natural* context of communication. As we saw above, and like the anthropologists of his day, Dewey associates speech with tool-using, calling language the tool of tools (**EN** 168).[16] We know that "the neural delay required when some extra-organic tool is interposed between stimulus and response probably had much to do with the first ability to use symbols as the start of language."[17] A kind of mediation, or foresight, goes with the carrying of a stone- or bone-weapon, since it involves a reference today to what might be encountered tomorrow. Events once named, says, Dewey, turn into objects, or things with meanings (**EN** 166); in communication, they begin to lead "an independent and double life, and they become subject to imaginative manipulation. When communication occurs, all natural events are subject to . . . revision; they are re-adapted to . . . the requirments of conversation, whether it be public discourse or that preliminary discourse termed thinking."

First, we note that Dewey thinks of an object as more than a thing; it is a thing *for* or *to* us. An object for Dewey, as in Peirce, is something *significate*. And this is part of the approach within which Dewey distinguishes between commonsense objects, aesthetic objects, objects for use, scientific objects, and so on. Thus, a scientific object is often a reconstructed commonsense object, as much as Cézanne's apples or Turner's riverscapes are artistic reconstructions of commonsense objects. The scientific characterization locates an object in the order of science, namely, in an order within which it can be related *deductively* to other scientific objects. Not only is H_2O not the kind of thing tap-water is, but H_2O in 1903 is not the recontructed scientific object which H_2O is in 1993.

Secondly, we note that Dewey has overlooked something of which Mead and Buchler have made us aware, namely, that in the reciprocal relation between them "communication" *presupposes community*. It is not communication that makes community possible, but community which creates the condition that makes communication possible. While Dewey recognizes that "soliloquy is the product and reflex of converse with others (**EN** 170)," he also says: "society not only exists *by* transmission [of culture], *by* communication, but it may fairly be said to exist *in* transmission, *in* communication (**DE** 7, **MW**9). The social in Dewey is of course more than association; but he thinks that for the association to constitute a society, there must exist a common interest among its members (**PIP** 353, **LW**2). Dewey is not wrong in pointing out that all communication and all social life is educative, but common beliefs or ends are not a sufficient condition of community.[18] On the one hand members of a group do not have to perceive the consequences of their joint activity or be concerned with "the contribution of each of its members to it," for the grouping to be a community, but on the other hand there is no community if members of the class are not "procepts" for each other, in Buchler's terminology.[19] Thirdly, the explicit emphasis on the *dialogism* of all thought and speech which we find in Peirce, Mead, and Buchler is, we note, rather missing in Dewey.

But meanings should not be hypostatized into objects of thought, as prior or independent forms of things; for, this forgets the fact that the import of logical and rational essences is the consequence of social interactions, of companionship, working together, direction and cooperation in fighting, feasting or labor. The insight that things, meanings, and words correspond says Dewey, was perverted "by the notion that the correspondence of things and meanings is prior to discourse and social intercourse" (**EN** 171f.). This notion gives rise to a belief in ideal essences, and, when these are related systematically or deductively, to a wishful belief in "the unity of science" so-called. "Thus," says Dewey,

> the greatest single discovery of man, putting man in potential possession of liberation and of order, became the source of an artificial physics of nature, the basis of a science, philosophy, and theology in which the universe was an incarnate grammatical order constructed after the model of discourse.

This, in turn, led to the failure of the moderns to recognize that the world of 'inner experience,' so-called, is entirely dependent upon the extension of language—a social product—to it; this is "the subjectivist, solipsistic, and egotistic strain in modern thought (**EN** 173). Like Mead, Dewey is insistent that "the human being is participative. The latter puts himself at the standpoint of a situation in which two parties share. This is the essential peculiarity of language or signs."

There are plenty of precedents in nature for the fact that association of things confers new properties upon the assemblage and its members, releasing untapped energies in them. So, the human phenomenon of *significance*, resides not in the bare fact of association (**EN** 175), but in the consequences that flow from the distinctive patterns of human association. In this case, "th[e] assemblage of organic human beings transforms sequence and coexistence into participation." Here, it worth pausing to note that Dewey's detailed analysis (**EN** 178) of how two people understand each other's gestures is thoroughly Meadian. The characteristic of B's understanding of A's movement and sounds is that he responds to the thing indicated from the standpoint of A; he does not only respond egocentrically. "Similarly, A . . . conceives the thing not only in its . . . relationship to himself, but as . . . capable of being . . . handled by B. He sees the thing as it may function in B's experience. Such is the essence and import of communication, signs and meaning. Something is . . . made common in . . . two different centers of behavior." As we shall see, this is the process described, in Buchler's theory of human judgment, as "proceptive parallelism."

"Because of converse, social give and take," says Dewey, organic attitudes become an assemblage of persons . . . conferring with one another, exchanging distinctive experiences" (**EN** 170). As in Mead, the functioning and very emergence of mind is a consequence of social interaction. In communication "things . . . acquir[e] representatives, surrogates, signs, implicates, which are . . . amenable to management . . . more permanent and . . . accommodating than events in their first estate." Learning comes into being. "Even the dumb pang of an ache achieves . . . significant existence when it can be designated . . . it ceases to be merely oppressive and becomes . . . representative" (**EN** 167). . . . "through speech a person dramatically identifies himself with potential acts and deeds: he plays many roles . . . in a contemporaneously enacted drama." Within his naturalist's emphasis, Dewey is also saying that communication is *a kind of sharing* of experiences. "Social life," as he says in *Democracy and Education*, is identical with communication" (p.8).

In Dewey's philosophy what is not shared is made sharable by communication, by "language" (**AE** 244). Language according to the *Logic* is the necessary and sufficient condition of communication (**LTI** 46). But to talk this way Dewey has to take language "in its widest sense," as including

> "speech . . . gestures . . . rites, ceremonies, monuments and the products of the industrial and fine arts. A tool or machine, for example . . . says something, to those who understand it" (**ibid.**).

Well-intentioned as Dewey's emphasis is here, his choice of words is misleading. Tools and machines, when they find *interpretants*, are indeed signs. As human products, they do come under Buchler's conception of utterance or contrivance. But they do not themselves *state* anything, except metaphorically. And the metaphorical sense in which they or a proud locomotive, say, "make a statement" is the exact sense in which they have an *exhibitive* effect, or constitute an exhibitive judgment. Dewey's formulation is also too broad to just the extent that it stipulates that "language" shall now mean "all kinds of signs," namely, anything that has an interpretant.

Now, one of Dewey's ongoing projects was to advance and get acceptance for an imaginative understanding and use of the scientific method for purposes of democratic organization. In historical retrospect we can see the contrast in matters social of Dewey's project with Santayana's—and the parallel, in matters imaginative. Santayana did not grow into a national community which he could call his own, or of which he was not a detached observer. So, where Dewey was an involved and thoroughly integrated member of his own country, Santayana's home was intellectual only, in the bosom of the Western tradition as a whole. But Dewey was like Santayana in believing that "the only test and justification of any form of political and economic society is its contribution to art and science—to what may roundly be called culture" (**MW** 10, 197).[20]

(v) *The Importance of Art*

In the context of his concern for the expressive arts, Dewey begins by making a useful distinction between "statement" and "expression," a distinction which has been neglected—to their detriment—by workers in the field of communicative interaction, such as Habermas.[21] Expression is a completive or consummatory activity for Dewey, and contrasts with statement, which is directive, as in experimental science, and transitive. Statement only leads to an experience; expression constitutes or is one. Scientific symbols don't express meanings, they state them. Poems and paintings guide attention, but they do not operate in the dimension of *directive* or scientific statement; they operate in (or as) experience itself. Poetry deals as directly as possible with the qualities of situations, in such a way as to express their meanings, and to create in us an unhindered response informed by just these meanings.[22]

Scientific symbols, in semiotic terms, are dicent thirds, and not iconic, except incidentally or in a sublated way. They abstract from the manifest qualities of things and processes, in such a way as to protect the experimenter from the emotional factor in his effort to get nomothetic (theoretic) and technological control over objective conditions. While there is no thinking without feeling in both scientific inquiry and art, in inquiry the technique consists in the use of symbols that neutralize emotion. In poetry, however, in artistic thinking or construction, the symbols used or invented transform and inform, i.e., express, the feelings generative of (and generated by) the productive or exhibitive activity of the artist, whether literary, visual or musical.

Dewey brings good insights to his explanation of poetic communication. "Prose is set forth in propositions. The logic of poetry is superpropositional even when it uses what are, grammatically speaking, propositions. The latter have intent; art is an immediate realization of intent" (**AE** 85). The logic of poetry is animistic (**EN** 181ff.). With words or signs, we relate to or prepare to act upon, things indirectly. But because signs can also represent the traits or consequences of things which make them interesting to us, signs are also used to act upon things, as if they were *unmediatedly* responsive to human purposes. They are called upon or addressed directly, animistically. What has happened is that properties of communicative interaction between humans, have been made properties of the way humans interact with things.

However, the way in which the individual's primary or gross experience becomes reflective gets described by Dewey in connection with problem-solving *only*. So, for Dewey, the process of experiencing is one in which the individual copes with problems encountered as s/he interacts with his or her world. Experience is both a doing and an undergoing in Dewey, structured mainly by a funding of the conscious and active manipulations, or means, by which the individual has previously solved his problems or attained his ends. It is only occasionally, among his adaptations or interactions, that an experience occurs in which its phases are harmonized into a meaningful whole, by or for the individual. These are the experiences which Dewey calls "consummatory." Consummatory experiences are the outcomes of successful expression, expression being a *transformation* of materials in which materials become the *medium* within which the constructed meaningful wholes are realized.

The reader will find a considered critique of Dewey's conception of experience in the chapter on Buchler below. But a difficulty that may at once by mentioned is pointed out by the latter in **TGT** (xxxv). This is that it is not clear in Dewey why *any* experienced event is not integral in its own way.[23] The difficulty is compounded by the fact that an experience, other than a successful experiment, gets its integrity, for Dewey, from felt qualities, and these are said to be indescribable. Buchler's criticism is addressed to Dewey's concept of experience as over-emphasizing the conscious and instrumental phases of it, where I am concerned, besides, with the incompleteness in his account of art and expression of these *as reflective* processes.

For, there are plenty of non-routinized *methodic*—and, therfore, reflective—activities (among them artistic and political activities) which are not attempts to solve problems. And it is rather in artistic activity that we may find the prototype for these other kinds of experience. Not all tasks to be accomplished are problems to be solved; not all explorations are inquiries. Much query is not in terms of formulated principle, namely, not all interrogation of nature or society is hypothetico-deductive. The shaping of materials, or completion of a work, may include some problem-solving but are not primarily problem-solving activities. Some adaptations may be as much a matter of drift, as of anything else. The impulse toward self-development, like the process of intellectual discovery or growth, involves much more than problem-solving and does not occur only at the level of consciousness. The learning of a language is, in some of these respects, like the effort of an individual to achieve his potential. Most important, it will be noticed that all of the above kinds of activity, are both communicative activities and presuppose what we may call the socio-existential matrix of individual life.

And if, as Dewey says (**EN** 128), "thing[s] are more significantly what [they] make possible than what they immediately [are]," how much the more is this function of perceptivity present in objects of artistic contrivance, built as these are out of allusiveness and suggestion. If what a 'cognitive' object 'portends' is its practical consequences, and if this is also, as Dewey says, "the first step away from oppression by immediate things," then when these are manipulated "so as to render them contributory to desired objects," as in art, then their artistically developed significance must be all the more liberating and all the more sharable. We see again, that once Dewey has (correctly) conceptualized communication as sharing rather than as linear transmission of discrete bits of information, he cannot consistently maintain that "language" is what makes communication possible without widening it to mean all kinds of signs, as in semiotics.

Art as Experience was an outgrowth of the ten lectures he gave at Harvard as the first appointee of the newly-instituted William James Lectureship in 1931. But it was published at a time when Dewey, true to his social conscience as well as himself, had been rewriting his portion of the Dewey and Tufts *Ethics*, preparing the new edition of *How We Think*, and involved in the affairs of Local No.5 of the American Federation of Teachers (which the communists took over, and from which he resigned).[24] Dewey's thinking about art had been stimulated by his friendship with Albert C. Barnes who, nine years earlier, had established the Barnes Foundation, with Dewey the main speaker at its dedication in 1925. Both Barnes and the Foundation's educational director, Violette de Mazia, attest to Dewey's influence on Barnes. The latter was first impressed by Dewey's *Democracy and Education* (1916); and Barnes dedicated his 1925 book, *The Art in Painting* to Dewey. Earlier fruit of Dewey's reflections on art can, of course, be found in the central chapters of **EN** (published in 1925) from which we have been quoting. W. Shack tells us, in *Art and Argyrol* (p. 191), that Dewey actually led a Barnes Foundation student group through the museums of Madrid, Paris, and Vienna in 1926. Barnes thought so highly of Dewey that, as of 1940, he granted him a pension of $5000 a year for life (**AA** 315).[25]

Now, Dewey's lifelong concern was to combat in their *cultural* or *institutional* forms, the overstated antitheses which occur as conceptual dualisms in rationalism and empiricism. And one greatly disturbing such distinction was the one, now almost defunct, between "fine art" and "useful art." He saw that it was "based simply on acceptance of certain existing *social* conditions" (**AE** 33).[26] So, when Dewey is accused of "sociologism" because of such contextualism and because of his finding that all psychology is *social* psychology (**EN** 84ff.), we have to say in his defense that Dewey's contextualism is not reductive, for it does not *explain away* the integrity of the objects, events, or texts he is analyzing. Because Dewey's experimentalism or, better, his *transformationism* is that of a social observer and critical analyst of human institutions, his history of philosophy is never polemical but always dialectical; it is rehearsed with a view to the *applicability* of the insights to be gotten from it. We note, also, that abolition of the distinction restores the *continuity* between human activities, which are only different in being worthwhile in different respects. It is clear that Dewey, in his philosophy of art as much as in his other work, was trying to have an effect upon the life of the existential communities upon which his thinking impinges.

More generally, we can now see that Dewey's words—that all of his works—are the concomitants of his *activist*, lifelong effort to *change* undemocratic or uncreative social arrangements; and that, for Dewey's pragmatism, philosophies, as reflective thinking are not simply the products of different "cognitive styles," but imaginative or ingenious rational responses to *existential* problems encountered by reflective individuals who, in trying to solve them, give them as intelligent and consequential a formulation as possible. As a categorization of philosophic activity, Dewey would have found the notion of "cognitive styles"—invoked by both 'analytic' and 'pluralist' philosophers—to be one which wrenches philosophy from its proper focus upon the problems of socio-intellectual culture. I believe we can say that Dewey would have found the notion superficial, and the kind of philosophizing which bred it just that kind of theorizing which, for Dewey, qualifies as less than intelligent practice. For, Dewey's distinctions are not theoretical, but between kinds of *practice*. As he says (**EN**, **LW**1 268f.), "it would then be seen that science is an art, that art is a practice, and that the only distinction worth drawing is not between practice and theory, but between those modes of practice that are not intelligent . . . and those which are full of enjoyed meanings."

It is unfortunate that readers of Dewey and other classic pragmatists, who come to them from other traditions, continue to believe—or act as if they believed—that pragmatism is neutral in relation to the cognitive importance of art. It's as if, to these traditions, the human and intellectual data gatherable from art and the aesthetic experience could be safely omitted from the initial phases of philosophic reflection about human experience or culture. Now, that this could be done has long been a belief of positivism. So, to this extent, current orthodoxies and the neo-, or para-pragmatist readers of Dewey are still dualistic in the sense of perpetuating the central misleading *discontinuity* between the arts and the sciences which Dewey and the classic American thinkers have made it their business to overcome.[27] Perhaps the time is near when Dewey will be re-read, and understood, (i) in the light of his change of emphasis in the later works from the misunderstood "method of experience" to "the method of cultural analysis," and (ii) in the context of the failure of other philosophic traditions to deal adequately either with art and the human sciences or with the relations of these to the natural sciences and social practices.

The above-mentioned inability to deal adequately with the phenomena of art is a corollary of views which hold that art is a kind of representation, and that the core of representation is *reference*, a dyadic relation which gives rise to meaning. One such view of art is Nelson Goodman's for whom 'reference' is the term which subsumes all the sorts of 'symbolization,' namely, "all cases of standing for" (**MOM** p.55), and for whom also reference is *dyadic* (**LA** 143).[28] 'Denotation' for Goodman is that subspecies of reference in which "a word or picture or other label [is applied] to one or many things (**ibid.**). And the labels that may be applied to an artwork (the properties that may be attributed to it) may be either "literal" or "metaphoric;" so that, when the denotating or exemplifying is "metaphorical," then the 'reference' is said by Goodman to be an "expression."

A symphony, for example, may 'express' certain emotions (metaphorically), but does not 'express' its own properties literally.

Literal, or 'instantiating,' reference can be illustrated by the texture or color of a piece of cloth. But since "not all the countless features of the work matter . . . but only those qualities and relationships of color or sound, those spatial and temporal patterns, and so on [matter] that the work exemplifies," the work has to be selective in referring to them (**MOM** 60). And there will be variation in the properties of the artwork selected to give it meaning, self-referential as this kind of reference ultimately is. And this is what creates ambiguity of expression in the metaphorical exemplifications of which art or symbols consist.

Even if art-symbols, for Goodman, are allowed to create in some sense their own reference, what, in his theory, accounts for the kind of referring that the symbols perform? For him, it is the practice of those who use the symbol system that determines the correlations with 'the field of reference.' In this view, it is the historical (and codifying?) practice of composition that determines—it is supposed—what literal properties or labels are appropriate in a musical expression. A passage could be said to be "mocking," for instance, or "pleading" only by contrast with some presupposed *literal* description in terms of key, tempo, and rhythm. But this does not get at the fact that it is *the way in which* the musical labels or terms are taken or read that actually determines the composition's expressive nature. Identification of 'metaphorical exemplifications' of 'labels' or 'properties' cannot do the job of grasping how the composition is shaped or hangs together as a qualitative communicative act. There is already in the key chosen, the tempo selected, and the rhythm mandated, an initial determinacy that Goodman's category of 'reference' as a 'standing for' completely misses.

This, in other words, is an aesthetics that cannot account for what is artistic about art.[29] We have digressed to consider it because it also fails to account for expression, for the nature of metaphor, or for the difference between propositional and qualitative, or medium-bound thinking. It is fairly certain that a view of 'denotation' which claims that "unicorn" or "Pickwick" denotes nothing will certainly not be able to account for literary or poetic meaning. Not only is it *not ordinal* in its view of the *existence* of material and imaginative objects, it also has no sense of the *interpretive* dimension of semiosis. And it is shot through with dualisms, discontinuities, and elisions. Thus, for example, to take appropriateness as a matter of arbitrary convention or codification is to split phenomena from perception; for, appropriateness is controlled by the attributes of the phenomenon, the design of the artist, and the values and assumptions of the maker and perceiver. Works-of-art are (at least) dicents, not things; but in treating them as so many objects, Goodman, does not adequately distinguish between kinds of objects either. Nor, without a theory of interpretation and with a dyadic view of reference, can he account for the meaning of objects when they have it.[30] Given that the *Languages of Art* is statedly *not* concerned with the aesthetic aspects of art, it can claim to be dealing with art at all only within the *pervasively reductionist* and dualistic habits of thought or climate of opinion first introduced by positivism.

The problem of the identity of the work-of-art will find its solution in Buchler's account of human products and the identity of natural complexes in their many integrities (in Chapter IV). Here we will look at what Dewey has to say about the expressiveness of works of art, and about them in their relation to culture. Works-of-art are constructed signitive complexes. And meanings, for Dewey, are qualities of objects when they are caught up in shared responses. Meanings are a function of human behavior in which objects are dealt with cooperatively or responded to participatively. And an experience is artistic when it is a response to an event having form, duration, and consummation.

Dewey is no emotionalist about art or in his theory of expression, as some of his latest readers seem to want him to be. Emotion, in Dewey and in psychology generally, is any activation or agitation of the human organism. This has to be made clear because, in covering everything that emotion is not, Dewey forgets to tell us what it is. But it also has to be remarked that in Dewey, interested as he was in the continuities among observable processes, emotion is more than just physiological. It seems to be the stage in the process by which sheer response, or energy, becomes feeling, and feeling foreshadows conscious awareness. So he considers that emotional discharge is perhaps a necessary but certainly not a sufficient condition of expression. He insists, however, that as a discharge, emotion to become available to expression must be expended *indirectly upon* objective materials.

But emotion or energy is not all that is aroused in the manipulation of objective, resistant materials. There is also a "qualitative . . . transformation of energy into thoughtful action. . . ." Things in the environment become, "are seized upon" as "means, media" to some end in the light of their possibilities (**AE** 60). Artistic construction, and appreciation, are for Dewey "as much a case of genuine thought as that expressed in scientific and philosophical matters" (**AE** 116). There has to be, in creation, "administration of subjective conditions"; hence emotion is always *about* something objective, or *to* or *from* it.[31]

Emotion, in other words, is *from the first* and increasingly intellectualized. Emotion is always implicated in a situation. Short of complete panic or blind thrashings and dischargings, excitement will utilize motor channels of action already worn by dealings with objects and will envelop such objects as it finds to the purpose with its own developing quality (**AE** 66-67). The fallacy which Dewey is exposing here is "the notion that an emotion is complete in itself within, only when uttered having impact upon external material" (**ibid.**). For example, team elation in a victory, or sorrow upon the death of a friend, cannot be understood except as interpenetrations of selves with objective conditions:

Save nominally, there is no such thing as *the* emotion of fear, hate, love. The unique, unduplicated character of experienced events and situations impregnates the emotion that is evoked. Were it the function of speech to reproduce that to which it refers, we could never speak of fear, but only of fear-of-this particular-oncoming-automobile, with all its specifications of time and place. . . . A life time would be too short to reproduce in words a single emotion. . . . poet and novelist have an immense advantage over even an expert psychologist in dealing with an emotion. For the former build up a concrete situation and permit it to evoke emotional response. Instead of a description of an emotion in intellectual and symbolic terms, the artist "does the deed that breeds" the emotion (**AE** 67).

There are, then, no singular or atomic emotions-in-themselves; emotion is always individuated or differentiated by reference to its objects.

The question which arises, however, is whether emotion is causally operative in the process of artistic production, and whether some other factors are not also operative. In Yvor Winters' poetics, for instance, the feelings in a poem are motivated by concepts; he says that any rational statement will govern the general possibilities of feeling derivable from it, and that the task of the poet is to adjust feeling to motive with precision. "He has to select words containing not only the right relationships within themselves, but the right relationships to each other" (**IDR** 367). Winters' position is—in his words—both that the motive for the poem is its rational meaning, and that a work of poetic art is a statement about an experience in which special pains have been taken with the expression of feeling (**IDR** 363, 491).

The contrast with Dewey's view is more apparent than real; the latter preferred to say that the poem *is* an experience, but he too explained judgment as a kind of adjustment. Dewey maintains, as a result of his observation, that emotion is pointedly operative; that, for instance, "the determination of the *mot juste* . . . is accomplished by emotion" (**AE** 70). In line with his emphasis on quality, Dewey also finds that emotion works to effect continuity of movement and singleness of effect amid variety in artworks. But it is harder see that, by itself, emotion is also *selective* of material and directive of its order and arrangement, unless we are allowed to stipulate that the kind of emotion within which works-of-art are generated is necessarily highly processed, and already reflective—else it would not be able to discern latent appropriatenesses and associations. If this qualifier applies, however, then the position is not so different from Winters'; for Winters is also aware that emotion and reason are simultaneously and inextricably operative in any statement or expression. His intellectualism—except for his belief that poetry is "statement"— then becomes as indistinguishable from Dewey's emphasis upon the role of intelligence in the task of creative selection as emotionalized intelligence is from intellectualized emotion.

For there to be expression, according to Dewey, the primitive or "raw" material of experience has to be reworked. By expression, however, he means the double process, the interaction, by which the artist, with (i) his store of already worked experience and (ii) his exploratory or constructive intent, transforms materials into a work-of-art. Dewey notes with respect to the physical materials that everyone knows that they must undergo change, but that it is not so generally recognized that a similar transformation takes place on the side of "inner" materials—images, observations, memories. The design itself of the work changes, in so far as it is emergent and modified, as the work is carried forward to completion. And, Dewey insists "the work is artistic" only "in the degree in which the *two* functions of transformation are effected by a *single* operation" (**AE** 75). In expression,

> everything depends upon the way in which material is used when it operates as a medium . . . it takes environing and resisting objects as well as internal emotion and impulsion to constitute an expression. . . . The act of expression that constititutes a work of art is a construction in time, not an instantaneous emission . . . the expression of the self in and through a medium, constituting a work of art is itself a prolonged interaction of something issuing from the self with objective conditions, a process in which *both* . . . acquire a form and order they did not at first possess. (**AE** 63-65)

The better to note the characteristic anti-dualistic emphasis which Dewey puts on the observation that expression is a *double transformation*, it is worth quoting another passage (**AE** 75):

> whether a musician, a painter, or architect works out his original emotional idea in terms of auditory or visual imagery or in the actual medium as he works is of . . . minor importance. For the imagery is of the objective medium undergoing development. The physical media may be ordered in imagination or in concrete material. Only by progressive organization of 'inner' and 'outer' material in organic

connection with each other can anything be produced that is not a learned document or an illustration of something familiar.

The emphasis on the continuity between inner and outer implies that the personal pole of the process of expression may not be isolated from the expressiveness of objective materials. It is also typical of Dewey, as it was of Peirce, that he insists on the objective reference of the feelings operative in expression. Human or psychic energy is called up and thrown into commotion by some need or some condition of the environment, and would without an expressive act of some kind brim over. But in the expressive act energy is put to work on objective materials; it is a little as if the waters themselves were put to work in building the very dams and breakwaters which make them usable:

> Unless there is com-pression nothing is ex-pressed. The turmoil marks the place where inner impulse and contact with environment, in fact or in idea, meet and create a ferment. . . . Hence it is not mere excitement that is expressed, but *excitement-about-something* (**AE** 66,my italics).

The thing expressed, Dewey says, is wrung from the producer by the pressure exercised by objective things upon the natural impulses and tendencies. For example, raging is distinct from expressing rage in a series of sharp-edged phrases. The human being has to become aware of the intent implicit in his impulsion. Only then are the attitudes of the self informed with meaning. As already noted, when energy is generated so are meanings called up, at the same time, from past experience:

> The quality of what is seen and heard varies with past experience. The scope of a work of art is measured by the number and variety of elements coming from past experience that are organically absorbed into the perception had here and now (**AE** 123).

Expression will, in general, consist of the fusing of emotive ideational "materials" with more sensuous and physical materials, of the suffusing of a medium with developed quality, feeling, or allusiveness. In art as in science, according to Dewey, "there is emotionalized thinking, and there are feelings whose substance consists of appreciated meanings or ideas" (**AE** 73). So that, in general the real *work* of art is the building up of an integral experience out of interactions of the human psychosocial organism with environmental conditions and energies.

Dewey is pointedly sensitive to the distinctive nature of meaning in the arts:

> Thinking directly in terms of colors, tones, images is a different operation technically from thinking in words. . . . If all meanings could be adequately expressed by words, the arts of painting and music would not exist. There are values and meanings that can be expressed only by immediately visible and audible qualities, and to ask what they mean in the sense of something that can be put into words is to deny their distinctive existence (**AE** 73-74).

In everyday practical semioses which carry no self-reference, the sign or symbol points to or stands for something other than itself. Dewey's view here is that meaning belongs to the sign only by convention, not in its own right. Art lets us see that:

> there are other meanings that present themselves as directly as possessions of objects which are experienced. Here there is no need for a code or convention of interpretation; the meaning is as inherent in immediate experience as is that of a flower garden (**AE** 83).

Dewey's views on art and expression will not be understood if we do not appreciate that, like Peirce, he believed feeling to be cognitive and proto-poetic, as we might put it. Thus his view that expression is a clarification of turbid emotion is intelligible by reference to his account of the process as one in which emotion is polarized about selected materials which are reformed, informed, or transformed in the light of the artist's expressive design, and which are used to exhibit what he has to express. The artist, by feeling about things in certain ways, makes something out of them. And the validity of what he makes of them is not to be judged according to standardized criteria, for the reason that the context of signification in which he is developing his plastic or acoustic ideas, allows for the interest by going beyond *old* criteria of meaningful expression. If any standards are to be applied they must be those of purely felt sequentiality and aptness, and ultimately of the kind of consummatoriness that the experience affords. And this is so because the context in art is a search for the kind of satisfaction which supervenes, without further action, upon realized meanings.

If emotion, attitude, suggestion, and interpretation are the personal contribution of the artist, what he expends upon his materials and what they draw out of him in given contexts, then expression is *inventive*. But insofar as the created significance is shared by others, there is communication. Thus, expression is also a social process and functions as *discovery*. The artist has indeed "made something intelligible" in the two important senses of these words.

For Dewey and for pragmatism, qualities are brought out from nature in the same sense, say, that gasoline is derived or produced, by human industry, from raw materials. Dewey no more *imputes* qualities to nature than gasoline is imputed to crude oil. Nor is gasoline any the less discovered in crude oil because it has to be manufactured or extracted from it. Just as in inquiry, attributes belong not to the problematic things inquired into (what Dewey calls the "subject-matter" in the *Logic*), but to the *objective* of inquiry, i.e., to the "objects of knowledge" which are the consummation of inquiry— so, in the process of art, it is the *outcome* of expression, i.e. the work-of-art, which exhibits the qualities felt to be immediate or moving. The way J.H. Randall puts it in Chapter 10 of *Nature and Historical Experience* makes Dewey's meaning clearer, namely, that one of the things works-of-art do is to "immediatize" experience as well as order it. Works-of-art, Randall says, "qualify" the human pole of the aesthetic transaction with "immediacy."

Because the experience of art is shared and immediatized, it puts the participants into a special relation with their surroundings. The creative or selective transformation of the material drawn into experience both enhances the vitality and consciousness of the interaction which human living is, and reveals unsuspected possibilities and continuities in it:

> The moments when the creature is both most alive and most composed and concentrated are those of fullest intercourse with the environment in which sensuous material and relations are most completely merged (**AE** 103).

Now it is this merging of the ideational with the emotional, of the sensuous with the relational, the motor with the sensory, that constitutes the expressiveness of objects. But the expressiveness of objects is generally overlooked in quotidian and practical contexts. Routine "apathy and torpor conceal this expressiveness by building a shell about them" first, and then lull us into believing that the form we take them to have in our practical intercourse with them is fixed and necessary:

> The conception that objects have fixed and unalterable values is precisely the prejudice from which art emancipates us. The intrinsic qualities of things come out with startling vigor and freshness just because conventional associations are removed (**ib.**95). . . . Art throws off the covers that hide the expressiveness of experienced things; it quickens us from the slackness of routine and enables us to forget ourselves by finding ourselves in the delight of experiencing the world about us in its varied qualitative form (**ib.**104).

Dewey, like Aristotle, rightly distinguishes art, which they both consider a knowledgeable and *productive* activity, from contemplation. Where the Aristotelian corpus deems contemplation a high point in the theoretical or knowledge-seeking life, for Dewey it is simply aesthetic in the original, etymological sense of "aesthetic," and affective only (**EN** 356). Art, for both of them—as it is for every artist—is an affair of practice, a point which too many aestheticians forget. But this is not the contrast in which modern thinkers are as much interested as they are in Dewey's opposition of expression, as terminal or completive activity and consummatory interaction, to statement, which is directive, as in modern experimental science, and transitive, as we saw above. Expression, unlike statement, constitutes an experience, *is* one. Accordingly he observes that poems or paintings do not operate in the dimension of directive or scientific statement, but in the dimension of experience itself.

The poet, as we said above, deals directly with the qualities of situations in such a way as to express their meaning, and to release in us a response informed only by these meanings and otherwise unfettered. The scientist deals with things at one remove, through the instrumentality of symbols that stand for qualities or properties indirectly, but which are not themselves immediately significant. Scientific symbols do not possess the qualities they stand for. Scientific symbols do not express meanings, they simply state them, and are of the nature of directions couched in such a way as to protect the agent from interference by the emotional factor in achieving the control which he seeks, for scientific purposes, over objective conditions. While there is emotionalized thinking in both science and art, as noted earlier, in science the technique consists in the use of symbols that neutralize emotion.

In poetry, on the contrary, in artistic thinking or construction, the symbols used or invented are such as will express the emotion in which the productive activity is involved. We saw that the logic of poetry, as Dewey propounded it in *Experience and Nature*, is animistic: words are used, as if magically, to act directly upon things in order to bring about a revelation of their latent powers. Things are invoked, or events conjured, as if they were amenable to human purposes. And the extraordinary thing about poetic communication is—that things do answer, are made to answer by it. And this is a consequence of the direct transfer of properties of the social situation of communication between persons, to an immediate relationship of things to a person. The expressiveness of things is developed for the sake of the immediate—not unmediated, but not instrumental— satisfactions which things or events may yield. Not only is an intent participated in by the reader, but an experience is enacted by him, either as poet or in the footsteps of the poet.

Like mimetic-making in Aristotle, expression for Dewey is a process directed towards a certain end, but the end is not something fully resist spiritually crippling conventions in search of fresher and freer coherences. "Creation," he says,

> is like civilization: it supposes an uninterrupted tension between form and matter, between evolution and the mind, history and values. If the equilibrium is destroyed there is dictatorship or anarchy, propaganda or formalist fantasy. . . . creation, which coincides with rational freedom, becomes impossible (p.270f.).

That art and civilization are not separate enterprises, as both the existentialist and the pragmatist are saying, cannot be repeated too often and should not be neglected in our smaller scale cooperative undertakings. We do almost all we do by art or culture. Man has, instead of biological speciation, his cultural adaptations or arts. And of these it has ever been said that the intellectual arts are those that free men most to be themselves.[34] The arts are not the fine late flower of civilization, as Dewey and Véron inistently remind us, not the fugitive bloom on civilizations as they emerge into the sun, but the very germ and active principle of culture-building from the ground up.[35]

Man and his arts were born together, however long they may have been aborning; the human process of adaptation is fundamentally artful. The global large-scale maladaptations which now threaten us, like our local ecologic and political devastations, are negative proof of the point that, without art—without thoughtful or humanizing contrivance—the process of living itself breaks down. Art must come out of "the beauty parlor of civilization," as Dewey said (**AE** 344), and into our factories, bureaucracies, and enterprises—not to mention our politicized, nepotized, and neglected universities—before either our *culture* or our *society* can be secure or even healthy.

For Dewey (as we know), it is a failure of education when the culture, in its transmission, is *not renewed*, and when the democratic culture does *not*—on the ideal model of self-correcting science and the constructive accumulation of artistic techniques—*correct* itself. Given that the general theory of education does not at bottom differ, for Dewey, from what we call philosophy, the measure of the failure foreseen and preconceive—as any artist we may wish to consult wil tell us. It has often been remarked that the greater the art the greater is the unexpectedness—and memorability—of what the art works out.[32] It should be noted, however, that art has not just the effect on us of discovery, but is itself a process of discovery. The work-of-art does not exist until it is made; and this is true even when the artist is in possession of the power to make it before he actually does so. But it will also be true of the artist that every work-of-art he makes is, in some way, a development of his powers.

Expression is not of objects of knowledge. These are instrumental and entirely conventional, the objects of scientific statement. It should be noted, all the same, that the first formal and well-formulated assertion of a scientific hypothesis may have, as discovery, much in common with an artistic expression. The expressive object is an object of, and for, creative experience, the enactment of an integral response in a given medium formally reworked. It is the outcome of a constructive process in which the qualities of the environment or of any objective material are immediatized, and in which therefore the significance of these qualities requires—it is worth repeating—no code or convention of interpretation in order to be appreciated. The similarities as well as the differences between the objects of science and the objects of art are, perhaps, best caught in the following insight of Dewey's:

> We are aware that thinking consists in ordering a variety of meanings so that they move to a conclusion that all support and in which all are summed up and conserved. What we perhaps are less cognizant of is that this organization of energies to move cumulatively to a terminal whole in which the values of all means and media are incorporated is the essence of art (**AE** 172).

It is heartening that the French activist and thinker Albert Camus thought, like Dewey, that art as a technical activity should be the model for those who seek freedom in free societies.[33] He too saw that the way in which the artist brings refractory thematic materials and resistant physical materials to expressiveness in genuine stylistic unities, is quite analogous to the procedures of creative revolt which of today's philosophy to be doing one of the most important tasks that falls to it is, in Deweyan terms, enormous: a tidal wave of a failure, and a gaping breach-by-omission of the intellectual ramparts of civilized humanity itself.

Notes

1. For a development of this point, see T.Z. Lavine "John Dewey and the Founders: Human Nature and Politics," *Works and Days* Vol.3, No.2 (1985); p.53-75.

2. "John Dewey's Metaphysics of Experience," *Journal of Philosophy* LVIII (1961); p. 5-14. Don't those who claim that Dewey's is a metaphysics of experience thereby negate their recognition of Dewey's characteristic contextualism as socio-existential? "Metaphysical description and understanding," he says in "The Inclusive Philosophic Idea" (**LW**3, 42), "has to do with the widest and fullest range of *associated* activity"; and by "associated," here, Dewey means relationally involved and locatable in more than one context.

3. John Dewey, "Body and Mind," **LW**3, 25.

4. John Dewey, In "American Education and Culture," (**MW**10, 197).

5. Malinowski's cited phrases are given as being from his article "Culture" in the *Encyclopaedia of the Social Sciences*, Vol.4.

6. Lavien, "John Dewey and the Founders: Human Nature and Politics;" *op.cit.* p.71.

7. See, for example, H.F.May *The End of American Innocence 1912-1917* (N.Y. Knopf 1959); D.W.Noble *The Progressive Mind 1890-1917* (Minneapolis: Burgess 1981); J.Weiss, Ed. *The Origins of Modern Consciousness* (Wayne State U.P. 1965), with John Higham's essay "The Re-Orientation of American Culture in the 1890's." For the deep background, see e.g., W.O.Clough *Intellectual Origins of American National Thought* (N.Y. Corinth Books 1961), and R.Hofstadter *The Progressive Historians* (N.Y. Vintage 1970).

8. Morton White, *Social Thought in America: The Revolt against Formalism* (Boston: Beacon 1957)

9. See A. Berleant "The Eighteenth-Century Assumptions of Analytic Aesthetics," in Lavine & Tejera *History & Anti-History in Philosophy* (Dordrecht: Kluwer 1989), and, e.g., T. Adorno *Against Epistemology A Metacritique* Tr. W.Domingo (Cambridge: M.I.T. 1983), in addition to Peirce's famous but unheeded "Concerning Certain Faculties Claimed for

Man," and "Consequences of Four Incapacities." Dewey's most concentrated critiques of Empiricism are in *Human Nature and Conduct* 1922 (**MW**14, p.3-24), and "An Empirical Survey of Empiricisms" 1935 (**LW**11, p.69-83).

10. See also James Gouinlock *Excellence in Public Discourse: John Stuart Mill, John Dewey and Social Intelligence* (N.Y.: Teachers College Press 1986); p.110-151.

11. For Machiavelli, cf. Chapter 8 of **CSFWPT**; for Shakespeare, "Santayana and the Western Tradition," *Papers of The 1992 Intl. Conference on Santayana*, Avila, Spain.

12. In his Introduction to *Experience and Nature* **LW**1, p.xiv.

13. Note the temerity of some of Hook's phrasing, "Dewey . . . as I would revise him," or "Dewey would have done well in my view to modify his conception of metaphysics and . . ." (ibid. p.xvi and p. xiv). Dewey does *not* in fact believe that metaphysics "is an independent discipline that gives us knowledge of the world that we cannot reach by any other study," as we shall see. He does believe "that what it gives us knowledge about are generic traits," but *not* that they are "discoverable in any subject-matter or every universe of discourse" (ib.). The last four cited words belong, in fact, to the Hutchinsite attack on Dewey's contextualism. See especially L. Hahn "Dewey's Philosophy and Philosophic Method," in *Guide to the Works of John Dewey*; R. Sleeper *The Necessity of Pragmatism: Dewey's Conception of Philosophy*; and the critique of Hook's interpretations of Dewey to be found in my "Hook's Interpretation of Dewey."

14. In Peirce's and Santayana's sense of speculative. Does the subjectivist view of experience or culture have to be met here with the reminder that institutions are themselves existences, so that Dewey is not in conflict with his other claim that metaphysics studies the generic traits of existence?

15. Let it be noted here that it is not good history of philosophy to speak (as some do) of "Dewey's break with British Empiricism." While Dewey was "empirical," "experiential," and "existential" in the senses explained, he was *always* a critic of that particular -ism, never a part of it. So, Lovejoy confuses Dewey's demand for 'direct' *observations* with 'direct experience,' and Dewey's '*experimental* empiricism' (**MW** 13, 389) with a 'principle of immediate empiricism" (cf. **MW** 15, 350). "Not safely," said Dewey, "can an -ism be made out of experience" (Apdx. to Experience and Nature, **LW** 1, 367). (Cf. also Dewey's "Empirical Survey of Empiricisms," **LW** 11, 69-83.)

16. As we know, teamwork makes intellectual demands of the same order as those made by language. Psychologically it may, in fact, be difficult to distinguish between the two. Cf. e.g., Hebb and Thompson in Lindsey's *Handbook of Social Psychology* (Addison-Wesley 1955).

17. J.N. Spuhler in *The Evolution of Man's Capacity for Culture* (Wayne State U.P. 1958).

18. Cf. B.J. Singer "Dewey's Concept of Community," *Journal of the History of Philosophy* 23, No.4 (1985); p.555-570.

19. See Chapter IV below, and Buchler on 'community' and 'proceptive parallelism' in **TGT**, p.33-45.

20. About Santayana, Buchler says "He revolutionized naturalism by giving it a new freedom of expression and a new vocabulary . . . widening the scope of its inventiveness. . . . He was a powerful analyst . . . of structures . . . and of grand and intricate structures. . . . In helping naturalism out of its starkness and rigidity, he showed what it was in other traditions that was available to liberal understanding," in *Animal Faith and the Spiritual Life*, ed. J.Lachs (N.Y. Appleton-Century 1967).

21. Cf. "Community, Communication, and Meaning in the Theories of Habermas and Buchler," *Symbolic Interaction* 9:1 (1986); p.83-104.

22. See especially especially Ch.5 of *Art as Experience*, "The Expressive Object." See also my *Art and Human Intelligence* Chapters 3-8, for a fuller account of art as expression, and expressiveness in art. I repeat what is stated in *Semiotics From Peirce to Barthes*, that though these chapters, like Dewey's, don't make explicit the distinction—now basic to classic American philosophy—between exhibitive, active, and assertive judgments, they are quite compatible with Buchler's way of categorizing artistic meanings in **TGT, NJ** and **ML**. Buchler's way of distinguishing artistic from scientific judgment is fully ontological, as we shall see. Dewey's distinction is generic only, applying to selected orders (discourse and other signs), not to whatever is. In Buchler, everything discriminable has an *exhibitive* dimension, though it need not be an exihibitive judgment; and all discourse is inclusively either assertive, active, or exhibitive judgment.

23. As Dewey himself says, "no experience of whatever sort is a unity unless it has esthetic quality" (**AE** 47).

24. As Jane Dewey and G. Dykhuizen tell us in, respectively, PJD and LMJD.

25. Laurence Buermeyer was another philosophical beneficiary of Barnes. He was (along with Dewey and Thomas Munro) an Associate of the foundation and author of *The Aesthetic Experience* (The Barnes Foundation 1924), a book that could be no closer to Dewey's *Art As Experience* without being an exposition of it, such as T. Alexander's excellent *John Dewey's Theory of Art, Experience & Nature* (1987). **AE** was published ten years later in 1934. See also L.J. Dennis "Dewey's Debt to Albert C. Barnes," in *John Dewey: Critical Assessments III*, ed. J.E. Tiles (New York: Routledge, 1992).

26. Further aspects of the distinction are dealt with in **AHI** (Chapters 3 and 4), **HAH** (218-19, 223), and my "The Intellectual Content of Hellenistic Alienation," *Proceedings of the International Association for Greek Philosophy*, Rhodes 1992; ed. K Boudouris (Athens: 1993 or 1994).

27. Cf. "The Centrality of Art in Classic American Philosophy," *American Studies* 31.1; Spring 1990; p.83-90.

28. Where we are (rather truistically) told: "A symbol system consists of a symbol scheme correlated with a field of reference."

29. See R. Arnheim "Painted Skies and Unicorns," Review of N. Goodman *Languages of Art*, in *Science* Vol.164, (May 1969); p.697-698; and A. Marsoobian "Rethinking Meaning in the Arts," in *Nature's Perspectives* ed. Marsoobian, Wallace, Corrington (SUNY Press 1991).

30. Nor can he possibly account for the integrity of the work-of-art if, as Rudolph Arnheim points out, a consequence of such theorizing is that the identity of a musical work is not violated when a funeral march is played at the speed of a polka, because of the notational vagueness of tempo in the score. In line with this, it would also follow that there is no such thing as the misreading of literary work. Such a view can find the integrity of a work only in the printed score or printed text of the work.

31. The reader is referred to my *Art and Human Intelligence* for a fuller account, with illustrations, of the relation between emotion and expression in Dewey's aesthetics, and for a fuller exposition of the aesthetic topics covered in this chapter.

32. The performing arts are a test case, here. See, for instance, Mary Drage, "The Dancer," in *The Arts, Artists, and Thinkers*, ed. by J. Todd. (New York: Macmillan 1958). The composer or author in performing arts necessarily gives others an opportunity to contribute creatively, but within limits, to the realization of "his" artistic product. There is a lesson here for reading theory, if we can see reading as a performance.

33. *The Rebel* (N.Y. Knopf, ed. of 1961); pp.268-275.

34. From Aristotle to Mark Van Doren (*N.Ethics* Bk.X, and *Autobiography*, N.Y. Harcourt 1958).

35. Eugène Véron *Aesthetics* Tr. W.H. Armstrong (Philadelphia: Lippincott 1879)

References & Bibliography

T.Alexander	*John Dewey's Theory of Art, Experience & Nature* (SUNY Press: 1987)
Associates	*Essays in Honor of John Dewey* (N.Y. Holt 1929)
J.A.Boydston	*Guide to the Works of John Dewey* (S.Illinois U.P. 1970)
L. Buermeyer	*The Aesthetic Experience* (Merion: The Barnes Foundation 1924)
S.M.CahnEd.	*New Studies in the Philosophy of John Dewey* (University Press of New England 1977)
J.Campbell	"Rorty's Use of Dewey," *The Southern Journal of Philosophy* Vol.22, No.2 (1984)
	"Dewey's Understanding of Marx and Marxism," *Context over Foundation*: Dewey and Marx, ed. W.J. Gavin (Dordrecht: Reidel 1988)
	The Community Reconstructs (U. of Illinois Press 1992)
	"Democracy as Cooperative Inquiry," *Philosophy and the Reconstruction of Culture*: Pragmatic Essays after J. Dewey ed. J. Stuhr (SUNY Press 1993)
	Understanding John Dewey (Open Court 1995)
N.Coughlan	*Young John Dewey* An Essay in American Intellectual History U. of Chicago Press 1975)
John Dewey	*Early Works* 1882-1898, 5 vol. Ed. J.A.Boydston (S.Illinois U.P. 1972)
	Middle Works 1899-1924, 15 vol. Ed. J.A.Boydston (S.Illinois U.P. 1983)
	Later Works 1925-1952, 16 vol. Ed. J.A.Boydston (S.Illinois U.P. 1989)
	J.Dewey and A.F.Bentley A Philosophical Correspondence, Ed. by S.Ratner, J.Altman, J.E.Wheeler (Rutgers U.P. 1964)
G.Dykhuizen	*The Life and Mind of John Dewey* (S.Illinois U.P. 1973)
D.F.Epstein	*The Political Theory of the Federalist* (Chicago U.P. 1984)
N.Goodman	*Languages of Art*: An Approach to a Theory of Symbols (Indianapolis: Bobbs-Merrill 1968)
	Of Mind and Other Matters (Harvard U.P. 1984)

L.Hickman   *John Dewey's Pragmatic Technology* (Indiana U.P. 1990)

R.Hofstadter   *The American Political Tradition and the Men Who Made It* (N.Y. Knopf 1948)

S.Huntington   *American Politics: The Politics of Disharmony* (Harvard U.P. 1981)

C.Lamont   *Dialogue on John Dewey* w. J.T.Farrell, J.Gutmann, A.Johnson, H.M.Kallen, H.W.Laidler, E.Nagel, J.H.Randall, H.Taylor, M.H.Thomas. N.Y. Horizon Press 1959)

T.Lavine   "Pragmatism & the Constitution in the Culture of Modernism," *Transactions of the C.S.Peirce Society* XX, No.1 (1984); 1-19.
                "John Dewey and the Founders: Human Nature and Politics," *Works and Days* Vol.3, No.2 (1985); p.53-75.
                "American Pragmatism: Transference and Aufhebung," *Transactions of the C.S.Peirce Society* XXIV, No.4 (1988): 469-486.

H.F.May   *The Enlightenment in America* (Oxford U.P. 1976)

Morgenbesser   *Dewey and His Critics* (N.Y. *The Journal of Philosophy* 1977)

H.Niles   *Principles and Acts of the Revolution in America* (New York 1876)

C.RossiterEd.   *The Federalist* (New American Library 1961)

A.Ryan   *John Dewey and The High Tide of Liberalism* (N.Y. Norton 1995)

P.A.Schilpp   *The Philosophy of John Dewey* Libr. of Liv. Philosophers (Northwestern U.P. 1939; N.Y. Tudor 1951)

R.Sleeper   *The Necessity of Pragmatism: John Dewey's Conception of Philosophy* (Yale U.P. 1986)

A.H.Somjee   *The Political Theory of John Dewey* (N.Y. Teachers College 1968)

J.E.Tiles   *Dewey* (N.Y. Routledge 1988)
                John Dewey Critical Assessments 4 vol. (N.Y. Routledge 1992)

V. Tejera	"The Human Sciences in Dewey, Foucault, and Buchler," *The Southern Journal of Philosophy* XVIII.2 (1980); 221-235. "Cultural Analysis and Interpretation in the Human Sciences," *Man and World* Vol.12, No.2 (1979); 192-204. "The Centrality of Art in Classic American Philosophy," *American Studies*, 31.1 (Spring 1990) "Community, Communication, and Meaning in the Theories of Habermas and Buchler," *Symbolic Interaction* 9:1 (1986); p.83-104.
J. Todd	Ed. *The Arts, Artists, and Thinkers* (N.Y. Macmillan 1958)
S.J. Tonsor Ed.	*America's Continuing Revolution* (American Enterprise Inst. 1973)
R. Westbrook	*John Dewey and American Democracy* (Cornell U.P. 1991)
I. Winters	*In Defense of Reason* (Denver: Swallow 1947)
G.S. Wood	*Creation of the American Republic, 1776-1787* (Inst. of Early American History and Culture: U. of N.Carolina Press 1969)

Abbreviations

TGT	=	Buchler	Toward a General Theory of Human Judgment
NG	=	" "	Nature and Judgment
ML	=	" "	The Main of Light
JDAD	=	Westbrook	John Dewey and American Democracy
DE	=	Dewey	Democracy & Education
EN	=	" "	Experience & Nature
EW	=	" "	Early Works
MW	=	" "	Middle Works
LSA	=	" "	Liberalism & Social Action
LW	=	" "	Later Works
PIP	=	" "	The Public and Its Problems
AE	=	" "	Art as Experience
LTI	=	" "	Logic: The Theory of Inquiry

PJD	=	Schilpp, ed.	The Philosophy of John Dewey
AI	=	Tejera	Art and Human Intelligence
HAH	=	" "	History as a Human Science
CDFWPT	=	" "	The City-State Foundations of Western Political Thought
MOM	=	Goodman	Of Mind and Other Matters
LA	=	" "	Languages of Art
NHE	=	Randall	Nature and Historical Experience
IDR	=	Winters	In Defense of Reason

Philosophy as a Spiritual Discipline in Santayana: Aesthetics, Metaphysics, and Intellectual History

(i) *Literal and Symbolic Knowledge: Signs, Symbols, and 'Essences'*

In a positivist century in which the mechanicism of the new popular science magazines was not felt to be incompatible with the popularized idealism of the older home journals, Peirce (b. 1839) had found it necessary both to refute the determinist version of mechanicism (1.405-410) and to remind his readers that ideas are of the nature of living things (6.270). That they are so, his younger contemporary George Santayana (b. 1863) had known from the beginning; but Santayana was also to make it his practice to let *his* ideas wear *their* vitality and connectedness on the sleeves, so to say, of their promenading best, as if thinking was as much a well-ordered festivity as a ramified search. So it is relevant, as Richard Robin has pointed out, that Santayana, says "I remember and have often used in my own thought, if not in actual writing, a classification [Peirce] made that evening of signs into 'indexes' . . . 'symbols' and 'images' [i.e. 'icons']."[1] Santayana recalled the same off-campus lecture for Max Fisch, because of its "view that all ideas . . . are signs," adding, "But I have never studied his published works. . . . If he had built his philosophy on signs (sic) I might have been his disciple."[2]

About "works of the human imagination" in general, Santayana had since boyhood felt that "they are good, [and] they alone are good" (**PGS** 7). But about the claims of some systems and thinkers to be in possession of the literal truth, he says:

> As in my younger days in respect to religions, so now in respect to all experience and all science, critical reflection has emancipated me from the horrid claim of ideas to literal truth. And just as religion, when seen to be poetry, ceases to be deceptive . . .[or]. . . odious, and becomes humanly more significant than it seemed before; so experience and science, when seen to be woven out of essences wholly symbolic, gain in moral color and spirituality what they lose in dead weight. The dead weight falls . . . from sensuous images and intellectual myths [on] to the material fatality that breeds and sustains them" (**PGS** 29).

The full reasoning behind this assertion can be found in Santayana's 1918 essay on "Literal and Symolic Knowledge."[3] There he showed that the difficulties that purportedly keep human intelligence from achieving reliable knowledge, arise from false conceptions of what would be success in science or the pursuit of knowledge. One of these false conceptions is that

> knowledge of existence ought to be literal, whereas [in fact] knowledge of existences has no need, no propensity, and no fitness to be literal. It is symbolic spontaneously, and its . . .[moral]. . . function is perfectly fulfilled if it remains symbolical. . . . religion, language, all the passions and science itself speak in symbols; symbols which unify the diffuse processes of nature in adventitious human terms that have an entirely different aspect from the facts they stand for" (**OS** 135).

The scale of the object of knowledge is too often not the scale of our senses (**OS** 126, 133). The biological basis of thought and our mortal condition make *complete* knowledge of anything impossible, if we include all the natural and ideal relations of that thing (**OS** 132). The scientific objects H_2O, $NaCl_2$ and $2\pi r$ are not what is intuited or found *in* nature, but are abstractions—intellectual derivatives—*from* it. They are not what appears to us: they are objects of knowledge, not 'essences' in Santayana's sense. Essences are the 'primitive' terms in any description and, as such, must remain undescribed within that description and left to intuition (**OS** 128).

Now intuition, in Santayana's approach to knowledge and the world, is nothing arrogative or mystical. What intuition intuits Santayana calls essences; as 'images,' 'icons' or sheer possibilities (Peirce's firsts), they are *intransitive*. Perception and belief, on the other hand, are *transitive*. We can be sure of what we see or feel as a visual or sensuous term, as the phaneron that it appears to be, if we take it as what it is and don't think beyond it: if we take it as what Santayana dubs *an essence* and only an essence. What the essence might be the term *for*, what it might *refer to*, however, is not certain. "We might almost say that,"

> sure knowledge, being immediate and intransitive, is not real knowledge, while real knowledge, being transtivie and adventurous, is never sure (**OS** 129).

An intuition, while "choos[ing] its object in the act of determining itself . . . asserts no existence of that object. For it is not the object of knowledge that produces the intuition; it is only the appearance (the essence) that does so. Rather, "the intuition [is] determined in its existence and quality by underlying organic processes, [it] chooses its [immediate] object[4] and lends it for the moment a specious actuality. . ."

Essences are not to be equated with the 'Ideas' of the platonist or Hellenistic systems of idealism. A neoplatonist 'idea,' in fact, is the opposite of an 'essence,' because the Idea is not only what makes the existence of the thing that copies it possible, the platonist's 'Idea' when fully grasped is also our knowledge of the object. From the neoplatonist point of view, in fact, the 'ideas' *as essences* can be said to have been downgraded to less than the status of the *eikasia* on the

Divided Line of the ironically virtuoso Socrates of Plato's *Republic*. The *eikasia* are at least conjectural, but an essence is only what it is, a mere term waiting to be applied.

So it is of essences that *literal* knowledge is possible. In acquiring reference, so to say, the pure rheme becomes 'symbolic' as Santayana says, or 'dicent' or 'legisignitive' as we might say in Peirce's language, and part of a 'symbol' or 'argument.' Improving upon two of Santayana's examples, we might say that until 'rainbow' became a dead metaphor or lexically standard legisign, it was hypoiconic. The 'Great Bear,' remains symbolic, a metaphor; but as a sheer pattern in the sky it was at first an essence, becoming a 'dicisign' as the pattern took on an Ursine aspect. The astrophysical characterization of it is, as a Peircean 'argument,' even more symbolic and indirect or non-literal. But the point of such dicent or argumental categorizations of the phaneron is that they are *functional*. They eventually give us some control over, or get some use from, the objects categorized. "Knowledge of nature," says Santayana, "is a great allegory, of which action is the interpreter" (**OS** 140).

This is wording, we note, that makes visible the affinity between his critical realism and Peirce's pragmaticism. As he says elsewhere, "our ideas are signs, not portions, of what exists beyond us; and it is only when experiment and calculation succeed in penetrating beneath the image that . . . we may gain some more precise, though still symbolic, notion of the forces that surround us" (**BR** 59). In **RM**, moreover, we find a sympathy for *synechism* and *tychism* that would have delighted Peirce.

On the one hand: "Action, when rational, presupposes that the transformations of substance are continuous. . . .(**RM** 42); on the other, "[the] secret flux [of matter]"

> involves at least as many contrasts and variations as the course of nature shows on the surface. Otherwise the ultimate core of existence would not exist, and the causes of variation would not vary. . . . Substance if it is to fulfil the function in virtue, [of] which it is recognized . . . must accordingly be for ever changing its own inner condition. It must be in flux (**RM** 15). . . . there is no assurance that law is constant "(**RM** 111).⁵

Once perceived this affinity is a good safeguard against that hypostatization of essences to which so many of Santayana's readers are prone. Under the hypothesis of continuity, in which the psyche, consciousness, and even spirit are explained as manifestations of matter, there is no "gulf that is digged between matter and essence" in Santayana, as Randall claimed (**AFSL** 99); nor does he hypostatize essences any more than Peirce hypostatizes firsts, qualisigns, icons or rhemes. And there can be no mistake that Santayana's repudiation of the neoplatonists' Ideas, mentioned above, operates with equal force in his sublation of Locke's 'simple' and 'complex' ideas.[6]

(ii) *The Pursuit of Ideal Meanings*

Looking at the sum of his works, we see that much of Santayana's original thinking was done hand in hand with interpretive recapitulations of Western intellectual developments related to the problems he was thinking about. Like Peirce who lectured on "Lessons from the History of Science," and was deeply-read in the philosophers of the past, like Royce who wrote a history of California and who shared with Dewey a Hegelian awareness of the continuity of the present with the past, like Mead who wrote chapters on the history of nineteenth-century French thought, Santayana practiced philosophy under a clear awareness of the history of his subject and his continuity with it, as well as of his place within it.[7]

More than that, his philosophizing is often simultaneously a practice of intellectual history which both advances his subject and makes it clearer than otherwise to the reader. It is the success of this practice that makes Santayana not only a transmitter of the Western intellectual tradition but also a renewer of it.[8] This is worth noting, at a time of spiritual illness in which, as Solzhenitsyn has said, "the spiritual axis of life has grown dim," in which "a denial of any and all ideas is considered courageous," and in which

> we can see that behind . . . ubiquitous . . . seemingly innocent experiments of rejecting 'antiquated' traditions there lies a deep-seated hositility toward any spirituality.[9]

When Santayana addresses the changes in belief that make up our intellectual past, he also takes note of the socio-existential antecedents that precipitated the changes, and to which they were a response. In analysing the adequacy of the response to the need that called it out, Santayana not only helps us to understand it in terms of its own assumptions and relations to the opinions it was displacing, but he also highlights the human questions to which the new doctrines hoped to be answers. He then as a philosopher takes up the same human questions or reformulates and tries to answer them in his own hopefully more enlightening and modernly relevant terms. As the free, transplanted spirit that he found himself to be, Santayana fixed his intellectual home in the bosom of the Western tradition. As a wide-ranging explorer of all things human, he became a reflective (and so a critical) practitioner of the life of reason, a critic, namely, of the understandings of ourselves to be found in the poetry, science, practices and institutions of the West, and of the ideal significance possible to or expressed by them.

And this pursuit of significance was the motivating intellectual content of Santayana's own life: the pursuit, in history and in life, of what he called 'ideal meanings,' namely, "the apprehension of that element in the past which was vital and which remains eternal" (**IPR** 106). "In imagination, not in perception," runs one of his lemmas, "lies the substance of experience . . . knowledge and reason are but its chastened . . . form" (**RCS** 49).[10] "Everything natural," runs another more famous dictum, "[has] an ideal development, and everything ideal has a natural basis"(**RCS** 28, 18). Santayana is not deprecating the life of action; he is considering how it has and can be made rational. But, on top of that, he shows how the lives and the histories which are all that humanity has, can (more than understood) come to be accepted and enjoyed in the consummatory or liberating mode of spirit.

"The *contemplative* force of spirit," he wrote in a note on Aristotle, "does not lie in not acting, but in *living* when you act" (**AFSL** 304, my emphasis). Spirit may require or institute detachment when it operates, but its function is *to illuminate* our human involvements and their material context and circumstances. As an intensity of consciousness, pure spirit is that dimension of living, that "life beyond life" where Milton embalms our intellectual treasure as between the covers of "a good book" (*Areopagitica*). It is the ability to take the point of view of other things as centers of being. Reason *mediates* among goods or else among interests and passions, and informs human action; but spirit is pure unmitigated *understanding*, in the sense of an *appreciation* of all forms of goodness wherever they arise. "Thought," wrote Santayana in response to a review of *The Life of Reason*, "[also] has an esthetic or ecstatic quality. This function, inefficacious as it is, would suffice to make thought the most important thing in the world."[11]

But now, if you are looking at the intellectual phases of human history synoptically and at the cosmos in both its vastness and microstructure, you have insensibly moved on, from the plane of special-science or poetic interrogation of what-there-is-or-might-be in existence, to the plane of metaphysics: to reflection upon your poetic or nomological reflection itself, *as well as* upon what you have observed. This, we note, is the very sense in which the turn into metaphysics was unavoidable for Peirce too. But it is from Santayana's example that later Americans (such as Randall, Schneider, Lamprecht, and Buchler)[12] were to proceed in metaphysics, with an explicit deliberateness and wide-angled focus that bring more clearly into its ken the explorations of art as well as the inquiries of science. The deep background of this, the historian will note, is Aristotle's *Metaphysics* as constituted by the treatises that were his *ex post facto* reflections on the sciences in their outcome.

(iii) *The 'Realms of Being'*: A Monumental Protreptic Meditation

If *Scepticism and Animal Faith* (1923) was the intellectual exercise by which Santayana sought to freshen, clarify and "restore his sense of life at first hand,"[13] the *Realms of Being* can be said to be a monumental protreptic meditation that would become an end-in-itself, given that systems of nature or philosophy could no longer be asserted in the way that scientific propositions are asserted. The world, Santayana had ironically shown in "Three Proofs of Realism," *signifies* less than all of itself *to* our *interpretant* thought.[14] But *Scepticism and Animal Faith* is positive that our interpretant thought does—mediately—signify what we need to know of the world both to survive in it and to enjoy it. Its dryly consistent, thoroughgoing application of skepticism discredits both solipsism and the excessively stringent criteria of knowledge uncritically instituted by Cartesian rationalism. Knowledge does not have to be absolutely *certain* to be knowledge; nor can it be knowledge of material existence, if it is *immediate*.

But Santayana's rejection of the Cartesian view of knowledge (like Dewey's and Peirce's) has a positive, anti-subjectivist outcome. Since knowledge should *not*, as he shows, have been grounded in the structure of powers of human consciousness, philosophy is now free to start from where it *should* have started, namely, the activities and **practices** of human life in the natural and social world. Hostile as both these worlds are, the effort of the human being to survive—and to survive with a certain quality of life—requires that he act on beliefs that the environment does not sanction with death or failure, on beliefs namely that he doesn't inspect apriori but that he trusts himself to act on, beliefs therefore that the environment can be said to justify. So situated, humankind cannot help having what Santayana calls 'animal faith' in the ways and regularities it encounters in the world.

Accordingly, Santayana's project in the *Realms of Being*, as stated in **SAF**, is to give "everyday beliefs a more accurate and circumspect form;" and he naturally begins by untangling what these tenets of animal faith are. Here, as with Plato's Socrates and Peirce—who tells us "not to doubt in philosophy what we do not doubt in our hearts" (**5.264**)—honesty begins at home:

> I stand in philosophy exactly where I stand in daily life; I should not be honest otherwise. I accept the same . . . witnesses, bow to the same . . . facts, make conjectures no less instinctively, and admit the same encircling ignorance (**SAF** vi). . . . I am talking of what I believe in my active moments, as a living animal, when I am really believing something (**id**.305).

That he does this so readably and picturesquely, even while asserting that the scale of the world is not picturesque and that when *he* is "reading books belief in me is at its lowest ebb," should not detract from the effort at intellectual honesty.

There is no paradox because Santayana is not offering a choice between artificial theories. His criticism, he says, "is the discipline of my daily thoughts and the account I actually give to myself from moment to moment of my own being and the world around me. I should be ashamed to countenance opinions which, when not arguing, I did not believe" (**SAF** 305). It would not be said of philosophy today that "it is dead," if its practitioners undertook it as the feasible *personal* intellectual discipline which it is in Santayana. Nor would it have become the inanimate application that it is now, of computerizable logics to just those subject-matters that lend themselves to axiomatic-deductive formalization, a turn which leaves everyman—with its exclusion of other methodic approaches to human subject-matter—unaided and uncounselled in the personal business of giving form and clarity to his own dianoetic activity.

Not that we can all follow in Santayana's expressive footsteps; but we all have expressive needs that would be better served were they informed by the systematic practices of self-examination, disambiguation, intellectual levelling, disciplined meditation, rememoration, cumulative commentary and criticism of which Santayana is the great secular example. So let us follow Santayana's lead in the enterprise of uncovering what we presuppose and of giving form to what we seek. His example just may teach us how to go about getting at what we ourselves really believe, and formulating the principles upon which we act and decide our priorities.

(iv) *The Realms of Being, the Sense of Life, and the Reason for Art*

We learn from *The Life of Reason*, as we would have to infer from any such historical account, that it is reason, and the attempt of mankind to live rationally, that gives meaning to history. But in Santayana's philosophy, it is only a good intelligibility that mind confers upon things *if* that mind is in love with the good. Science, which begins with observation, puts reason to the test of facts, as we say; but art, which molds observation into perceptivity, is the culmination of reason and of the sense of life. Never mind the split which bourgeois consciousness sees between the art and the quality of life of so many artists: that the particular living arrangements of artists, when they are not at their art, can look chaotic to that consciousness does not negate the achievement of art as art. The exception that confirms the rule here is that it is precisely by *living*, intellectually or spiritually, *in* their art, that artists are able to tolerate the material discomfort they must live *with* in philistine societies that do not favor their pursuits. And so it is, perhaps, with an intellectuality like Santayana's that can also function as an antidote to the discomforts of *existence*.

Fully to appreciate *Realms of Being*, then, we have to be able to see the work, not only as a technical achievement in the conceptualizing tradition of Western school philosophy. We have to see it also as a meditational masterpiece in the pursuit of an understanding of the world that could be the basis of psychic health and honest practice in the face of the potentially tragic facts of life and the limitations of knowledge. *Realms of Being* is, more than a great theoretical work, a *vade mecum* for people of intellect in search of sane or holistic responses to the existential challenge of the world into which we have been cast. Nor will the academic people who call themselves philosophers fail to find that "Santayana's categories, properly understood, are powerful instruments of conceptual orientation," as John Lachs has said (**GS** 61).[15]

Having, in **SAF**, helped skepticism to do its deconstructive best Santayana found (**PGS** 18), that he could no longer honestly begin from any "knowledge of fact," that "nature, history, the self" had become mere notional presences, and that

> the being of these images [had] become . . . purely internal to them; they exist in no environing space or time; they possess no substance or hidden parts, but are all surface, all appearance. Such a being, or quality of being, I call an essence; and to the consideration of essences,

composing of themselves an eternal and infinite realm, I have . . . devoted much attention.

Now, the discipline that focuses on the different sorts of being with which, and within which, we live is called ontology, from the Greek *on* ('being': neuter of the masculine participle *ôn*, feminine *ousía*). Whatever we discriminate in experience is, as Parmenides first said, not nothing.

But well before we have done any ontology, we have already felt that some things are not "real" at all or "less real" than others, that some things which are "not material" are "more real" than some which are—as our purpose in getting somewhere was "more real" than the actual or alleged obstacles seen or said to "exist" in our path. We may even have asked, are some things "really" more real than others thus, again, presupposing either degrees or kinds of "reality." Hence the need for a consistent practice which can distinguish between sorts of being, and which can answer whether there are or are not degrees of existence, reality, and being.

The distinction Santayana makes between what exists and what is real is a key to his ontological practice. It's important to note that 'non-existent' in Santayana does not mean 'not real;' it means, rather, 'non-existential' in the sense of 'non-material.' So when he says that some things, namely, essences are the most real of beings, he means that they are *the least conditioned* of beings. Since they exist, existences are not less real than essences, but they *are* existentially less stable, more precarious and not repeatable like essences. Essences are not non-existent, since they are real in the orders of sensation and discourse; they are, rather, 'non-existential.' They are determinative only of *what* we discriminate in existence, not of existence itself.

Like William Blake's "eternal identities,", as R.C. Lyon notes,[16] Santayana's essences are not abstract; each is perfectly individual. And they are not *prior* except in the sense that they are the condition of possibility of truth, of the activity of spirit, and of the being of whatever comes into existence in the realm of matter. And this real, non-existential realm of possibilities and forms of definiteness is not "a chunk of existence" or "portion" of the world, as Lachs is at pains to insist (**GS** 64ff.), but a mode of being, a distinguishable and irreducible aspect of what there is.

Like Peirce's approach to the phaneron, Santayana's perhaps too elaborate elucidation of essences, obviates the epistemologist skepticism of both the Cartesian and British empiricist traditions. But then, the problem of philosophy for Santayana was not "Do I really know what I know?" but rather "How may human beings best live their lives, given their natural endowments and the precarious natural conditions into which they are born?"

So it is to the study of these conditions that Santayana turns in *The Realm of Matter*. How, he asks, are we to penetrate the inner flux of material existence (**RM** 280), of which Kratylus and Herakleitos had said we can have no knowledge (Arist.Met.**A**,6. 987a29f.)? Aesthetic, moral, mathematical, and scientific descriptions of it are all merely symbolic, sketchy and clearly biased. But "existence,"

> in ourselves and in the objects in our own plane *encountered in action*, existence is a strain and an incubus, particular, self-centered, substantial. It is in terms of such existence, unstable but burdened and concrete, that an unsophisticated natural philosophy might conceive the realm of matter (ibid.).

We note that Santayana is calling his speculative metaphysics 'natural philosophy.' He seems to have disliked the term 'metaphysics.' But natural philosophy is either cosmology, a special science, or metaphysics, a *speculative* inquiry which is rhetorical (as in Peirce) or poetic (as in Parmenides), or both as in Santayana himself. We also pause to note that the usage which makes the term interchangeable with 'natural philosophy' is the standing symptom of the indefeasible compulsion philosophy has ever been under, since Herakleitos, to tell its auditors about 'the way things really are.'

In any case, and because of the inadequacy and non-literalness of knowledge, what Santayana is after in *The Realm of Matter* is, as he projected in *Reason in Science*, that "suitable attitude toward [nature] . . . which reason would dictate were knowledge complete" (**RS** V.122).[17] For, as he has already established (and does not tire of repeating), scientific knowledge is the best we can get when it is a matter of acquiring material control over natural processes for purposes of survival. And this is not a frivolous conclusion since, to reach it, Santayana had to refute the various apologetic approaches which, in explaining away the negative consequences of science for dogmatic credos, warp or weaken the rational—and pragmatic—understanding of the scientific enterprise.

What Peirce called habits or regularities in nature, i.e. laws, Santayana calls 'tropes.' Tropes are the repeatable patterns or essences of events. The driving force of nature, the principle of continuity in natural processes he calls *substance*. Formless matter, the undetermined *other* of essence, as Santayana defines it, since it is no less a mode of being or category than essence, is therefore not to be confused with substance. Matter is existence *in potency*, and existence is sheer material presence; but this presentness results from the determinacy lent to matter by an essence.

> Matter is no model devised by the human imagination . . . but is a primeval plastic substance of unknown potentiality, perpetually taking on new forms; the gist of materialism being that these forms are all passive . . . while the plastic stress of matter is alone creative and, as far as we can surmise, indestructible (**RM** 100).

It is to avoid "the confusion between essences and facts which makes quicksand of all philosophy" that Santayana gives the separate name of 'trope' to the essence of any event *as distinguished from the event itself*. An event differs from the trope it exemplifies in being enacted; events, like things, are contingent and compound, whereas essences are eternal and indissoluble. The whole trope cannot be realized in any particular moment of the flow of the event, only the order in which these moments arise and vanish can be realized.

> This order is the trope . . . the essence of that sequence seen under the form of eternity; and since existence, in this event, has realized that essence, that essence has descriptive value in respect to this world. It belongs to the *realm of truth* (**RM** 102).

Since simplicity is not a property of either substance or essence (RM 108), neither is it of tropes; it is only a semiotic condition of our perceiving them: the regularities we call laws are simplifications captured through the "sieve" of "distance and theory." So, in calling tropes laws we must not forget that they are approximative or statistical only; otherwise the plausibility they acquire in successful practice will turn our reliance on them into a myth which "erects Law into a metaphysical power compelling events to obey it" (RM 109).[18]

But the reality of law, such as it is, does not obviate the "contingency, substantiality, originality of fact everywhere"; while the assumption that "whatsoever spontaneously happens once will have spontaneously happened before and will spontaneously happen again, wherever similar elements are in the same relations," is simply the postulate called the uniformity of nature (RM 102). And this postulate is no more than the modern, bombastic equivalent for "the ancient naturalness of nature":

> In so far as the law is more rigid than a habit, it is a human artifice of notation. In so far as it indicates a co-operative march of events mutually generated and destroyed, it is another name for the ways of nature or of God, for *the forms which existence can show to spirit* (RM 110, my emphasis).

Natural science, then, is only the science of causes in the sense of being able to answer the question of what follows upon what; it cannot answer the question of why.

This, however, does not make Santayana a nominalist any more than Peirce was. "Everything cannot be merely imputed. Imputation itself must exist actively, in centers and on occasions which are not imputed but actual" (RM 105). We are not entirely duped by nature in our habits and interests; these "are themselves tropes that must have been . . . victorious . . . if living creatures defined by those tropes" have been able to survive in, and survey, the flux of nature. This would also imply, from the semiotic point of view, that Santayana thought of habits and beliefs as *indexical*; so that, because we use them indicatively, "if in the region indicated by these nam[ings] in perception and by animal faith—there is anything at all, it must possess the essence which it possesses, of which these names are partial suggestions; although . . . the true essence of that substance need not . . . resemble the images which, in using these names, may occupy a man's fancy" (**RM** 105).

Santayana's critical realism no less than pragmatism thus salves the gap between belief (or theory) and practice which plagues the epistemologies of the European tradition.

In retrospect, then, Santayana's skepticism can be called creative because, like Socrates's skepticism and his own metaphors, it doesn't block inquiry but leads to further perceptions. And this is relevant to the discourse of speculative nature-philosophy or metaphysics because, in going beyond the special sciences to speak of matters at the limits of knowledge, metaphysics cannot help resorting to metaphor.

Above, in connection with the descriptive value of essences and the forms which existence can take, Santayana invoked in passing both the notion and realms of *truth* and *spirit*, the two remaining dimensions of his categorial system. Now truth in Santayana, whatever else we may find it to be in his technical philosophizing, is an object of *reverence*. Likewise, certain essences for this thinker can be objects of *consummatory* intuition, namely, of spirit.[19] The valuative connotations of these terms tip us off to the fact that the *reality* of the realms of truth and spirit is human: non-material but existential in the case of truth; in the case of spirit, non-material *and* non-existential, but human in the sense of cathartic and completive, or liberational. Truth is existential as that part of the realm of essence which has "interesected with," or is being exemplified by, existence.

Insofar as truth operates in existence, it has the functional reality, the non-material effectiveness, of a standard (**RB** 841, **RS** 287). Its reality is like that of essences; it is posited by an honest skepticism that honors what it can't avoid presupposing. And what any knowledge-seeker assumes is

that there is some real object or event to be known or reported, prior or subsequent to the report that reaches us. In other words, we presuppose existent facts about which our affirmations may be false or true (**RB** 831, **RS** 277).

It is the principle of realism that, as far as it goes, our knowledge of facts is true, "if we have access to them and discount the relativity and partiality of our perceptions and theories"; more than that, "it is the first presupposition of intelligence and sanity" (ibid.).

Similarly, Santayana is brought to the realm of spirit by his skeptical rejection

> [of] all hypostatized myths . . .[and]. . . all affectation of disbelief where life and action render belief inevitable and perpetually renew it. I posit therefore that the realm of matter is animated by spirit . . . as far as my sympathies avail to conceive that animation spontaneously, or my experience, reflectively to confirm my divinations. . . . In regard to the extent and detail of the realm of spirit, then, all must be hypothesis and literary fiction, to be indulged in by poets, historians, and critics as their genius may prompt or their prudence allow (**RB** 832, **RS** 278).

The actual or lived moral history of spirit, on the other hand, is constituted by the traditional languages of poetry and religion in which the capable spirits among us have recorded its essential fortunes. These precedents are there to impress "each new soul" anew; "yet they count spiritually only in so far as they are confirmed or rediscovered in each case. Spirit cannot live except alone" (ibid.). Nonetheless, it is clear that Santayana's monograph on spirit is also a recovery, for our benefit as well as his own, of the spirituality possible to a modern sensibility that accepts but keeps in perspective the advances of natural science, and that is content to underpin its consummatory insights, not with the dogmas of a chosen religion, but "by [its] fellowship with what is perennial in [the human] heart" (**RB** 833, **RS** 279).

This, we see, is Santayana's response to the *ontological anxiety* asserted by existentialists to follow necessarily upon the disappearance of theological legitimation for our human projects, in combination with the knowlege that death is inevitable and existence inhumanly contingent. And this does not make Santayana's approach to the reflective life at all liable to the same charge of cosmic "defiance" as readers levelled at Bertrand Russell's famous essay "A Free Man's Worship."[20] For, Santayana does not believe that "the tie" which "unites us with our fellow-men" is the "common doom" of death. Yes, Santayana would agree with Russell, "omnipotent matter rolls on its relentless way," depriving us of our loves today and our lives tomorrow.

But "the world that [our] own ideals have fashioned" is not just a construction that we must Atlas-like "sustain *alone*" by sheer strength of "weary but unyielding" will. Rather it is based, like Peirce's discursive universe of search, in the community possible to humans: the reflective community which, when rehearsed and renewed by its transmission, is an ideal dwelling-place sufficient in its dianoetic variety to give form to the most unexpected spiritual needs and provide responses to the direst of physical challenges. Santayana's implicit faith in a tradition which he saw as pluralist—as self-correcting in respect of survival, as creatively skeptical in respect of knowledge, and both tolerant and exploratory in respect of nature, values and human differences—is stronger by far than that of the less historical Russell or the rebellious Nietzsche. But it is not less well-informed or less healthily skeptical. And, as a more cherishing piety toward both the natural and cultural sources of our existence, it is an attitude which is not just deconstructive but also reconstructive.

Death, of course, cannot be overcome physically. But put to the only use that Ortega y Gasset says it can be put, namely, to the service of life, the consciousness of it becomes the opposite of paralyzing, and not alienating. So, in the transition that is often dramatized by association with his reported "change of heart" or *metanoia*, from the life of reason (and involvement in human history and experience) to the realms of being (and the experience of synoptic detachment),[21] Santayana's subject—experience—has not really changed.

As he had said in 1906, "my subject . . . is experience viewed at a certain angle, in the measure in which it torments or educates spirit" (**RS** viii).[22] Santayana's development of the notion of spirit, and of all that it presupposes, is his extended answer in expressive practice to the torments of mortality. But it is also, minor quibbles aside, a representation of the last phase of the career of an exemplary human being, working—with an audience-consciousness inevitable to his kind of intellectual—to realize his best possibilities as a spokesman, if not for everyman, then for the tradition in which civilization *is* the condition of redemption for everyman. Detached he may have become, but he was not ever, in his communicativeness, alienated.[23]

Not only does spirit, in its ability to take the point of view of what is *other*, honor the universal aspiration to justice by choosing "for all others that which their nature, in each case, demands." Spirit, in taking the point of view of the other, has also found a non-alienating, non-anxious way of thinking death, and the death of its own mother-psyche. Since no psyche can be other than itself, it follows that if spirit can identify with the project of another self or center, it can negate the project of its own mother-psyche. And this negation is a way of figuring my own death: the world as it might be without me. It would still, however, be the world seen in human terms, as if it mattered to humanity though no longer to me. Operating here as well is Santayana's notion of truth, the revered object of spirit

[Truth] is tragic even in comedy, since it looks to the end of every career and every achievement. The very movement of . . . exploration that discloses truth, thereby discloses also the relativity, limits, and fugitiveness of this exploration. It shows life under the form of eternity, which is the form of death. Life then becomes an offering, a prayer, a sacrifice offered up to the eternal; and though there may be incense in that sacrifice, there is also blood.

It dawns on us that this is the Dionysan element in Santayana's account of philosophy's contribution to human redeemability. Since we're bound to bleed anyway, it is better to bleed expressively than non-expressively, laughing, groaning, praying, dialoguing, and *dramatizing together*. I say dialoguing because it has turned out here that our relation to an indifferent universe is in the end made bearable, for Santayana, by the dianoetic quality of our relations to each other.

That Santayana's thinking on death is an improvement upon Heidegger's and Sartre's, gives us the sense in which his vision of life and history is existentialist. The overlap between the function

Santayana has here assigned to spirit, and Sartre's humanistic account of art is notable even when not complete. For Sartre, when consciousness makes the world intelligible, it is trying to understand or constitute it *as* a totality; consciousness seeks to recover the world not only *as it is*, but also *as if* it were compatible with the purposes of free men;

> the creative act aims at a total renewal of the world. Each painting, each book is a recovery of the totality of being. . . . For this is the final goal of art: to recover this world by giving it to be seen *as it is*, but *as if* it had its source in human freedom (**WL** 37).

Spirit, in the resumptive function that Santayana assigns to it, opens into the vastness of the realm of essence knowing that, though infinite, it is the locus of *determinacy*: "the realm of truth . . . is the total history and destiny of matter and spirit . . . the enormously complex essence . . . they exemplify by existing" (RB 834, RS 280).

And spirit knows that, in seeing even inhuman processes in human terms, it is in permanent if implicit rebellion against their inhumanity. As the being that questions its own being (in both Sartre and Santayana), human being creates itself by developing *artistic* or *spiritual dominion* over the disproportion between itself and the indifferent, transhuman cosmos. Finally, just as "metaphysics," for Sartre,

> is not a sterile discussion about abstract notions which have nothing to do with experience. It is a living effort to embrace from within the human condition in its totality" (**WL** 217),[24]

so, for Santayana, *Realms of Being* is his address to the reader on how a free spirit can best understand and most creatively address his situation in the world.

Now , "the proper goal of spirit is an impartial enjoyment of the innocent form of all things" (AFSL 30), and "the freedom proper to spirit . . . [is] . . . the fact of being sometimes liberated from distraction and permitted to be pure spirit" (RB 837, RS 283).[25] And this understanding of spirit is, naturally, continuous with the function of reason in **LR**, but with a difference of emphasis. Where the reflective quality or rationality of art had, in **LR**, produced works of great enlightenment and solace, and was the creative principle of civilization itself, in the realm of spirit (**RB**703, **RS**149),

> [c]ivilization is a . . . growth, like the mechanism of animal bodies; the achievement is wonderful, but the advantage to the spirit thereby elicited is problematic: there will be much new experience and much new suffering.

Spirit in **RB** is the dimension of this rationality *made fully conscious*; it is *unmixed* with the anxiety of achievement, and *untroubled* by the obstructions which medium-bound thinking must contend with when it gives form to its insights in the sensuous media of the various arts.

But to be able to "consecrate itself to its essential vocation" spirit must have chastened itself with a sense of the besieging realities that limit its "initial" tendency toward "omniscience . . . perfect freedom and happiness . . . even absolute power" (**RB** 526f. **RT** 120f.). Moreover, the "moral warmth," idiosyncratic, and "synoptic character" of spirit "are encouraged by the aesthetic . . . fertility of mind, when once an organism has flowered into consciousness, and begun to dream." The principle of spirit, then, is different from the principle of art. Spirit is pure consciousness, pure perceptivity untrammelled by even the human interest; whereas the principle of art, while seeing what-there-is *as it is*, cannot help addressing the human condition *as if* it was not absolutely desperate or hopeless.

And this must be why spirit is renunciatory of the world, but art is a reappropriation of it—in the exhibitive mode and in the human interest. A noteworthy difference between the two principles emerges here: when art captures an essence, it is not pure essence but a meaning conveyed in a medium. Doesn't entertaining a mediumless essence, as spirit does, imply that we have deeply internalized the *substance* of which it is the form? In this case rehearsing the essence is one with its evocation in us of what it was the essence of. Clearly, the intuitions of spirit are more intense and rarified than the dianoetic effort involved in art, and this explains why the insights of spirit are intermittent and harder to sustain.

So there is a difference between giving preference to moments of spirit as the entelechy or perfection of consciousness and giving the preference to the peak-experiences which art affords. And the difference accompanies or gives rise to different life-styles as exemplified, in fact, by the difference between Santayana's own earlier worldly, intellectually successful life and his later, partly circumstantial reclusiveness. Both preferences of course were operative in both phases; and this is the clue suggesting that Santayana's ever-latent restlessness about, and dissatisfaction with, life was over-determined by the *spirit* generating his insights, as opposed to to the *poetic power* or gift informing the expressive dimension of his life.

It's as if Santayana's *unconscious* project and realization was, as Theognis and Sophocles say, that it is better never to have been born;[26] but that, having been born into a hostile world with unsatisfactory bodies, we should both embrace what there is to enjoy in human life and never forget that cosmo-circumstances make life a false friend; for, in the end, it betrays us into death. I say this, however, with the explicit qualification that, like all psychoanalytic verbalizations of motive, it is inevitably an over-statement and verges on caricature.

We have to grant, on the other hand, that well-adjusted and dedicated to philosophizing as he was,[27] Santayana's victory is intellectual and literary. Only Plato, among men with great conceptual talent, is more literary in his own way than Santayana. Nor is the switch from the point of view of spirit to the aesthetic point of view at all like the lapse from from the point of view of spirit back into that of the anxious, driven and conflicted psyche. For, both the aesthetic and the point of view of spirit are harmonies, and a kind of accepting, yea-saying "dominion" over the flux of matter and the tensions of the psyche.

The kind of "dominion" Santayana is talking about is, of course, not dominationist. It is perhaps best illustrated by the sense in which an artist becomes a master of his medium, acquiring ever greater freedom and virtuosity within it as he lovingly—coolly or heatedly— assimilates and manipulates his materials, while letting himself be guided by the leads they suggest to him. The difference between spiritual or artistic "dominion" and dominationist mastery may not be easily visible in our dominationist culture, where non-dominationist responses are automatically misread as submissive. But the difference is a huge one, and may be measured by the contrast between the *liberation* which art and spirit effectuate for their practioners, and the oppressiveness which pervades both sides of a dominationist relationship.

But the ordinary reader may also have to grant that, in so far as Santayana's triumph is spiritual, he has not fully understood it. For, if pure spirit is free to rehearse and enjoy its perceptions *selflessly*, what has happened to the enjoyment and liberation received from art and literature which the perceiver gets by identifying with the rhythms of the creator's perceptivity, and from identification with the humanity of its protagonists? It is to be feared that only a soul who has achieved a spiritual emancipation equal to Santayana's, over and above the intellectual emancipation which a good reading of his work provides, only such an emancipated soul can truly appreciate his discipline or meaning on this point.

(v) *Epiphenomenalism and the Realm of Truth*

In Santayana's critical realism, the truth is surely something we help to make—or 'constitute,' in the technical terminology. Compatible with pragmatism as this is it is still not pragmatism. Santayana would certainly not deny that the meaning of a proposition is to be found in its consequences, as pragmatism proposes. But the truth of a proposition, he would say, is not exhausted by its practical consequences, even though he also agrees that the test of the validity of propositions about existence is experiential. Human action, as already stated, is the interpretant and test of ideation.

But, as "the standard comprehensive description of a fact," the truth about it includes all the other essences that articulate that fact, and the relations that radiate from it.[28] Moreover, valid propositions, for Santayana, originally arise from, and reflect, successful action rather than guide or direct it, in Dewey's sense of 'direct.' What concomitant or ensuing consciousness does is to theorize *the interpretant action*; it finds the correct formulations for the processes humanly bent to the sought-for end. And consciousness, so viewed, does not appear to be an intervening or material power. In Santayana's terms, it does not have 'causal efficacy.' This is the view that is called "epiphenomenalism," in the technical term for *the theory that causation occurs only in the physical world.*[29]

I have never understood the deprecatory tone that positivists or idealists who are also physicalists (and cannot therefore disagree with epiphenomenalism), take toward it or Santayana when the term is applied to him. Perhaps they fear that epiphenomenalism banishes mind from the world; but what they show is that they have not read Santayana, and that it is their—not his—epiphenomenalism that either banishes mind from matter physicalistically *and* reductively, or else, is animistically turning ideas into agential powers. A reader of Santayana's brilliant rehearsals at book-length of the realities of essence, spirit, and truth, who also knew his Peirce, would find rather that Santayana's epiphenomenalism is as non-dualistic and has the same starting point (in the phaneron or appearances), as Peirce's phenomenological synechism or affirmation of the continuity of mind with matter.

As Paul Conkin points out,[30]

Almost as much as Dewey, Santayana emphasized the role of formal thought (logic or dialectic) in scientific inquiry. In fact, he . . . used the term science to encompass dialectics as well as physics, since animal faith is involved in both. In mathematical reasoning . . . intent is not directed to. . . substance impinging upon the body, but to a term of discourse entertained. . . . mathematical reasoning relates an essence present in intuition with one absent and involves both faith and risk of error. As much as cognitive thought, dialectic originates at the level of experience and here finds its first terms. . . . Dialectic, truistic in itself, free to take any deductive pattern it prefers, provides the form . . . of all scientific theory. It is . . . indispensable . . . for any broad explanation and . . . suggests such guiding ideals in science as unity and simplicity. Inspired by a perfect logical universe, man tries to find an existent one.

But Santayana completes this behavioral or pragmatistic approach to truth with an account which takes cognizance of "the consequences of refusing to think humanly when we are human" (**RT** 64). If we omit the human dimension, thought is reduced to a mechanical notation of details; and such unselected, uninterpreted records would be mere echoes or *binary indexes* to other parts of the world of which they are only parts too. Truth must be more than behavioral because action, as the individual's interpretant response to the world, is itself signitive or a *sign*. A human action, in Buchler's terms, is an active judgment.

The "instrumentalities and" impersonal "procedures of science" do indeed "lie in the realm of matter," and, as indexical, are existential. But "science in act" is "a category of spirit" (**RT** 65); as such it is an interpretant third: a discursive and systematic interpretant when theoretical, a teleological or final interpretant when experimental. And this is what allows Santayana to take it that "the being of truth" consists "in the fact that facts exemplify essences and have relations." Organic processes and interactions in the realm of matter would have remained blind forever, if possibility—in the form of alternative possible responses to given stimuli—had not arisen and, in arising, turned indexes into symbols, or essences calling for interpretation.

Now, the *realm* of truth is "that segment of the realm of essence which happens to be illustrated in existence" (**RT** viii).

> Truth is but the complete character of the universe seen under the form of eternity; and essence, in its infinity, is but the field of all the complementary characters that any given character excludes. Both this infinity and that eternity transcend mutation, transition, and local emphasis, and therefore transcend life" (**RB**839, **RS**285).[31]

The question whether a particular claim is true, in this context, is the question whether a proposed idea belongs to the existentially embodied segment of the realm of essence. And this question has "tragic" importance for a human being "intent on discovering and describing what exists . . . has existed, or [will] exist in his world," because his survival and the quality of his survival depend upon it. The nature of truth should, however, not be inflated: "there are no eternal tenets: neither the opinions of mankind, nor mankind, nor anything existent can be eternal; eternity is a property of essences only" (**RT** ix). In its relevance to action "truth is . . . a household presence: not the naked nor the divine truth, but truth . . . dressed in homespun" (**RT** 139).

In considering the love and hatred of truth in our socio-intellectual tradition, Santayana finds that the first thing we meet is not the love of truth, but the dismissal and disguising of it because it runs counter to the belief that mankind is the measure of all things. Self-assertion is such that, even while nominally recognizing "the ideal authority of truth," we do violence to it. A philosophic instance of this violence is *Occam's Razor*, presumptuously invoked as a criterion of truth (**RT** 104). No grounds are to be found in nature or history for believing simple rather than more complex truths. Thus, Santayana finds modern physics not only "respectful" of "the profound complexity of things," but that it is also more modest than school philosophies in "admit[ting] that [its] conventions are largely arbitrary and symbolic" (**RT** 105).

Pre-rational morality, likewise, fetishizes and asserts aesthetic or political sentiments in defiance of the human truth, with a barbarian courage that is blind and ferocious.[32] But, in speaking of truly great individuals who are able to invoke the authority of "destiny" understood as the truth, Santayana fails to stop at just that related fallacy which political theorists and historians know as the appeal to Destiny. As the twin-brother of *fanaticism in fairer guise*, however, we do find this form of delusion condemned in many other of Santayana's writings.

Close as he ever was to the data of history, Santayana suggests that the strongest spring of truth is prudential, namely, the experience that

> *there can be no peace in delusion*: [it is] in this negative and moral guise the idea of truth first insinuates itself into the mind. No . . . interest in the truth . . . for its own sake: [but] only discomfort in uncertainty, uneasiness about things, and a prudent concern for the future (**RT** 107).

Without an intellectual notion of the truth, people still want "to be armed to face the obdurate facts" and avoid being mistaken. And this leads only to a "specialized sagacity . . . remote from the love of truth," generative of complacent slanders, party tenets, or superstitions. "The more these self-indulgent minds fear and hate the truth, the more insistently they give the name of truth to the mask that hides it" (ib.). The ideal authority of truth has no power against pleasant fictions, and only irks the more, the more convenient the fiction or convention it would unmask. The love of power, or novelty, or ideas easily overrides the pursuit of truth. The example Santayana gives here of the philosophic empiricist turns out to be a critical sleeper: it anticipates a great lapse of Post-Modernism: empiricism when partisan, thorough, and (I would add) theoreticist, ends by allowing *all* theories to be "true," thus "collaps[ing] into idiocy, as if nothing could be true. In contrast, the martyr ready to die for some false opinion has, at least implicitly, set up the category of truth" (**RT** 109).

Since Santayana takes ethics as "a descriptive science of manners" (**RT** 67), ethical truths would not be different from truths in other special sciences. This study would collect "large material and historical facts on the human scale." But the only kind of moral *judgment* that his material could admit is whether moral judgments were as a matter of fact passed, and whether they were general or lasting or passionate (**RT** 68). For, if *morality* is limited, as it should be, "to actual allegiance in sentiment and action to this or that ideal of life," there is nothing in reference to which "any type of morality could be called *true*." Truth and error are only possible in morals, as truths or errors in *self-knowledge*, and as answers about whether the choice in question responded to a moral illusion or not, or was true to that person's best self.

> In moral willing as in knowing there is a good deal of substitution and representation. Moral passions carried by words and ideas . . . may be deceptive . . . they may tragically misinterpret. . . the inmost . . . allegiance of the soul. Such . . . judgments . . . may be called false, since . . . they deceive us about our own fundamental needs and demands (**RT** 69).

Integrity is achieved and preserved by being true to oneself in his or her choices. Similarly, other *representations* of seated interests—e.g.

political interests—may be said to be true or false according as to whether they "pursue true or false *aims*, in the sense of being or not being in line with the . . . permanent interests of the people."

But ethical truths, even the most basic, cannot become moral commandments; for they neither inspire nor negate natural moral preferences. Take the belief, for instance, that we should

> Value others for their own sake, because they too are centers of life and of values. Consider them . . . always as ends and never merely as means. In fact and by nature they are ends to themselves as much as you are . . . to yourself. Here, in respect to all living beings . . . we reach a necessary truth, since life means precisely the power in organisms to grow and to propagate, as if they loved their own being (70).

It cannot be a rule governing behavior, because it is saying "that life in one form can adopt, or morally ought to adopt, the interests of life in every other form." But "this would . . . be the death of all morality, not the perfection of it" (**RT** 71). The will of the other "cannot be weighed in the balance against the constitutive will and radical virtue of one's own being."

It would not be rational, but a betrayal to abdicate impulses of one's own soul "in a a brotherly compromise with cobras, monkeys, idiots, sophists and villains." It would (like Post-Modernism) "solve the moral problem only by dissolving all goods, all arts, all species and all individuals" (**RT** 71). "There is," Santayana points out,

> a mystical insight proper to spirit within ourselves—spirit not being specifically human—that perceives the universal innocence of life in the midst of universal war: but this insight cannot impose on the psyche in . . . ways contrary to her native ways: nor has impartial spirit any reason for wishing to do so.

The moral judgment that life is good is an inevitable presupposition of the organism that is maintaining and defending itself. The phenomenon of rational suicide is the seeming exception that, for Santayana, clarifies the rule.

> Even when in some tragic moment reflection turns against instinct
> and prefers physical death to life, not everything in life is judged to be
> evil; for . . . this . . . renunciation . . . of life is regarded as a . . . victory
> and liberation for spirit; and what is spirit but the quintessence of life
> here purified into tragic knowledge, into clear loyalty to what is felt to
> be best (**RT** 73)?

The recognition that moral judgments are neither true nor false,
restores our moral intuitions to their legitimate field, the field of
intuition (**RT** 74). On the model of Socratic self-knowledge which
Santayana identifies as 'expressive' and 'moral' not ethical or scientific,
"we might f[in]d . . . *moral truth* in the discovery of what one ultimately
wants and ultimately loves." And this is no easy discovery; for "the
inmost oracle of the heart" too often proves to be disconcertingly
ascetic and disillusioning." Santayana suggests that perhaps it was
Socrates' sense of this disillusion that rendered him "so endlessly
patient, diffident, and ironical, so impossible to corrupt and so
impossible to deceive."[33]

Now psyche, as Aristotle and Santayana reiterate, is the hereditary
principle of organization in the body or of direction in the will (**RT**
75). And preference is always individual, even while the demands of
psyche are variable. Hence the negative aspect that passion wears at
different times or for different individuals, cannot be taken for an
argument that passion is elsewhere "false" or wicked. Like
omnisicience, moral truth is impossible to reach; for it would have to
be a perception of "the aspirations of all souls at all moments"; it
would have to "confront. . . these aspirations with their occasions . . .
[and] . . . measure their relative vanity and physical compatibility"
(**RT** 76).

So, *moral dogmatism*, as a tyrannical stretching of moral community
"beyond the range of natural organization," is *spiritually sinister* in
oneself, and an offense against spirit everywhere. Yet in political society
moral dogmatism and morality itself are not distinguished, because
of the adjustment required of the political animal. Socially divisive
dogmatism becomes war and spirit becomes the enemy of spirit, each
side imagining that it represents morality *in general* and, therefore,

wishing to annihilate all (other) *particular* moralities. But, as the expression that it is of animal bias, all morality is particular. The paradox is that to renounce one's moral bias would be to renounce life, just because there is no 'morality in general.' The unheeded philosophical truth is that "moral truth . . . even at its purest, by no means bestows moral authority over alien lives" (**RT** 78).

This same relativist lesson we learnt also, on historical grounds, from *The Life of Reason* which showed that "morality" can be rational when it is an art of compatibilizing and maximizing human satisfactions. And reason, like spirit in its different mode, is individual. But an individual nature, in Santayana, is both the complete set of determinate capacities, passions, and tropes of the psyche, and the human being in process of becoming rational. Consequently, the good is relative and differential; it is determined by the particular nature whose good it is or is to be, and is different from individual to individual and society to society. And, as Lachs points out, the real good of any individual is *a system* of fulfillable desires and compatible satisfactions (**GS** 97). A stable self and a rational life are a function of each other. They develop out of the ability to distinguish more permanent from short term goods. Reason itself, Santayana reminds us, is an optional desire; but, as the desire whose object is the harmonizing of desires-in-conflict which are, therefore, 'seconds,' and which began as impulses or sheer 'firsts,' reason as a rational desire or rational passion is a *third*, in useful Peircean terms.

Since the good is "the perfection of life for each creature according to its kind," we cannot do without a modicum of truth and self-knowledge. But, just as there is a penumbra of ignorance encircling our knowledge, so moral control of our passions and moral judgment of our actions seems both to girdle and go beyond the truths we rely on in natural life (**RT** 139). Thus, on the one hand, "it w'd be inhuman and fanatical to set up the truth as the only good" (**RT** 140), so, on the other,

> charity, a disinterested sympathy with [all] spirit . . . cannot be impartial in all directions and at all removes. . . . universal and unbiassed charity would abet contrary impulses and . . . utterly dissolve the too

sympathetic soul. Truth cannot dictate to love. Will and aspiration move . . . beyond the actual, and forbid the human spirit to attune itself to truth only. Nearer and lovelier things also solicit us.

Intellectuals devoted to the pursuit of truth in their special fields should remember that "truth proper is indifferent to being praised or possessed (**RT** 137), and not confuse the seeming love of it which is stimulated by the hope of glory, with the passion for achievement. And it is the part of the generalist, or philosopher who might desire a knowledge covering all existence, to remember that "finitude [is] not . . . error, if we assert no more than we know, and privation is not suffering if we are willing to be ourselves" (**RT** 136).

Truth, as its chosen object, is indeed the good of the intellect both in its impersonal inclemency and in its dramatizing or humanizing function (**RT** 134). But there are limits to the devotion to and satisfactions of truth; so that when we go beyond the truth proper, into myths which humanize the harsh realities (**RT** 137), we know that they are not of the same kind as the truths by means of which our material survival is to be secured. The practical ballast of the latter kind of truth leads Santayana to say that "happiness in the truth is like happiness in marriage, fruitful, lasting, and ironical. *You could not have chosen better, yet this is not what you dreamt of.*" There is a Nietzschean irony, and an echo of 'the eternal return,' in this affirmation of intellectuality as a possibility of the human condition.

Notes

1. As reported by J.Buchler in "One Santayana or Two," The *J. of Philosophy* Vol. LVI (1954); p.54.

2. Cited in the preface to his *Classic American Philosophers* (N.Y. Appleton-Century-Crofts 1951). In his "Santayana & Philosophy at Harvard: Wasted Chances in the Creation of 'The Great Department'," The Santayana Conference, Avila, Spain 1992, R. Robin reminds us that President Eliot was as consistently hostile to Santayana as he was in rejecting Peirce. His unfavorable attitude to Peirce can be traced in J. Brent's *Charles Sanders Peirce A Life* (Indiana U.P. 1993), to Santayana in *Persons and Places* (Crit.Ed. M.I.T. Press 1986).

3. G. Santayana, *Obiter Scripta*, ed. J. Buchler and B. Schwartz (New York: Scribner's, 1936), 108–50.

4. Santayana's 'object' here is, obviously, Peirce's *immediate* object as distinguished from the dynamoid or effective object of the sign or essence. "What qualities," adds Santayana, "shall be found in or attributed to an object is . . . determined by the structure of the organ, not by that of the object" (**OS** 145).

5. The big difference from Peirce, of course is that existence as a whole and as such for Santayana is an absolute contingency, not as for Peirce, a process in which there is an emergent 'reasonableness': "the fatality that first adopted this constitution for the universe may have adopted it . . . for a time only, to be exchanged, after so many revolutions . . . for a different rhythm" (**AFSL** 141). But this is a difference in their speculative cosmologies, not in the understanding of how metaphysics relates to the arts and sciences.

6. It's interesting that Peirce, independently and in speaking of the ideas and constructions of mathematics as actualizing possibilities or firsts, has no qualms about the 'Reality' (his term) of a first Universe of Experience "compris[ing] all *mere* Ideas those airy nothings to which the mind of poet, pure mathematician, or another *might* give local habitation and a name. . . . Their very airy-nothingness; the fact that their Being consists in mere capability of getting thought, not in anybody's Actually thinking them, saves their Reality" (**6.455**). "Real," he has just told us at **6.453**, "is a word invented in the thirteenth century to signify having Properties, i.e. characters sufficing to identify their subject, and possessing these whether they be . . . attributed to it . . . or not."

7. J. Royce *California A Study of American Character* (N.Y. Houghton 1886). G.H. Mead *Movements of Thought in the Nineteenth Century* (U. of Chicago Press 1936). J. Buchler's work as an intellectual historian and editor is embedded, from 1942 on, in his teaching of the Contemporary Civilization courses in Columbia College, and his editing of the historical texts and sources into usable manuals. A handy edition of these rather massive manuals is the one-volume *Man in Contemporary Society* (Columbia U.P. 1962). Previous two-volume versions were titled *Introduction to Contemporary Civilization in the West*, and *Chapters in Western Civilization*. More hidden from notice is how in the Contemporary Philosophy courses which he taught, Buchler was, like Santayana, simultaneously substantive and historical in his analyses. We could say that just as Royce determined in his *California* "to write from the sources" (p. vii), so Buchler "generalizes from the documentary sources of contemporary Western thought"; see Chapters IV and V.

8. In his writings about America as distinct from the rest of the West, Santayana is unique in communicating a sense that "the mixture of what we have inherited from Europe with what we have invented for ourselves has," as J. Barzun puts it, "nothing fixed, nothing final about it," but is ever

as renewable as the plastic human nature of its teachers and thinkers, anchored as they are in a New World tradition of productivity and experimentation. And if, by Santayana's sixties (the twenties of the century), America had not yet learned that productivity is not enough, it had by the post-Depression era begun to criticize and repudiate sheer material increase and unrelieved standardization. Cf. J. Barzun *God's Country & Mine* (N.Y. Random 1954); *George Santayana's America* Ed. w. Intro. by J. Ballowe (Illinois U.P. **1967**); and *Santayana on America* Ed. by with Intro. R.C. Lyon (N.Y. Harcourt **1968**).

9. New York *Times Book Review*, Feb.7, 1993; pp.3, 17.

10. The page numbers given for volumes of *The Life of Reason* are those of the Triton edition of Santayana's works; the italics are mine.

11. *The Journal of Philosophy*, III (1906); pp.410-412. Reprinted in **AFSL**.

12. Authors, respectively, of: *Nature and Historical Experience* 1958, *Ways of Being* 1962, *The Metaphysics of Naturalism* 1938-1967, *The Metaphysics of Natural Complexes* 1966 & 1990. Cf. also my, "The Centrality of Art in Classic American Philosophy," *American Studies* Spring, 1990.

13. In H.S.Levinson's words, *Pragmatism, and the Spiritual Life*, p.207.

14. *Essays in Critical Realism* ed. by Durant Drake 1920, (N.Y. Peter Smith 1941); p.163-186.

15. What Santayana says about non-usable technical philosophies is worth quoting: "Professional philosophies, sincere and . . . impassioned enough in controversy, are often but poor hypocrisies in daily life. . . . I am addressing those only who are willing, for the time being, to accept my language. . . . [In contrast to the realm of matter, the realms of truth and essence] are proposed as conceptual distinctions and categories of logic; as one of many languages in which the nature of things may be described. Anyone who wishes is free to discard these categories and employ others. The only question will be how he will get on; what sort of intellectual dominion and intellectual life he will achieve; also whether he will really be using other categories in his . . . successful contacts with the world, or only a different jargon in his professional philosophy" (*The Realm of Truth*, book 3 of *The Realms of Being* [New York: Scribner's, 1938], 47f.).

16. In "The Spirit's Alchemicana," p.11, with reference to Blake's "A Vision of the Last Judgment," *1992 Intl.Conf. on Santayana*, Avila, Spain.

17. References with an uppercase Roman numeral after the title's initials are to the Triton edition of Santayana's works. In the footnote to **RS V.**73, while rehearsing two or three senses of 'matter,' Santayana anticipated having to return to the subject of 'matter.' **RM** did this 25 years later, in 1930. The passage from **RS** quoted above is part of that which J.H. Randall quoted to

begin his famous review of **RM**, "The Latent Idealism of a Materialist." Useful and eloquent as this review is, it mistakenly takes Santayana to be hypostatizing—instead of merely positing—essences, and sees dualism where Santayana, on the contrary, was reaffirming the continuity between mind and matter.

18. Note the anti-formalist intent of this description of law. As bearing upon the nomothetic-deductive model of explanation that was to become fashionable in logical-empiricist circles, it anticipates the critique that disallows the applicability of this model to such disciplines as history. See my *History as a Human Science* The Conception of History in Some Classic American Philosophers (Lanham, Md.: University Press of America, 1984); Ch.2: "Narrative and Nomology." Santayana's view of history is rehearsed in Chapter 3.

19. Cf. A. Kerr-Lawson, "An Abulensian Pragmatist?" *Bulletin of the Santayana Soc.*10, Fall 1992; p.17-21.

20. And that I. Singer raises in his *Meaning in Life* (p.73); Russell's 1903 essay is reprinted in *Mysticism and Logic* (N.Y. Norton 1929).

21. This "detachment" should be seen to be really composed of *acceptance* made sharable, or, else, as a creative assimilation and witnessing.

22. Cited by Kerr-Lawson in "Toward One Santayana: Recent Scholarship," **TCSP** XXVII, 1 (1991); p.15; not found in the Triton edition.

23. Cf. **RT** 66: "We live in this human scene as in a theater, where an adult mind never loses itself so completely in the play as to forget that the play is a fiction. . . . So in the medium through which we see the world we may learn not to see the world falsely but to see ourselves truly; and the world in its true relation to ourselves. With this proviso, all the humorous and picturesque aspects of experience may be restored to the world with dramatic truth. The near is truly near, when the station of the speaker is . . . accepted as the point of reference. The good is truly good, the foreign truly foreign, if the absoluteness of the judgment is made relative to the judge. And this judge is no vagrant pure spirit. He is a man, an animal, a fragment of the material world. . . ."

24. *What Is Literature?* Tr. B. Frechtman (N.Y. Philosophical Library 1949)

25. Corey's 'innocent,' in this citation, calls for a reminder that it is their 'moral significance' that distinguishes *great* works of art for Santayana (**RA** 216). 'Innocent' in the context of aesthetics puts too much emphasis on the perception of surface-form.

26. Theognis 425: *Pántôn mèn mê phûnai epichthoníoisin áriston,* "Of all, the best earthly lot is never to have been born;" *Oed.Col.*1225: *mê phûnai tòn hápanta nikâi lógon,* "Not to be born overcomes any rationalization."

27. Cf. **AFSL** 168: "There are three traps that strangle philosophy; the Church, the marriage-bed, and the professor's chair. I escaped from the first in my youth; the second I never entered, and as soon as possible I got out of the third."

28. "A comprehensive desciption (of any fact) includes also all the radiations of that fact . . . all that perspective of the world of facts and of the realm of essence which is obtained by taking this fact as a center and viewing everything else only in relation with it" (**RT** viii).

29. Cf. D. Corey "Notes on the Deliberate Philosophy of Santayana," **AFSL** 31, where Corey points out that thinkers who also "accept, on other grounds, the causal inefficacy of consciousness in nature," are inconsistent when they impute to Santayana a gap between thinking and behavior or ethical conduct.

30. P. Conkin*Puritans and Pragmatists* (N.Y. Dodd, Mead 1968), p.438f.

31. This passage lets us see that while Santayana's realism is as much a humanism as Dewey's, it succeeds in contextualizing the human into the wider background of cosmographic nature and social history, in distinction from Dewey's anchoring of human conduct in biology alone and social responsiveness.

32. Rational courage, Santayana reminds us, is courteous.

33. Santayana's reference, here, has to be, as in the American or dialogical tradition of Plato-interpretation, to the Socrates of Plato's dialogues, not Xenophon's or D. Laertius's or some de-dramatized, ideological or idiosyncratic composite. Cf. F.J.E. Woodbridge **SA**, J.H. Randall **PDLR**, and my **PDOBO**.

References & Bibliography

J.Brent   *Charles Sanders Peirce A Life* (Indiana U.P. 1993)

J.Buchler   "One Santayana or Two," The *J. of Philosophy* LVI (1954); p.54.

P.Conkin   *Puritans and Pragmatists* (N.Y. Dodd, Mead 1968)

M.Fisch   *Classic American Philosophers* (N.Y. Appleton-Century-Crofts 1951)

J.Lachs   *George Santayana* (Boston: Twayne 1988)**GS**

S.Lamprecht   *The Metaphysics of Naturalism* (N.Y. Appleton-Century 1967)

A.Kerr-Lawson "Spirit & the Materialism of Old Age," *1992 Intl. Conference on G. Santayana*, Avila, Spain
"Toward One Santayana: Recent Scholarship," *Transactions of the C.S.Peirce Society* XXVII, 1 (1991); 1-26.

H.S.Levinson *Pragmatism, and the Spiritual Life* (Chapel Hill: U. of N. Carolina 1992) **PSL**

R.C.Lyon "The Spirit's Alchemicana," *1992 Intl.Conf. on Santayana*, Avila, Spain

J.H.Randall *Nature & Historical Experience* (Columbia U.P. 1958)
"The Latent Idealism of a Materialist," in *Animal Faith & Spiritual Life*.
Plato: Dramatist of the Life of Reason (Columbia U.P. 1970) **PDLR**

R.Robin "Santayana & Philosophy at Harvard: Wasted Chances in the Creation of 'The Great Department'," *The Santayana Conference*, Avila, Spain 1992.

B.Russell *Mysticism and Logic* (N.Y. Norton 1929)

G.Santayana "Lotze's Moral Idealism," *Mind* vol.15, no.58 (**1890**); pp.191-212 (Digest of G.S.'s **1889** Ph.D. thesis)
The Sense of Beauty **1896**, Critical Ed. II, ed. Holzberger & Saatkamp, Intro. by A. Danto (M.I.T. Press 1988)
Sonnets and Other Verses (N.Y. Stone & Kimball **1896**)
Lucifer: A Theological Tragedy **1899**, (N.Y.: Irvington, rpt. 1975)
Interpretations of Poetry and Religion **1900**, Critical Ed. III, ed. Holzberger & Saatkamp, Intro. by Joel Porte (M.I.T. Press 1989)
The Life of Reason, or the Phases of Human Progress **1905-1906**, 5 vol.: I.
Reason in Common Sense II. *Reason in Society* III. *Reason in Religion*. IV. *Reason in Art* V. *Reason in Science*.
The Life of Reason One-Vol. Edition Revised (N.Y. Scribner's 1954)
Three Philosophical Poets: Lucretius, Dante, Goethe (Harvard U.P. **1910**)
Winds of Doctrine: Studies in Contemporary Opinion (N.Y. Scribner's **1913**)

G.Santayana *Egotism in German Philosophy* (N.Y. Scribner's **1913**)
    Character and Opinion in the United States With Reminescences of W.James, J. Royce and Academic Life in America (N.Y. Scribner's **1920**)
    Soliloquies in England and Later Soliloquies (N.Y. Scribner's **1922**)
    Poems: Selected by the Author and Revised (N.Y. Scribner's **1923**)
    Scepticism and Animal Faith: Introduction to a System of Philosophy (N.Y. Scribner's **1923**)
    Dialogues in Limbo **1926**, w. *Three New Dialogues* 1948 (N.Y. Scribner's)
    Platonism and the Spiritual Life (N.Y. Scribner's **1927**)
    The Realm of Essence Bk.I of *The Realms of Being* (N.Y. Scribner's **1927**)
    The Realm of Matter Bk.II of *The Realms of Being* (N.Y. Scribner's **1930**)
    The Genteel Tradition at Bay (N.Y. Scribner's **1931**)
    Some Turns of Thought in Modern Philosophy (N.Y. Scribner's **1933**)
    The Last Puritan: A Memoir in the Form of Novel (N.Y. Scribners' **1936**)
    Obiter Scripta: Lectures, Essays and Reviews Ed. J. Buchler & B. Schwarts (N.Y. Scribner's **1936**)OS
    The Realm of Truth Bk.III of *The Realms of Being* (N.Y. Scribner's **1938**)
    The Realm of Spirit Bk.IV of *The Realms of Being* (N.Y. Scribner's **1940**)
    Realms of Being **1942**, One-Vol. Edition, w. New Intro. (Cooper Sq. rpt. 1972)
    Persons and Places **1944-1953**, Critical Ed. I, Holzberger & Saatkamp, Intro. by R.C. Lyon (M.I.T. Press 1986)
    The Idea of Christ in the Gospels; or, God in Man: A Critical Essay (N.Y. Scribner's **1946**)
    The Philosophy of George Santayana Ed. P.A. Schilpp (Northwestern U.P. **1940**)PGS
    Dominations and Powers: Reflections on Liberty, Society, and Government (N.Y. Scribner's **1951**)
    The Poet's Testament: Poems and Two Plays (N.Y. Scribner's **1953**)

G.Santayana   *The Idler and His Works*, Essays Ed. Daniel Cory (N.Y.
               Brazillier *1957*)
               "On the False Steps of Philosophy," Pref. by D. Cory *J.of
               Philosophy* LXI (**1964**); pp.6-19.
               *Animal Faith and Spiritual Life: Unpublished & Uncollected
               Writings of G.Santayana*, w. Critical Essays, Ed. by J.
               Lachs (N.Y. Appleton-Century **1967**)
               George Santayana's America Ed. w. Intro. by J. Ballowe
               (Illinois U.P. **1967**)
               The Birth of Reason and Other Essays Ed. by D. Cory
               (Columbia U.P. **1968**) **BR**
               Santayana on America Ed. by with Intro.R.C. Lyon (N.Y.
               Harcourt **1968**)
               Physical Order and Moral Liberty Unpublished Essays Ed. J.
               & S. Lachs (Vanderbilt U.P. **1969**)
               Lotze's System of Philosophy G.S.'s Harvard Dissertation Ed.
               by P.G. Kuntz (Indiana U.P. 1971)

J.P.Sartre   *Being and Nothingness* Tr. H. Barnes (N.Y. Philosophical Libr.
               1956)
               What is Literature? Tr. B. Frechtman (N.Y. Philosophical Libr.
               1949)
               Literary & Philosophical Essays Tr. A. Michelson (N.Y.
               Criterion Bks. 1955)

H.Schneider   *Ways of Being* (Columbia U.P. 1962)

B.J.Singer   *The Rational Society* (Case Western Reserve U.P. 1970)
               "Naturalism & Generality in Buchler and Santayana,"
               Bulletin of the Santayana Society No.3, Fall 1985; p.29-37.

I.Singer   *Meaning in Life* (N.Y. Free Press 1992)

V.Tejera   *Art and Human Intelligence* (N.Y. Appleton-Century 1965)
               Plato's Dialogues One By One (N.Y. Irvington 1984)
               PDOBO
               "Spirituality in Santayana," *Transactions of the C.S.Peirce
               Society* XXV, No.4 (1989); pp. 504-529.
               "The Centrality of Art in Classic American Philosophy,"
               American Studies Spring, 1990; pp.83-90.
               "Santayana, and the Western Intellectual Tradition," *1992
               Intl. Conf. on Santayana*, Avila, Spain

V. Tejera   *The City-State Foundations of Western Political Thought* 2 rev. ed. (Lanham: U.P.A. 1993)

"Santayana's Whitman Revisited," *Bulletin of the Santayana Society* No.10, 1992.

"On the Classical Origins of the Concept of Happiness," *Intl.Soc. for the Study the Classical Tradition*, Boston; March 1995.

FJE Woodbridge   *The Son of Apollo* (Boston: Houghton 1929) **SA**

W.B. Yeats   *The Autobiography of William Butler Yeats* (N.Y. Macmillan 1938)

Abbreviations

GS	=	George Santayana:	Lachs
PGS	=	The Philosophy of George Santayana:	Schilpp
OS	=	Obiter Scripta:	Buchler & Schwartz
BR	=	The Birth of Reason:	Lachs
AFSL	=	Animal Faith & Spiritual Life:	Lachs
SAF	=	Scepticism and Animal Faith:	Santayana
LR	=	The Life of Reason:	"
PGS	=	The Philosophy of G. Santayana:	"
RCS	=	Reason in Common Sense:	"
RS	=	Reason in Socety:	"
RR	=	Reason in Religion:	"
RA	=	Reason in Art:	"
RSC	=	Reason in Science:	"
IPR	=	Interpretations of Poetry & Religion:	Santayana
RB	=	Realms of Being:	Santayana
RE	=	The Realm of Essence	"
RM	=	The Realm of Matter	"
RT	=	The Realm of Truth	"
RSP	=	The Realm of Spirit	"
WL	=	What is Literature?	Sartre

CHAPTER IV

Buchler's Metaphysics:
The Dimensions of Reflective
Activity

(i) *Experience and the Human Process*

A good way to take Buchler's introduction to the revised edition of
his *Toward a General Theory of Human Judgment* is as a clarification,
upgrading, and replacement of Dewey's notion of 'experience' with
the idea of 'proception.' Just as John Dewey had, in both his 1917
essay on "The Need for Recovery in Philosophy" and his Preface to
the second edition of *Experience and Nature*, criticized and revised
the notion of "experience" in the traditions of European rationalism
and empiricism, so Buchler revises, contextualizes, and replaces
Dewey's conception of experience—in *Toward a General Theory of
Human Judgment* and *Nature and Judgment*—with the broader, more
determinate conception of "proception."[1] And this is a key-term in
Buchler's philosophy, or *analytic* contextualization, of the human
process. Buchler's metaphysics, his philosophy of natural complexes,
corresponds to the second of his two great concerns, namely, the

coordinative categorization of both human and natural processes in such a way that the continuity between, and distinctiveness of, both are respected and made intelligible.

One thing wrong with the inherited notion of experience is its unexamined reliance on the opaque contrast between "inner" and "outer" experience. The distinction is not metaphoric, nor can it be made more precise; it blocks inquiry, and biases discussion of the topic towards dualism. The traditional conception of experience at once excludes too much and is too oriented to knowledge in a narrow cognitivist sense. Nor does it succeed in giving a satisfactory account of the assurance that experience can and does give us in making connections, namely, in our reasoning.

The acceptance of the term ranges from that of a bio-extended unit of "reference," as when we say, "that was a dreadful experience," to a matter of degree or court of appeal: as when we say, "your experience as a carpenter is greater than mine," or "experience shows otherwise." Given, further, that it is taken to be something that we are both *involved in* and *pervaded by*, and that, on the other hand, it is taken to consist of little more than a succession of sensations such that neither Hume nor Kant were able to give a satisfactory, non-apriorist, non-dualistic account of how it is that these sensations produce knowledge. Given, finally, that experience has also always been used meaningfully and basically in phrases that equate it with human history or the human process, as in the usage, "that is what dramatists have found important in human experience," it is no wonder that Dewey felt the conception needed clarification.

Most broadly Dewey (in Buchler's interpretation) reconceived experience as a kind of relation. But he also

> combines a Hegelian-type emphasis on the continuity and movement of consciousness with a Peircean-type emphasis on thought's response to what is recalcitrant (TGT xxx).[2]

In the transaction between organism and environment, there is an alteration both of the world and the organism. This is *experiencing*; but there is also experience that feels like, or emerges as something unified, what Dewey calls "*an* experience." The two dimensions of experience are "doing" and "undergoing." And Dewey distinguishes between primary or "gross experience," and secondary or "reflective" experience. Like his colleague G.H. Mead who saw that experience is communicative, because constituted by social behavior, Dewey included both knowing and behaving in his conception of experience. With good historical insight Buchler points out that,

> what for Hegel is the experiential struggle of thought with its own depths and internal oppositions, is for Dewey and Mead the experiential process of *problem-solving*. Whereas for Hegel the focus of experience is the Idea, for Dewey it is *the situation* (TGT xxxii, my emphasis).

Under the influence of Darwin, *adaptive* man is now seen by Dewey as the problem-solving animal. Active experience (doing) is seen as a seeking of means to survival.[3] Dewey calls experience associated with the attainment of ends "consummatory experience." When there is a balance between doing and undergoing, according to Dewey, we may be said to have had *an* integral experience, as when we go through an aesthetic experience. But in spite of Dewey's repeated insistence that experience is one manifestation of nature: that it is precisely the *interrelation* in which nature is *joined with* human nature, Dewey's *best* critics—such as Santayana—have misread him as subjectivist, even though Santayana was not himself, as are most of Dewey's other critics, trapped within a subjectivist model of experience. This was because of Dewey's concern, in his metaphysics, with what Santayana called "the foreground" of man's interaction with the environment, rather than with his cosmographic or historical situatedness, as in Santayana's own philosophy.

But Dewey's account does not clarify why *any* event experienced is not integral in its own way. If the event, like an aesthetic experience, acquires its unity from the felt quality of it, then Dewey has still not explained matters, because for him qualities are "indescribable." It seems, I would add, that Dewey is unconsciously defining the unity of an experience as a function of its unitary object. And this object when it is a work-of-art is indeed more unified, and more inducive of coherence in the response to it, than ordinary events. But this was exactly the fallacy of those nineteenth-century books on feelings and emotions that distinguished them according to their objects.[4]

Buchler's bigger objection is that, aside from reflective experience such as that of art,

> the process of experiencing as such requires the individual to be an agent who consciously perceives and anticipates. . . . it follows that any individual whom events affect, but without his agency . . . awareness . . . assent or dissent, his choice or intention, is somehow excluded from an experience and from experiencing. If this is what the concept entails, then clearly another concept is required to fill the explanatory gap (TGT xxxv).

Because his focus is on *whatever is relevant* to the individual's *continuing course of life* (ibid.), Buchler has to disallow Dewey's claim that that "to have an experience, the action and its consequence must be joined in perception." Because of his concern with the social, ethical, and aesthetic aspects of human being, Dewey "confuses the traits of experience with the traits of morally important experience" (TGT xxxvii). Buchler concludes from his survey of the notion of experience that the concept is "from the philosophic point of view . . . functionally spent," and that a fresh set of concepts is required.

For an adequate metaphysics of the human process, these concepts need to overcome such sharp distinctions as that which Dewey saw between doing and undergoing, and the residual discontinuity which Dewey is unaware of between his *experiencing* and *an* experience. They will try to take account of the fact that even "doing" is not always instrumental behavior, and that experience *as problematic* is not primary; there **is** non-problematic and non-instrumental doing.

> Not even all *methodic* activity is an attempt to solve problems. . . . an artist *may* be engaged in problem-solving of [some] sort . . . he also may *not*. His methodic experience may be that of shaping materials through the cultivation of powers and propensities. The completion of his product . . . may wait upon the mere passage of time . . . the occurrence of an inclination, or . . . growth in perception. A task to be accomplished is not the same as a problem to be solved (TGT xxxviii).

Undergoing is not mainly affective sensory awareness, as in Dewey; nor is it, when it's gradual conditioning, mainly conscious. Undergoing can be diffuse, generalized, inarticulate and random as well as purposive, wasteful or even perverse. These are "aspects of . . . life" which "an adequate philosophic conception . . . of human life should be able to encompass [as] "reflected by the sciences and arts, by moral and religious attitudes, and by what takes place psychologically, socially, technologically" (TGT xxxix).

(ii) *Proception and the Human Process*

As a starting point for a philosophy of the human process, Buchler's idea of the individual in his multidimensional humanity and directional particularity, is poles apart from the notion of the human individual as a mere entity lost in the cosmic maelstrom that is common to both existentialism and positivism.[5] Buchler's search for an adequate account of the individual's embedment in, and practice of, communication, method, and reason (TGT 3), compels him to improve upon or replace such commonsense but partial concepts as "self," "character," "organism," "personality." We have looked at the difficulties caused by the term "experience;" Buchler's interest in "the status and meaning of individuality" finds further that,

> "experiencing" is not broad enough to include all forms of behavior, and "behaving" is not broad enough to include all phases of experience (TGT 4).

Functionally viewed, the individual not only has some kind of unity ("functions in a unitary way") but also has dimensions, and drift or direction. So Buchler sees that "the interplay of the human individual's activities and dimensions, their unitary direction," constitute "a process which [he will] call *proception*."

Buchler wants to stress that the whole individual is the *cumulative* representative of the moving individual. So the term proception is designed to suggest, a moving union of seeking and receiving, of forward propulsion and patient absorption. Proception is the composite, directed activity of the individual. Any instance of his functioning, any event in his history enters into the proceptive direction. Reciprocally . . . the way . . . an individual will act at any time . . . the way in which his . . . character will be modified, depends on his proceptive direction. Proception is the process in which a man's . . . self is summed up or represented.

The claim is that *the distinctive* human activities, *such as imagination, creation* or *inventiveness*, will become more intelligible when seen as properties of the proceiver rather than as properties of the thinker or feeler (TGT 5).[6] "It is the proceiver," the whole individual, "not some physiological or intellectual capacity, that wonders, asserts, interrogates. These are proceptive functions." Just as it is the hearing apparatus that determines what is heard, so the proceptive direction determines for the individual such things as his quality of conscience, his idea of the Gods, the limits of his tolerance, his hunger for Erôs, and his need for order, for reason, for art.

What we call the individual's world is, in Buchler's more precise terminology, his proceptive domain: "the content of the summed-up-self-in-process" (TGT 6). The character of this domain of course varies specifically from person to person. And *within* the process of proception the character of the domain is always alterable in kind and degree. "The proceptive domain is the ongoing representation of the human aspect of the human animal." Accordingly,

> Rationality in its most fundamental sense is a property of the proceptive process; a property predicable of the proceptive domain but not of every proceptive domain.

We will return to Buchler's renewal and clarification of the concept of rationality. For the moment let us note that proception is much more than the conscious life of the individual. It encompasses all that affects, and all that comes out of the individual human being in his life-cycle. We have to realize that Buchler is not only recategorizing the process called experience, he is "identifying a more inclusive process which has not previously been recognized as such," as Beth Singer first pointed out (ON 88).

While consciousness is only a part, and not a necessary part of the proceptive domain (NJ 109), neither are all the biological or physical events in a life proceptively relevant to the individual. The mentalistic and dualistic residues in Dewey's views of "experience" and "an experience" become visible as we come to understand that when occurrent complexes of nature involve an individual, it is *these* complexes that *constitute* his experience.[7] "[A] procept is the *existence itself*, the . . . fact, state, situation, or other . . . complex *in so far* as it is relevant to an individual as individual" (NJ 122-3). "Proception. . . . is a natural process, distinguishable in specific terms from other natural processes" (NJ 111).

> [A]t the risk of initial imprecision let "proception" suggest the inseparable union of process with receptivity, of movement in nature with impact by nature, of things shaped with events accepted. The emphasis is on historicity and natural involvement (ibid.).

The term "proception" aims to recognize conceptually the precise character of individual historicity. So, too, the term "procept" is needed to determine the status of a natural complex that enters, or is actualized by, proception.

The "questionable metaphysical assumptions" that Buchler's terms seek to avoid are (i) the implied opposition between "experience" and "nature" as contrasting existential orders, with the contrast constituting the principal problem of philosophy; (ii) the implied roping off of a "realm of experience," entailing that what is to be found in experience is not necessarily found in existence; (iii) the reductive inclusion of the "realm" of experience in a positivistically understood "realm" of nature.

The proceptive process is directed and propulsive in character. Birth and growth are the primary propulsive forces. They are what give rise to the individual's "natural commitments," as Buchler calls them (NJ 112), or to those "imperatives [that] are categorical in the sense that they are inevitably present in experience" (NJ 3). As Buchler says in the first sentence of NJ, "Man is born in a state of natural debt, being antecedently committed to the execution or the furtherance of acts that will largely determine his individual existence."

The *proceptive direction* is the result of the propulsions of the individual and the specific directions in which they lead; and it is, naturally, malleable by events and variable. The concept of the proceptive direction supersedes, in Buchler, the older idea of "funded experience" which did not allow clearly enough either for the fact that this fund can be qualitatively changed by a given addition to it, or that as a persistence of the individual it is a natural complex (a procept) "essential to the uniqueness of the total individual-in-movement" (NJ 113). The proceiver, indeed, is *not*

> anything separable from the plurality of traits and circumstances distinguishable in his history: it is quite enough to say that they make *a history* and are not just a plurality (*ibid.* my emphasis).

Being propulsive and directional, proception has to be cumulative; and this means that some potential relations are excluded from the individual's future, while others are included in it. This, in turn, is what facilitates the identification of repetitions or regularities in experience; events or things become instances because of their experiential character or their role in an individual's history. But the sheer recurrence of events is not the only feature in the primitive texture of experience (NJ 116), confrontations with oddity or brute newness are a part of it too. We see that the phrase "learning from experience" implies "all three of the factors . . . enumerated: many repeated instances of occurrence, a cumulative efficacy in these repetitions, and an integration of new instances with old." The phrase "sharing his experience with another," on the other hand, assumes that what one individual has assimilated may be communicated to another as a relative novelty in his life.

To proceive, says Buchler, "when it appears to be used transitively, is only an ellipsis for a more complex relational account" than is available in the locution "to experience" used transitively. "Nature proceived," he continues, "means, not the object of an operation, psychic or otherwise, but nature in so far as it is related to a given individual history" (NJ 124). Now, the proceiver is also a producer; so that an individual's judgment or utterance is necessarily one of his procepts; for, "what stems from him is part of that which makes him what he is" (ibid.). There are, of course, numerous complexes related to individuals, yet not related to them as procepts, such as for example the microorganisms in their shoes. There is nothing however, that may not conceivably enter into relation to some individual as proceiver.

Only at times does a modification or reinforcement of an individual's proceptive direction (a procept), depend upon awareness. "This truth," says Buchler,

> neglected by contemporary philosophers, is a commonplace to the older philosophers of the passions, to poets and storytellers since antiquity, and to almost all the . . . schools of modern psychology" (NJ 125f.).

The world to most empiricists becomes experientially available through what they call the "data of experience," where data are *mere* sensory *surfaces*. But the distinction that this gives rise to between "datum and object," "appearance and reality," "shadow and substance," is legitimate only when functionally invoked to distinguish between some *standard* configuration and an irregular, adventitious or unexpected, version of it. The distinction is philosophically inexcusable, for Buchler, because it asserts a bias (an ontological priority) in favor of one form of reality over all the others. But, in "a more comprehensive conception of experience . . . the one realm is as experiencable as the other, and each is a factor in any proceptive domain" (NJ 127). I will quote Buchler's aside here, because it is relevant both to many philosophers in the tradition, and to such Post-Modernists as Jacques Lacan.

> Those . . . for whom in monstrous but unwitting irony the real is the inaccessible, have succeeded not in sundering nature from experience

but in providing fodder for the philistines. They have, as Whitehead suggests . . . tried to make two natures, nature meant and nature dreamt. But what is intrinsically inaccessible cannot be meant; and a dream which has uninterrupted order and continuity, a dream to which there can be no alternative condition, is no dream at all.

On this approach "naive realism," and "representationalism," likewise become meaningless. For, in saying that our knowledge is of reality just as it actually is or that the structure of our knowledge is isomorphic with the structure of reality, they are denying or minimizing the distinction between appearance and reality in a way which does not abandon an ontological priority—whether that of the knowledge-process (as in idealism), or that of a prior reality which knowledge may match conceptually (as in positivism). Similarly, not only "a doctrine of intrinsically unavailable realities is avoided," but so is a doctrine of "internal relations," given that not all natural complexes are pertinent (as procepts) to the unique being of any given individual.

Also saved by the idea of proception are such usages of "experience" as are found in locutions which appeal to social experience; for example, as when we appeal to "the American experience of competition," or "country x's experience of parliamentary government" as a form of oligarchy. Buchler's terminology acknowledges that there are real similarities between one individual and another, between spans of one individual history and spans of other individual histories. This is proceptive parallelism; and proceptive parallelism makes social history and social experience possible.

There can be no community or history of a group without proceptive parallelism, because without it the group is reduced to atomized aggregates or masses with no representative or common traits. What we call "human experience" is not just a multiplicity of human happenings, but "the tissue of likeness in individual human histories." That which we appeal to when appealing to it is

what can be appropriated in some mode of judgment by one individual and another and still another. It would make no sense to what is available in one way to this individual, in another to that, and in no way at all. There is no social experience, and actually no social being, without community, and there is no community without proceptive parallelism (NJ 129).

What Buchler means by "in some mode of judgment" is key, and will emerge in the sequel; it is of strategic importance in Buchler's system.[8]

To the question of the relative weight of activity or passivity in experience, "sensationalism," "intellectualism," "rationalism," and "empiricism" have provided different answers. But none have given a sufficiently generalized account (NJ 131). So Buchler proposes replacing the old distinction between agent and patient with the concept of the bi-dimensional proceiver who is simultaneously manipulative and assimilative in whatever he does. We must not absorb conditions into results, or process into product; for, that is how manipulation gets thought of as only of objects "wholly available and controllable" (NJ 133).[9] To be manipulated is *not* to be *wholly* manipulated. While coping with obstructions is a regular function of the proceptive economy, this function "is not to be confused with the problem-solving process, than which it is far more rudimentary" (NJ 134).

Manipulation, in Buchler's account, is much more the perpetuation of the individual's functions than a piecemeal handling of objects. An individual manipulates the environment by giving form to complexes within it, whether these are behavioral or communicative processes. What is encountered by the individual are "elements in a gross framework of" of having to respond and having to formulate. Buchler emphasizes that, as an attribute of proception, manipulation no more entails awareness and is no more the result of willing than proception or than living itself is. Even intentional manipulations don't always have specific ends, while deliberative manipulations are always concomitant with other non-deliberative manipulations.

Buchler amends the old dictum that there is nothing in the intellect that wasn't first in the senses, to say: "there is nothing in the intellect or in the senses which is not first in the proceptive economy" (NJ 135). Moreover, the world that the individual manipulates is the same portion of the finite world that he accepts and endures; and supposedly wholly assimilable objects are never wholly assimilable any more than supposedly wholly accessible objects are wholly accessible or manipulable. The latter would be the complete destruction of the object, just as complete assimilation would be of the assimilating subject by the object. What cannot be assimilated at all is, of course, that which is no part of the individual's proceptive domain. On the other hand, when assimilation-manipulation is *methodic*, it becomes what Buchler calls "query" (NJ 140).

Buchler's "manipulation," then, captures aspects of experience that Dewey's too instrumentalist notion of "doing" does not do justice to. When I juxtapose two images in memory, or inhale more deeply, I need not be acting instrumentally. Nor, in the particular way in which someone might panic, is s/he acting instrumentally. Again, "undergoing" in Dewey is too much associated with "immediacy," "the qualitative," and at the other extreme with the "final," the "terminal," or the ineffable. Assimilation consists in receptivity, not just to things qualititative, but to the addition of every procept in the proceptive domain. What an individual assimilates is not just what he feels, but rather what he sustains (NJ 138); for example,

> when [one] is slandered by his neighbors, in the . . . absence of awareness on his part, great changes may take place in his possibilities and relationships, and the course of his subsequent experience altered; yet these occurrences are assimilated into his proceptive direction, sustained by his . . . related self, in utter independence of any "immediate qualitative experience."

Lastly, where assimilation and manipulation are co-occurrent, co-dimensional and continuous with one another, doing and undergoing in Dewey, can vary inversely with each other or actually suppress each other.

Now the ways in which an individual's environment is altered by him are to an extent determinable by his choice. And his methodic assimilation or methodic manipulation constitutes the process that Buchler calls *query* (**NJ** 140).

Choice is itself at once a shaping and an acceptance: a subject-of-query is manipulated because it can be sustained . . . as a procept, and endured or assimilated because it can be shaped to be the procept that it is.

In the rationalist-empiricist tradition which Dewey was attacking, however, the sole manifestation of *activity* in what that tradition called "experience," is "thinking;" and the sole manifestation of *passivity* was "sensing." From the points of view of classic American philosophy, this is a travesty, as if there was no assimilation in (the activity of) thinking, or no manipulation in (the receptivity of) sensing. The exclusive rationalist-empiricist concern with "knowledge" in its own special sense, only compounds the narrowness, since this sense has been dogmatized and overly circumscribed by its followers. Thus,

they have inadvertently left it to art to deal with experience in its proper breadth and to render exhibitively what they should equally have recognized and encompassed assertively (NJ 141).

Buchler wants us to see the experiential relation as an "object-object" rather than a "subject-object" relation.[10] In his view proception (or experience) is the diversified interrelatedness or involvement of manipulation and assimilation. Therefore, the judgments of the individual are   *not*—as might at first appear—instances solely of manipulation. He is *both* "a witness, a gatherer, a patient, a recipient of the complexes of nature," *and* "he is a shaper, a transformer, an initiator, an agent of these complexes." The role of the individual "implicit throughout the course of the permutations of proception," is that of "commentator on nature [and] his own nature" (NJ 142). And this commentary, for Buchler, is utterance or judgment:

Utterance is the succession of "positions" or "postures" in proception. Each . . . takes the form of a *product*, an instance of making, saying, or acting. And it is because every product is inherently a position in nature—inherently a pronouncement and appraisal—that it is a *judgment* (my emphases).[11]

In today's metaphysics of egocentrism, all the synonyms of "experience" not only signify "mental operations," but are derivative of a supposed subject-object relation: perceiving, feeling, knowing, and so on. And these are specialized forms of *involvement* which elide the natural historicity of the individual, whereas proception is the involvement of the whole proceiver in his history. "Involvement," moreover, Buchler adds, is in strictness *also* applicable to the complexes which are the individual's procepts, because "as related to [the] given proceiver, [involvement] expresses . . . the common presence and common relevance of all relata or determinants of proception, [as well as] the modification imposed by proception on all its relata" (NJ 144).

We should use the subject-object distinction, in other words, *only* as a functional one when discriminating situational differences between related complexes, namely, when one of the involved complexes is discriminated as proceiver and the other as procept. For, "proceivers are human complexes; their procepts may or may not be human. The experiential relation is a natural fact, like any other relation in nature, with describable differences between the complexes related."

The terminology of proception is tested by Buchler himself against two interesting problems that he brings it to bear upon, at the end of his chapter on "Experience." Let us see how it succeeds in clarifying the first, and in accounting for the second. Consider, first, some of the perplexities that plague the concept of the unconscious. How account for the disparity that is sometimes felt between the proceptive direction and a given seemingly unearned or baseless feeling—as, for instance, when an author reflecting upon a lifetime's work is overtaken by dissatisfaction with what looks, at the moment, like its futility? We would not want, with Buchler and psycho-analysis, to grant that *conscious* feeling always has the authority to approve or disapprove such a lifetime structure. The question becomes whether the occurrence of such a feeling is actually to be counted as evidence of experiential *continuity* or of fragmentariness and *discontinuity*. How can we deny that a feeling of great import is "extrinsic to the total burden of proception" (NJ 149)?

Because the judgments we produce are not wholly novel, and our habits cannot be discounted—anymore than the strong feeling in question can be—we have to look for concealed connections within experience to explain the appearance of discontinuity. But "the view that [the hidden] links lie in the Unconscious . . . blackens one half of the experience and renders most operative what is least intelligible. . . . a history half of which is intrinsically hidden would hardly seem by itself to explain the efficacy of hidden things." Buchler, on the other hand, can get at the identity of the factors of an individual history by invoking the proceptive process.

> Whatever is hidden in the individual is a natural complex that became a procept, that is, became relevant to him, in one respect (in its cumulative influence), but not in another respect (as a felt occurrence or as a cognitive object).

Having been *assimilated*, the proceptive past is no more or less accessible than the social past (NJ 151), different as the techniques might by which they are cognitively recoverable.

> The "unconscious," if it is to be preserved as a piece of functionally useful terminology, is best interpreted as a name of the pervasive structures of an individual past, its orders of coexistence and its orders of succession, and its continuing influence. What "lies in the unconscious" is something which is as yet a cognitively unrecovered situation of the proceptive process.

What is overlooked, then, when a *present feeling* appears wholly alien to a *total past* is that the two realities are not at the moment available in the same sense. The past, which is a whole order in a long process, has been shrunk into just one procept that can't compete with the presentness and nugatory strength of the new procept. But the latter can neither annul nor ratify a history, and as the result of a process, will likewise have its aetiology in the individual's history.

Another application that confirms the usefulness of Buchler's terminology is the clarification it brings to the philosophical idea of "the overwhelming recalcitrancy of natural fact" (NJ 146), which Buchler finds to be a result of misconceptions about human passivity and activity. On the one hand,

> we appear to be borne on a current that is independent of our productivity. Great portions of time and great phases of change seem to escape uncontrolled and . . . unencountered in the course of our existence. . . . they appear to be simply attended by us in a kind of inevitable passivity.

On the other, despite his helplessness, the individual

> is able to traverse vast domains of nature by the power of his thought. . . . thought is able to surmount the intransigency of fact, and to populate any number of worlds; and it is able, above all, to note and to represent to itself the whole scene, including its own helpless station.

On this view thought is passive, and inefficacious with respect to causality; but it is active as far as representation is concerned, while matter is in this respect passive.

And mind, the light kindled after a long natural evolution, is then thought of as illuminating the tragic nature of the human condition in an inhuman universe, rather than as working to insure the human quality of our survival.[12] From Buchler's point of view we see that "experience" has been conceptualized as mental life or a history of consciousness, not as a natural history. As "a history apart, rationally evaluating its irrational surroundings," it has been hardened into a separate realm of being. The assimilative and manipulative dimensions of the individual have been separated, the one being assigned to consciousness (Sartre's *pour-soi*, Santayana's *spirit*), the other to matter (Sartre's *en-soi*).[13] Consciousness is then rallied into a culminating moment in which "it" experiences a transcendent sense of liberation from or dominion over a blind material universe that cannot be present to itself.

(iii) *Query and the Metaphysics of Natural Complexes*

Before we can locate Buchler's analysis of the human process within the wider context of his ordinal metaphysics, we need to say something about the fresh understanding of *query* that it presupposes. Proceiving is not judging; but the human process, so far as it is distinctively human, is judicative—whether deliberatively so (*proairetically* so)[14] or less than deliberatively so. When "only" exploratory (*zêtetic*), it is already judicative because it is instating determinacies in reality. But "when pursued systematically or methodically, the process of ramifying judgments is the process of query" (NJ 58). Query is Buchler's term for all the forms of searching, reflection, inventiveness, or creation. It is the genus of which reasoning, as zêtetic, and as Locke reminds us, is a species (NJ 71).[15] It is "the process underlying those products that are of greatest consequence in the inventive life of man" (NJ 7).

In query the individual is engaged, at a minimum, in a process of reflexive, or self-directed, communication: he becomes an interrogator and his own advocate. In query leading to products, namely, to judgments—for every product is a judgment (**NJ** 8)—Buchler recognizes, in a far-reaching coordinative distinction, three actual *modes* of judgment. And these, as we by now should know,[16] are the assertive, the exhibitive, and the active modes of judgment. To these modes of judgment,

> we shall do well to recognize three corresponding types of process in which each . . . is potential. The **physicist's** concepts are assertive in the producing no less than in the product. **Works of art**, as exhibitive products, spring from exhibitive processes. **Political decisions** are acts fathered by a course of political action. Abstracting . . . shaping, and acting are thus names for a natural history preceding purposive judgment, not merely descriptions after the fact. The probing and the creating are in the same mode as the product (NJ 69).

In line with this, philosophy as a product gets categorized as mixed in Buchler's terms. Insofar as it formulates starting-points and its arguments draw conclusions, it is assertive; but the compounded structure of the ideas which it devises need not, as such, be assertive and may be deliberately exhibitive in design (as in Plato), or intendedly assertive (as in Spinoza or Wittgenstein)—and as oblivious to its own exhibitive edge as a structure, as dogmatizing propositionalists are to the dramatic and dialogical structuring of Plato's dialogues. There is indeed plenty of assertion in philosophic theorizing, but a philosophy also "shows" or points to certain traits of existence; it can "show by providing the means for [others] to look and find" (CM 167).

Because philosophic contrivance "takes the form of arranging categories into an order of judgments which compels as an order and not only as a means of assertion" (NJ 58), it cannot help being also an exhibitive form of judgment. "Like art, philosophy contrives to exhibit traits; like science, it aims to affirm truths" (**NJ** 59). In Buchler's own philosophy, then, we may expect a reasoned—exhibitive as well as assertive— development of the Buchlerian analogues of such central ideas as those of inquiry and method, meaning and truth, knowledge and rationality (not to mention those of experience, nature, and communication) *all of which have heretofore been construed only assertively.*

Using language about philosophic systems in general that Buchler used about Whitehead's system in particular, we may say that Buchler is *not* offering his work as a "new way of seeing." He finds that locution unsatisfactory, because[17]

> Besides perpetuating the age-old bias toward sight as paradigm, this expression is not more applicable to systematic than non-systematic invention in philosophy.

Major philosophic systems arise in Buchler's view "from . . . new mode[s] of discriminating complexes in nature . . . which intrinsically aim to translate [them]selve[s] into a discipline of generalization. . . . A system is kindled . . . not by a desire to give answers, but by a demanding form of awareness that requires conceptual ramification."

Thus, Buchler discriminates inquiry as only one species of query. Query itself, he finds to occur in three irreducible, but sometimes co-occurrent modes, namely, in the three modes of judgment. When it functions exhibitively for instance, and as just stated, "a philosophy judges or discriminates exibitively not through individual units or compounded units but through its categorial order" (MNC2, 193).

However, "Metaphysics is not the whole of philosophy" (MNC2, 207). The term "metaphysics" is not analogous to "aesthetics" or "ethics." It is not a subject-matter area in the same sense. It is, rather, one of the functions of philosophy. "The metaphysical function is to frame . . . 'the most fundamental and general concepts of a given subject-matter' . . . . It is not the breadth of the subject-matter that distinguishes metaphysics, but the breadth of the complexes discriminated in a particular subject-matter" (ibid.). So, because philosophy is not only metaphysical query, Buchler's reader can expect to find both assertive judgment and exhibitive judgment operating in his work.

Philosophy, as we are seeing in this book, is query as well as inquiry. Buchler's reader will remember, however, that philosophic assertions call for additional criteria of validation, and are not validated the same way that scientific assertions are verified. For, a philosophic structure does not compel assent in the same way that a scientific theory does. In general, the worth of an exhibitive judgment lies, as in poetry, in its being worthy of articulation (MNC², 212). And judgment in general becomes, in Buchler's system, what *creators in other fields* have always felt it could ideally be, namely, a matter of *communicative* power or *effectiveness* not just a matter of propositional clarity. As a practice, lastly, a philosophy is a form of active judgment responding to the questions of how much its achieved intellectual order can benefit the quality of life of its readers, and whether (as a multimodal discourse) it can satisfy their need for basic understanding as well as their tacit craving for perspectives or narratives that address the human condition at the level of art.

Buchler's naturalistic humanism, like Santayana's, is not Protagorean. There is no inference in his metaphysics that nature at large has the traits that characterize proception or experience as such. Where Dewey's philosophy would count as a philosophy of experience, in Randall's distinction between philosophies of experience and philosophies of being (NHE 273f.), and Santayana's as a philosophy of being, Buchler's is clearly a metaphysics of both natural and human processes. What is novel about Buchler's philosophic explorations is his formulation of the principle of ontological *parity*, his *ordinal* restatement of the problem of *identity*, his redefinition of change in terms of *prevalescence* and *alescence*, his disambiguation of the concepts of possibility and actuality, and his success in locating the inclusive human order, and human *utterance* or productivity, in relation to other inclusive orders.

Buchler was no doubt led to his principle of ontological parity by, among other things, the experience of poetry and art; perhaps, also by his democratic sense of reality. The way in which poetry, as productive query, discriminates its objects is already a tacit assertion of ontological parity. Whatever is and whatever is discriminated, in whatever way, is, in Buchler's systematic philosophy, a *natural complex*. Whatever is *for* us, is discriminated and has traits; but, of course, not all natural complexs are discriminated. Any complex is an order or complex of traits or subaltern complexes and traits. Nature is the presence and availability of complexes, the provision and determination of traits. Nature is providingness, but not providence or providentness.

The traditional terms "being," "existence," "reality" are beset by perplexities when they are applied to all conceivable discriminanda, as are the terms "thing" and "object" (MNC4-5). We cannot say that any of the expressions "*a* being," "*an* entity," "*a* reality," "*an* existence" is applicable to every conceivable discriminandum. So, Buchler introduces the concept of "natural complex." It

> permits the identification of all discriminanda generically, without prejudicing the pursuit and the analysis of differences, of further similarities within differences, of futher differences within these similarities. . . . [And] it permits various distinctions and categorizations.

And just because every discriminandum is complex, it is always subject to query. All complexes, when their ramifications are pursued, will be found to harbor both actualities and possibilities. For the same reason, natural complexes are unendingly interpretable or manipulatable in any number of orders. This last statement will sound, to many readers, like Buchler's version of the classic American philosophic principle of corrigibility.

A complex is seen as a trait when it is considered subaltern in a more inclusive complex. Every complex is an order of complexes and belongs to an order of complexes (MNC 13); and, as with traits, complexes may be located in more than one order of complexes. The point is the contribution this makes to the analysis of change: it enables us to speak justifiably of a complex as *the same*, even if not all of its traits remain the same. "Subaltern complex" means no more than "trait." Any complex has subaltern complexes, and is subaltern in some other complex.[18] The relations of a complex, its possibilities and powers, or potentialities, are also, it is to be remembered, traits or "constituents" of complexes but not necessarily in the sense of "parts" of the complex (MNC 15-16).

Nothing is perfectly simple, Buchler's ontology recognizes, because for something to be absolutely simple it would have to be single, unrelated, and unqualified (MNC 17). Simples are only conceptual; the adjective "simple" does no more than negate the plurality or multiplicity of a complex *in some respect.* An element or simple would, contradictorily, have to be *related* to the complex of which it is an element or simple; and this relatedness would, be a trait of something that by definition can't have traits. And there can be no possibility that is a simple, because possibilities cannot be relationless. Nor could a simple be known or manipulated, since it must remain *unrelated* to what would assimilate it.

The insufficiently analyzed notion of unanalyzable qualities, of "simple quality," does not evade the pre-category of natural complex any more than "simples" do. A quality is said to be simple because "it is the common denominator of nothing else,"[19] and because (it is also said) it has no "parts." But, in Buchler's terms, anything that has no ramifications or constitution, that has no integrity or is not an integrity, cannot be discriminated (MNC 20-21). In connection with feelings or colors alleged to be simple qualities, their "spread-outness," for instance, is just as much an integrity as their tone or hue. To be discriminable is to be a complex, is to be trait-constituted, namely, a differentiable integrity. And what is differentiable, of course, both has traits in common with other complexes and traits that are unique to it.

Now, a complex has an integrity for each order in which it is located; so Buchler calls the interrelation of its many integrities the gross integrity of the complex or, synonymously, the contour of the complex. "The identity," of a complex thus becomes definable as, "the continuous relation that obtains between the contour of the complex and any of its integrities" (MNC 22). The notion of "contour" recognizes that the many integrities and suborders are the integrities (complexes) of a more inclusive order. The more inclusive order is the continuity and interrelatedness of the subaltern orders, no matter what discontinuities they might also show (MNC 286); but the contour is neither prior to its constituents, nor closed to new ones.

Why do we need the concept of contour? Because a complex is not just the relatedness of its integrities to one another. The addition or alteration of an integrity only augments the contour of the complex; it does not change the identity of the complex. When given integrities of a complex are unrelated[20] they all belong to the same complex if they are determinants of the same contour of integrities. And we don't have to posit an "underlying substance" as what preserves the identity of the complex undergoing change.

There are two distinct and, it turns out, mutually exclusive modes of being that philosophers of "being," have failed to identify. Buchler discriminates them as "prevalence" and "alescence." As two generic aspects of natural processes, they are needed to bring out the senses in which complexes can be said to be. Prevalence and alescence are also needed for completion of the account of change and the sense in which identity is not sameness, or not sameness in the sense handed down by the Sophistic and cosmogonic interpretations of Parmenides.[21]

"A complex," says Buchler, "is prevalent in so far as it excludes traits from its contour. A complex is alescent in so far as it admits traits into its contour" (MNC 56). And, in so far as a complex prevails, its integrity is in that respect definitive. But an alescence also has an integrity; as a prevalence excludes variation and deviance, so an alescence is an integrity introducing them in the midst of some prevalence (MNC 57f.). Alescence, then, is difference within (relative to) an order; it is "relational variation" or "relational arising" (MNC 70). It is "the introduction of a different integrity within the contour of that complex" (MNC 72).

> It is that dimension of nature in which the specific integrities of complexes *initially* are what . . . and how they are, whether in time, within an organization of traits, or . . . an order of encounter. It suggests origination or nascence or incipience . . . of growth . . . irrelevance . . . oddity, or of deterioration; the incipience of ordinal relocation of or difference within an order (MNC 57).

It helps to begin by noting that, when an alescence is a coalescence a complex arises from a junction or intersection or novel configuration of complexes: "there is variation in the world without deviation from any prevalent complex in particular, and without any particular complex having to be augmented or despoiled" (MNC 57).

The three other distinguishable forms of alescence may be intermingled:

> In *augmentative* alescence a prevailing complex is extended, increased, or enhanced. In *spoliative* alescence there is loss or attenuation, expiration or extinction of a complex that has prevailed. . . . The fourth form, *vagrant* alescence, involves that which has a "chance" or "dangling" character (ibid.).

The only English term that comes near to being synonymous, *tabescence*, is defined (in Webster) only in its aspect as medical deterioration, without reference to the growth that replaces lost tissue or cells. *Alescere* is Latin for "to grow up," and appears in the English co-alescent, "growing together," from *coalescere*. That the word begins with an "a," and that "a" at the beginning of a word is so often a-privative, seems to confuse readers on first acquaintance with the term. But Buchler is identifying two co-occurrent modes of "being" that need to be distinguished, and in which the being of the one does not in nature negate the being of the other.

As aspects of natural processes, prevalence and alescence are equally generic and equally necessary for a good metaphysical understanding of change. However, Buchler tells us that, while every complex must prevail, not every complex must be alescent (MNC 60). There are complexes that are changeless in the order that locates them. But since natural processes abound in augmentations and spoliations as well as in constancies and regularities, in variations and coalescences as well as individuations, the differences that complexes make need to be categorized as both alescences and prevalences because, without alescences, there would be no beginnings and no endings, no coming-into-being or passing-away, no change. Natural and human processes would be impossible because there would be no actualization of possibilities; human processes would be impossible because no complex could become a procept, and a fortiori there could be no modification of the proceptive process, no assimilation or manipulation, no learning and no productivity.

Possibility and actuality, finally, are no less fundamental dimensions—modal aspects—of natural and human processes than are prevalence and alescence. The ordinal understanding of them which we find in Buchler's account will not only complete our comprehension of the new definitions of identity and change, ordinality and relation that he has introduced us to, but will allow us to ponder the success or value of Buchler's metaphysics as a categorial scheme or category-set. We might also be able to anticipate some far-reaching and illuminating uses of his system for the purpose of clarifying or renaming basic distinctions in such more special fields as poetics or politics.

(iv) *Possibility, Actuality, and Buchler's Ordinal Category Set as Metaphysics*

As a discriminable integrity, "an" actuality, like "a" possibility, prevails or arises in an order (MNC 131). Possibilities are always of or for a natural complex: that such-and-such will occur or get done. As such they are traits of a complex, subaltern complexes in an order (MNC 130). The parallelism between possibility and actuality as dimensions of nature means that neither is "prior," in any sense, to the other. When mistakenly conceived as apart or "by themselves," actualities get called "substances" and possibilities are seen as "essences;" but, in fact, each is inseparable from other complexes in the order. Possibility and actuality are each related to other possibilities and other actualities.

> A possibility cannot be said to arise if it is unrelated to any actualities, nor can an actuality be said to prevail or arise if it is unrelated to any possibility. Every complex that prevails as an actuality either arose under or is presently contingent upon . . . finite conditions. . . . it is an actualization. It derives from and reflects the possibilities of other actualities (MNC 133).

Traits of complexes are what count here, not "realms" of being.

> **A given trait** (of actuality) is inevitably connected with various and numerous other traits (of possibility). Conversely, a given [trait of] possibility reflects (belongs to an order of traits containing) an innumerable train of actualities.[22]

A complex, of course, may be modified either in scope or in its integrity. It is modified in scope only, for example, if the actualization is one more instance of a recurrence; but it is modified in integrity as well if, for example, the actualization is a deviation from a recurrence (MNC 134).

As Beth J. Singer points out, in her chapter on possibility and actuality, "logical possibilities" are merely complexes defined linguistically in accordance with the principle of noncontradiction, and occur *only* in the order of discourse. "Pure possibilities" would be as contradictory as "pure simples," because they are equally unlocatable in any order (ON 183). Similarly, a "realm" of pure possibilities, with no location among the orders of nature, would have no integrity, because it has no limiting conditions. It could, therefore, not be an order or complex; it could not prevail. Having no ordinal location, moreover, such a realm would have no determinable relation to the complexes of nature; it would not even be contrastable to nature-at-large.

While possibilities and actualities presuppose one another, there is an important difference in the way that they, respectively, prevail. As we have seen, in the orders in which actualities prevail, they exclude their contradictories. On the other hand, possible complexes that are mutually exclusive may prevail in the order of which they are complexes. In Buchler's own words (MNC 156),

> If mutually contradictory complexes are actual, they never prevail in the same order; if mutually contradictory complexes prevail in the same order, they are not actualities.

It is also the case that there are two ways in which the traits of a complex may function as determinants of its contour. The contour of a complex is defined by its constituent integrities; and "those subaltern traits which define or chart the 'prospect before it' are its possibilities. On this conception of what may be called *natural definition* every trait defines, and a possibility is one kind of defining" (MNC 162).

This natural process of delineation or definition is not verbal, and it is not particularly human; it is the delimitation in nature of the limits of a complex. The traits which define "the current situation" (the actual condition) of a complex are, of course, its actual traits. But the traits which are possibilities define or delimit the alternatives open to the complex. "A possbility," Buchler says, "is a *prefinition* of the **relevant** traits in the contour of a natural complex. . . . A possibility is an extension of a complex—an extension prefined" (MNC 165). "Embraced in the prefinition," naturally, is the scope as well as the contour of the complex. By contrast, "an actuality is that prevalence of a natural complex whereby certain traits are related (or, not related) to certain other traits." In counterpoise to the actualities of a complex, its possibilities are the constituent traits of its gross prefinition.

A possibility, then, prefines the extension or continuation of the traits of a complex. But, while a prefinition may include the signification of a complex, prefinition should not be conflated with signification (MNC 166). Prefinition is a matter of traits that may or may not have meaning for someone.

> A prefinition is therefore to be distinguished from a sign, which is indeed a trait but a far less comprehensive trait within a complex. A sign is the kind of trait whereby specific limits of the complex may be ascertained by present means. It is through signs that knowledge of the complex is extended by awareness of its possibilities, and by the association of known possibilities with their eventual or anticipated actualizations.

The prefinition is intrinsic to the complex as it prevails, to *that* complex, that order of traits. The *order*, with its makeup of traits, is what basically prefines. It is represented by its prefinitions or possibilities (MNC 167). In other words, a complex can be thought of as having had traits which it no longer has; it can also be thought of as having traits which it no longer will have; complexes may acquire traits as well as lose them. "No complex . . . can be said to be "complete" in all respects, because additional traits can be absolutely excluded only in so far as it ceases to prevail" (ibid.).

"Powers" or potentialities, notes Buchler, are often attributed to complexes insofar as they are unique as often as they are attributed to complexes insofar as they are typical. Subaltern possibilities of well-patterned complexes are called potentialities; and they are usually thought of as prevalent rather than alescent. But a potentiality could just as well be discriminated for its unrepresentativeness. Buchler finds it desirable to distinguish between a potentiality and a power. "A power is a possibility that has been actualized in some degree and can be recognized as that generic power in the next instance of actualization" (MNC 173).[23] A potentiality is "a possibility in a family of possibilities"; it is located within an identifiable set of associated, prevalent conditions. "A given power," on the other hand, "does not presuppose a family of similar possibilities to which it belongs, but it does . . . presuppose other possibilities to which it is related (MNC 173-4).

The example Buchler gives emphasizes the view that the powers of the human individual, e.g., George Washington, belong to him as a sociohistorical being; they are traits of an order that includes his relations and circumstances, the communities to which he belonged, and the events he took part in. Powers don't belong to agencies or human subjects in any simple way, because their traits or potentialities are inseparable from the orders in which they are implicated. It is necessary to remember that there are powers and potentialities that are not traits of individual agents at all; namely, an institution, a method, or a theory may also have powers.

> The power in which a method consists may be found in a single [person], or in thirty. . . . it also may not happen to reside . . . in any particular community of men. . . . A method of altering international relations, or the scientific method of acquiring knowledge . . . are each, as powers, indefinitely distributed and shared. The emphasis . . . on the might of a method as compared with the limitations of its practitioners makes perfectly good sense (CM 100).

Institutionalized or formulated in this way, a power becomes independent from any particular practitioner: it may, indeed, arise as the product of other powers, "For instance, the power to make various medical diagnoses is ultimately the product of the power to solve biochemical problems" (CM 140).

In line with this, knowledge is the power deliberately to invoke or employ a given judgment instrumentally and as needed. "To have knowledge," Buchler says in ML (149), is to have acquired a certain kind of power. For the gain is not a gain if it cannot be exemplified on more than one occasion." Knowing, he adds in MNC, is that process by which an organism gains from its own continuous living or from the world available to it the capacity to produce or to experience in different, unprecedented ways" (p.296).

Knowing . . . is the recurrent actualization, in various forms, of a possibility. In knowing, we must be able to make a comparison with, construct in an envisaged way, or act in a tried way toward a given complex (ML 149).

Specifically, our power of judging, in order to be actualized as cognitive, "must be one . . . required for the augmentation of the order in which it functions." The instances or actualizations must be dependable, and needed, not gratuitous. They must have an objectively compulsive character, rather than a merely wilful, character: the only thing that the individual-as-such decides, in the knowing process, is to initiate it, to seek knowledge. Thus, "the compulsiveness is the validity or 'objectivity' or efficacy that belongs to knowledge" (ML 150). Buchler points out, finally, that

> Every gain in knowledge is to some extent a loss in subsequent freedom of choice, but the elimination of untenable choices ultimately enhances freedom of judgment. The loss is the kind that makes possible further cognitive gain; and in this way the process of knowing continues (ML 151).

We are confirmed in the view, and the guidance, offered in Singer's *Ordinal Naturalism* that the way in which Buchler has defined possibility and actuality "cuts across all such traditional distinctions as those between being and becoming, and change, determinateness and indeterminateness." He does not make, as she says, "[any] distinction comparable to the traditional one between essence and existence (or being)"; and, most importantly, "his categories also cut across the conventional distinction between "being" in the existential sense, and the "being" of predication" (ON 173f.).

Buchler's conception of laws, and of universals goes beyond Peirce's and Santayana's, but is only in some respects incompatible with them. The old metaphysical problem of the reality of universals does not arise in connection with natural complexes, because these in themselves are neither particular nor universal. While no complex is absolutely unique because no complex is totally unrelated, any complex is unique in some respect. This is implied in its being individual. The common involvement of complexes in a relation is at least one respect in which they are similar; and complexes may be similar in other ways. For Buchler's metaphysics, this fact means that there must be universals; for, a universal is a possibility of similarity. So, like any other possibility, a universal is a natural complex that prevails as a trait of an order: it is "the possibility of different complexes having traits that are similar in a given respect" (MNC 180). Just as possibilities may not be actualized, so there may be universals that lack actualized instances, such as Peirce's ideal community of investigators, or the perfect work of art which deconstructionists posit in (belatedly) fussing that no work-of-art is perfect. It is the order of its location, then, that allows for and defines, or prefines, a universal— not its exemplification(s).

Laws are prevalences the very notion of which suggests scope or comprehensiveness, "entailing relatedness among complexes that have been independently encountered, complexes as yet unencountered, and complexes not encounterable except in the most indirect ways" (MNC 177). As a possibility with continuous or recurrent actualization (MNC 176), a law is one of the possibility-traits in an order: "It prefines and contributes to the gross (or collective) prefinition of relative limits in the order." But, as distinct from the conditions under which a possibility (a law) prevails as a possibility within an order, the conditions which *actualize* the possibility (the law) are typical or recurrent conditions within the order (MNC 177).

Buchler's examples are (i) a law of capitalist economy, which prevails as long as the conditions of capitalist order prevail; (ii) geological laws, which prevail as long as the earth prevails. Such laws themselves, despite their stability, may be alescent; for variations may arise in the regularly actualized possibilities of the economy or the earth. But alescence in the conditions under which a law is actualized (e.g. variations in the frequencey with which given conditions are present) does not affect the integrity of the law as a *possibility* (MNC 178); nor does it affect the integrity of its actualizations.

Buchler's last paragraph on law as an actuality and a possibility is almost a peroration. He notes that a law's actualizations are a class of

conspicuously similar complexes. They are marked by a *thematic* trait
where the actualization is continuous (as in the laws of motion), and
by a *rhythmical* trait where it is recurrent (as in the laws of heredity).
But in some cases, because of the pervasiveness of the order within
which the law or possibility resides, the instances seem less notably
similar. Such, for instance, would seem to be the law of
non-contradiction.[24] "And yet, upon reflection, the similarity of the
instances [i.e.] the repeated and continued absence of contrary
instances . . . is the more impressive. For in the case of this law,
unlike laws prevalent in other types of order, we cannot describe
conditions that would spoliate its integrity or diminish its scope,
though we can describe conditions under which it would not be
relevant" (ibid.).

(v) *Buchler's Metaphysical Distinctions as a Category-Set*

In his essay "The Nature of Categorial Theory,"[25] A. Edel begins by
examining Aristotle's categories as basic to the Aristotelian system of
metaphysics and reconceives them as a conceptual experiment in
distinction-making. Just as Aristotle studied the operation of the four
causes throughout his own works, he says (NP 130), so is he "applying
Aristotelian method to Aristotelian ideas."[26] Edel finds that "for
Aristotle the basic concepts enter into truths about the ultimate
character of what there is; in that sense, he is a metaphysical realist.
They are not simply conceptual *instruments*" (ibid.).

He finds further that, viewed in this way, the essence-accident
analysis was Aristotle's first great metaphysical experiment: "It
spawned the categories. It sent him into logical inquiries, clarified
large areas, formalized others, and got still others underway." Edel
concludes, however, that "the experiment was not wholly satisfactory."
In spite of successes in logic and biology,

> it failed to produce a coherent theory of natural movement in physics,
> and it came to an impasse in metaphysics in the central problem of
> the nature of substance. [He] therefore . . . shifted to his second great
> experiment—to see the world in the focus of potentiality and actuality.

Here, says Edel, Aristotle had greater success: "in psychology and metaphysics . . . for revisions in physics. . . . it helped avoid determinism in a deeper way . . . it help[ed] out against the Democritean atomism and solve[d] the problem of the infinite. And so on" (NP 131). We note that "treating categorial sets as great conceptual experiments" is Edel's way of taking metaphysics as hypothetical and exploratory (namely, as query), rather than as the assertive, doctrinally systematic inquiry which it has traditionally been taken to be. And this is already "progressive;" but we shall see that it is also a measure of how far ahead of his time Buchler's distinction-making is, even while it was developed against the background of traditional Western metaphysics.

In thus beginning to take Buchler's approach to metaphysics, Edel rightly says that "when a dichotomy leads us into an impasse it is the dichotomy that goes on trial." It is re-examined by being recontextualized in relation to "its grounds in human purposes and interests," and in relation to the state of knowledge in *other fields*, as prelude to the needed conceptual reconstruction. The big new problem that arises in all this, for Edel, is that of "furnish[ing] criteria for success" in the making of basic distinctions of the widest application across and within "fields of inquiry" (Edel does not adopt Buchler's wider term, query). Neither tests of theoretical "fruitfulness" nor sociological explications of given sets of categories, can postpone indefinitely the "unavoidable normative reckoning" to which they must be submitted. This, I will say, is rather neo-classistic of Edel; namely, and on the analogy of creativity in the arts, it is wanting to have rules about how to make a poem or a painting before you've painted or written it. Given that we would want our distinctions to apply to both the arts and the sciences (in the standard narrower senses of "art" and "science"), we should not prematurely import expectations about *human products* in special fields (such as mathematics) where the rules are given ahead of time (because of the deductive nature of the field), into our understanding of other fields of query where the "rules" are only ex post facto, and not rules in the same sense at all. In art, it's often been quipped, rules are made only to be broken.

Now, Edel is right when he says,

in metaphysics, as in science, we are in some sense *trying out* categories, we are *experimenting*. . . . the treatment of categories in relation to fields of application is not a mere afterthought when the analysis . . . is finished. It is part of the essence of their exploration, even of their construction. Hence metaphysics as a field of philosophy has to be carried out in intimate relation to the diversity of areas in which metaphysical concepts are being tried out.

But he is wrong, in his ten-page examination of Buchler's metaphysical work, in failing to perceive that Buchler's system is, in fact, a conceptual experiment in the very senses specified by himself. And the misperception begins with his failure to take note of the passages— few enough, to be sure—in which Buchler *does* "tell us . . . about how he proceeds" (NP 133). I have quoted these passages earlier, with the help, it must be added, of the enlarged edition of MNC which make these passages more easily available. Perhaps Edel's essay worked only with the 1966 edition of MNC; but perhaps it is also a matter of *the devotion* of a rival metaphysician and Aristotle specialist *to his own* and *Aristotle's formulations* blocking perception of what agreement there is between these formulations and those of others. It is surprising, however, that this otherwise brilliant commentator has not seen how his own view of what metaphysics should be, agrees, in general, with Buchler's extended practice.[27]

That it is this kind of blockage rather than anything else can be seen from the fact that while Edel appreciates Buchler's "emphasis on generality," he thinks that the "far-flung illustrations . . . from a variety fields" are both "juxtapose[d] deliberately" and a "casual procedure" (NP 133). More, Edel does not notice that it this part of Buchler's insistence "that an adequate category is 'to provide a just basis for distinctions, and not to blanket or transcend them'." (Edel NP 133, MNC 9).

In approving Buchler's view that metaphysics is "an attempt to discover fundamental traits," Edel unfortunately is thinking only of traits discoverable "in the process of experiencing," using words from *Nature and Judgment* (p. vii). This neglects the metaphysics of nature to be found in MNC, which had been out since 1966. About Buchler's "*minimal* requirement" that a philosophy "compel imaginative assent and arouse the sense of encompassment even where it fails of cognitive acceptance" (TGT 134, my emphasis, NP 134f.), Edel agrees that this does "not on the whole depart from Aristotle as traditionally conceived" (NP 134). But, as traditionally conceived, the Aristotelian metaphysics—whether in its Scholastic Latin version or among modern commentators—has always been tacitly taken as a composition in the purely assertive mode. Where the Scholastics insisted on reading it as compatible with Christian faith, the moderns work at compatibilizing the internal logical coherence of its parts (on a logicist, not a Peircean conception of logic).

   In connection with the conception of "experience," Edel wishes that Buchler had done what, in fact and ironically, he does do. "The history of the philosophic use of 'experience' might have been studied to bring out the lesson for a reconstructed meaning." So that Buchler's conceptual analysis of "experience," in enumerating and contextualizing the defects in the notion, does indeed "provide [the] causes" of and "cures for" its banalization, replacing "the straying category" with the concept of *proception*. Edel's criticism here seems to be that, in redefining old terms or providing new ones, Buchler "does not work out systematic criteria for responsibility [Buchler's term] . . . nor a systematic mode of testing the new categories, nor even the various dimensions of a process of justification" (NP 134). This again overlooks the fact that, insofar as philosophies are exhibitive constructions, criteria of their effectiveness may not, as in works-of-art, be providable before they have been reflectively worked out. And it overlooks the way in which Buchler has shown that validation of both assertive and exhibitive compositions is much more than, and occurs in more dimensions than, justification as verification.

   Another clue as to the cause of Edel's misreading is the epistemologism that he shares with the European tradition since Descartes. Edel takes Buchler's "proception" to be a concept, like Dewey's "experience," that is "distinctive[ly] . . . at home in both metaphysical and epistemological inquiries" (NP 137). But, in the first place, Buchler has shown that Dewey's "experience" is systematically ambiguous, not just occasionally so as Edel thinks (NP

138); and, secondly, "proception" is neither an epistemological term at all, nor does Buchler perform or want to perform any epistemological analyses in his systematic work. In fact, the great value of "proception," as a contribution to the anti-epistemological tradition of classic American philosophy, is its complete avoidance of, resistance to, and impenetrability by, epistemological analysis. And in this it is quite unlike the concept of experience it was designed to replace.

The remark that Buchler's naturalistic metaphysics "raises the question how far the results of scientific knowledge enter into categorial formation," is quite an understatement. Buchler has not only raised it and answered that, of course, they enter into the formation of categories, which categories may be of *a different level* of generality, but also has tried to meet the requirement that the categories arrived at should be adequate to the reflective processes operating in the production and practice of the arts as well as in human conduct. And this allows us to respond to Edel's unwarranted feeling that such of Buchler's concepts as proception or alescence "cannot bear the weight" in metaphysics that they are asked to bear. The feeling is hasty because these categories have been worked out in the context of their author's deep involvement with (i) historic systems—from Aristotle's through Locke's and Leibniz's to those of Whitehead and Peirce—that have failed (Edel's complacency about them notwithstanding) to solve the problems which Buchler's metaphysics addresses, and because Buchler's categories are also the product of his lifelong love of and involvement with (ii) music, poetry, and literature—including (once he got to Columbia) the documentary bases of contemporary Western socio-intellectual organization.[28] But it is Buchler's work as a whole, in both its assertive and exhibitive dimensions, that shows whether his categories do their work better than those of the Aristotelian corpus or those suggested by Edel—not my assertive summary of the metaphysics of natural complexes.

One frivolous aside or lapse in Edel's paper calls for comment, finally, because it is typical of the frivolities which the neopositivist philosophic environment not only tolerates but resorts to for refutative purposes. Edel has understood that "alescence" is not just deterioration, but he goes on to prove (*sic*) what Buchler has already amply shown "that 'alescence' is [also] not simply growth" (NP 139). The proof is a "Quinean substitution": "I cannot revise the poet's "Grow old with me, the best is yet to come" and say "Alesce old with me. . . ." This is not only supererogatory, it neglects what Buchler has said about prevalence and alescence in relation to grammatical transitivity. A poet could, in any case, say "*arise* with me." "Categorial novelty" does indeed need to be approached with "subtlety."

Buchler indeed does nothing more or less than what Edel desiderates for categorial sets. "Aristotle,"[29] says Edel,

> both derived his categories from the vital concepts that did the heavy work of analyzing and formulating questions in different scientific and humanistic disciplines, and returned the categories to these and other fields to continue the analyses and investigation (NP 141f.).

The traditional materialists, continues Edel, exported their categories from the physics of the day to other fields such as psychology and social inquiry. "Dewey applied his concepts of change and experience to field after field. . . . Santayana put his categories to work in his *Life of Reason* to assess society and religion, art and science." Not only are Buchler's categories derived by reflection from all these fields, Buchler does not simply "export" concepts from common usage or from one field to another, as we have seen; he formulates new concepts or, else, re-invents and redefines them if they are already in use. Philosophic and other readers should indeed try doing for themselves what Buchler's concepts are designed to do, namely, set Buchler's categories to work "in area after area." They will find that *many a phenomenon* (in education, politics, morals and the arts, in the experimental and theoretical sciences, in professional and leisure-time practices) *the account of which has been problematic*, will yield to the application of Buchler's distinctions. Buchler could not agree more with Edel's conclusion that "metaphysics" must be "validated" by more than "her own processes," and "the fruifulness of her constructions in the diversity of human inquiries" (sic); it must be validated, he implies, by its (now explictly) experimental nature and its (novel) non-isolationist involvement with all the other arts, sciences, and human practices.

Appendix:
Letter from J. Buchler to B. Singer
Dated 3/23/72

[On Justus Buchler Letterhead]

Justus Buchler

3/23/72

Dear Beth,

I don't know whether the "missing link" you are looking for can be found in philosophy proper. I'll explain this in a moment. In a sense, the philosophic influences that I absorbed stem as much from Plato and Aristotle, Spinoza and Locke, as from American thought. *All* of the influences are piecemeal rather than systematic: a specific insight here, an adaptable concept there, a mode of approach, an emphasis, a happy formulation. My flirtation or adventure with logical positivism came between 1937 and 1939 or 1940. The brevity of this phase is shown, for example, by the fact that my interest in Santayana was strong before this phase and continued strong after it (*Obiter Scripta* was prepared in 1935).

To return to our missing link. Perhaps you shouldn't think in chronological terms alone. Or if you do, look at the chronology broadly: In 1942 *Philosophy: An Introduction* appeared. In 1951 *Toward a General Theory* appeared. The decade between was crucial for me. In 1942 I began (a) teaching Contemporary Civilization, and (b) teaching Contemporary Philosophy. The teaching, reading, editing and (in 1950) administering of **CC** (the great staff, the discussions, the *esprit*) was the most fundamental intellectual experience of my life. On the other side, the teaching of contemporary philosophical trends gave me the first full chance to think recurrently about what were the better and the worse aspects of late 19th and early 20th century philosophy, especially American. By the late 40's *Toward a General Theory* was germinating. Peirce's theory of signs and Royce's theory of interpretation, which attracted me (both of the men idealists, be it noted), were gradually felt by me to be metaphysically inadequate.

CC was broadening my awareness, and I think it is true to say that without it I would not have arrived at my sense of what constitutes human *utterance*. Somehow I distinctly remember saying one day in the [contemporary philosophy] class (it included Bob Olson, Freddie Sommers, Willard Arnett, and God knows who else) that the pragmatists had tried commendably to understand "judgment" (assertion) in terms of action, but had failed to see that action as such was judicative. Royce's "interpretation" is man's cognitional rendering, in triadic terms, of the world's contents. What impressed me was his suggestion of its pervasiveness and ubiquity. My feeling in general was that sign-theory (Peirce, Royce, Mead, Cassirer) had to be superseded metaphysically by a theory of human production—the basis of our ubiquitous discriminativeness being the way we produce: or conversely, each of our products being our way of discriminating or selecting (judging). I also distinctly remember a CC luncheon (always on Thursday) in which I sat next to Randall and told him I was preparing (it was around 1950) a category that would or could, if necessary replace the notion of "experience"; that would take Dewey's great broadening and reconstruction of the latter notion for granted, while showing why Dewey could not avoid often lapsing into the views he thought he was abandoning. Randall, chewing vigorously but smiling, kept nodding his head and saying, "Yes, yes. . . ."

Nostalgically,

Notes

1. The conceptions of experience of Aristotle, Augustine, Locke, Kant, Hume, Hegel, and G.H. Mead are also reviewed in this Introduction.

2. Buchler is apposite here in pointing out that one meaning "experience" has in Peirce is "existentialist." This is the meaning in which experience is a matter of shock modifying the experiencer, but never totally assimilable (**TGT** xxix).

3. This is the process that goes by the name of instrumental rationality, in social theorists such as J. Habermas; cf. notably, *Knowledge and Human Interests* Tr. J.J. Shapiro (Boston: Beacon Press 1971)

4. Such as A. Bain's *The Senses and the Intellect* (London: Longmans 1894), *The Emotions and the Will* (N.Y. Appleton 1876), and J. Sully, *Sensation and Intuition* (London: King & Co. 1874).

5. A notion to which there is a perhaps self-pitying undertone. Not to be unfair to existentialism, however, it is (like art) concerned with the human condition, but addresses it too directly and too simplistically. Its elegiac note, in any case, is tempered with a Stoic or rebellious spiritedness (as in Camus) which contrasts favorably with the bland optimism of Comtean positivism or the end-of-history "cool" of deconstructive neopositivism.

6. "Here then," says Buchler in his chapter on "Experience" in *Nature and Judgment*, "we may augment our nomenclature, lest important traits be obscured by tenacious associations" (p.110).

7. They are *not* "presented to" experience, Buchler adds in parenthesis. It will not escape Americanist readers that Buchler, in emphasizing the continuity between the individual and nature, is no less synechistic than Peirce or Santayana.

8. In the meantime, anticipation about Buchler's notion of community can be allayed by his reference to it as a class of proceivers whose members are procepts for each other, for all of whom some natural complex functions as a dominant procept, and who jointly manipulate the same set of signs. Community is a pre-condition of communication, but community in one respect may conflict with community in another to inhibit communication (**TGT** 39).

9. In parallel with the way "experience" is linked only to the most available data of existence, such as sounds, colors, shapes and tastes.

10. MNC (p.23) articulates the concept further: "Utterance ranges from the primordial maneuvers and responses—those which men cannot help making and which are humanly taken for granted, but which nevertheless vary individually—to the most intricated methodic products. . . .utterance

may be seen as 'production' or as 'judgment'. . . . .Man produces [or judges] (a) by *acting* in relation to the integrities among which he finds himself, (b) by *contriving* new integrities, and (c) by *propositionally* structuring integrities in order to affirm or test his suspicions."

11. As if the gap between our humanity and the inhumanity of human nature were not just as "tragic" as that between inhuman Nature and mankind.

12. To say or imply that matter, as the pure potentiality that it is in Santayana, is passive, emerges as a technical slip of Buchler's here.

13. Aristotle's term, *Nic.Ethics* Bk.II.vi.

14. *An Essay concerning Human Understanding* I.i.10.

15. More than forty years later; **TGT** was first published in 1951.

16. J. Buchler, "On a Strain of Arbitrariness in Whitehead's System," *The J. of Philosophy* 66.19 (Oct. 1969).

17. Buchler himself notes that this way of putting things covers and neutralizes Anaxagoras's maxim: "Neither is there a least of what is small, but there is always a less . . . But there is always a greater than what is great" (DK 59B3).

18. Buchler notes that it is also claimed that: "The highest genus is 'simple' because it is the common denominator of everything else" (MNC 20).

19. As, for example, the marketable or the literary value of a novel is unrelated to the particle physics of it—if the parameters could ever be specified that would distinguish a book from other objects, and a given book from another with a different content.

20. Buchler agrees with the *original* Parmenides that: "no discriminanda can be consigned to 'non-being,' on pain of contradiction; for they have the being that enables them to be discriminated" (**MNC 31**). Here is Parmenides' fragment B3: *to gar auto noein estin te kai einai* = "for the same thing can be thought and can exist" (Tarán), or "Thought and being are the same" (Wheelwright), or "denn dasselbe is Denken und Sein" (DK). What is at stake here, precisely, is Buchler's principle of ontological parity. See my *Understanding Parmenides: The Poem, the Dialogue, the All* (in press).

21. The brackets and parentheses here are all Buchler's. Here is what the statement comes out as, if they are removed—which we may do because traits (like possibilities and actualities) are themselves complexes: "A given *actual* trait is inevitably connected with numerous and other *possible* traits. Conversely, a given possibility reflects an innumerable train of actualities" (my emphases inserted).

22. "Power" was defined in CM (100f.) as "a possibility that has been actualized in some degree and can be recognized as generic in the next

instance. . . . Power resides not in agents purely as such, but in a natural complex that embraces agents and other component complexes."

23. In Buchler's view, "the law of non-contradiction is not a 'stipulated' or 'legislated' law, any more than the laws of motion are" (MNC 178).

24. In *Nature's Perspectives: Prospects for Ordinal Metaphysics*, ed. by A. Marsoobian, K. Wallace, R.S. Corrington (S.U.N.Y. Press 1991); pp.115-144.

25. Edel illustrates: "For example, the *Parts of Animals* gives the material cause of animals . . . the *Generation of Animals* the efficient cause; *On the Soul* the formal cause; the ethical and political writings the final cause."

26. An end-note to Edel's essay indicates that it was written in 1974, the date of publication of the fifth volume, ML, in the original series. Edel makes no reference either to this work or to CM. The second edition of TGT did not appear until 1979, the enlarged edition of MNC until 1990. Edel's section on Buchler makes three references to MNC, in contrast to eleven for TGT and NJ together. The essay was in fact first solicited from Dr. Edel jointly by Douglas Greenlee and the present author for inclusion in a collection which we were editing, and which failed of completion because of Professor Greenlee's untimely death.

27. The reader may consult the Appendix to this chapter for a reference to this by Buchler himself.

28. We should not forget that the reference of "Aristotle," when it is a question of the *Metaphysics*, is to the Aristotelian-Peripatetic corpus, namely, to Aristotle's *hypomnemata* as put together by his Hellenistic, platonizing or stoicizing transmitters. Like other insufficiently guarded works of the post-classical period, the corpus was liable to manipulation, overwriting, and interpolation.

References & Bibliography

J.Buchler   "Charles Sanders Peirce, Giant in American Philosophy," *The American Scholar*, Fall 1939.

"The Accidents of Peirce's System," *Journal of Philosophy*, May 9, 1940.

"The Naturalism of G.Santayana," *Kenyon Review*, Spring 1941 [Joint Review of *The Realm of Spirit* and P.A.Schilpp's *The Philosophy of George Santayana* (Northwestern U.P. 1940)]

Charles Peirce's Empiricism (N.Y. Harcourt 1939)

J. Buchler   *The Philosophy of Peirce: Selected Writings* (London: Rout-
               ledge 1940) and J.H. Randall Jr. *Philosophy: An
               Introduction* (N.Y. Barnes & Noble 1942)

               "The Philosopher, the Common Man, & William James,"
               The American Scholar, Fall 1942.

               Review of *Symposium on The Interpretation of History*, *The
               Journal of Philosophy*, Aug.19, 1943.

               Editor: *Introduction to Contemporary Civilization in the West*
               2 vols. (N.Y. Columbia U.P. 1946) with J.H.Randall, &
               E.Shirk *Readings in Philosophy* (Barnes & Noble 1946,
               1950, 1972)

               Review of E.Cassirer *Language and Myth*, *The J. of Philos.*
               Oct.10, 1946.

               Review of P.A.Schilpp *The Philos. of E.Cassirer*, *The Nation*
               Aug.20, 1949

               Toward a General Theory of Human Judgment 1951 (N.Y.
               Dover. 2 Rev. ed. 1979)

               "What is a Discussion," *The Journ.of General Education*;
               October, 1954.

               Nature and Judgment 1955 (N.Y. Grosset, repr. 1966)

               The Concept of Method 1961 (Lanham: U.P.A 1985)

               Metaphysics of Natural Complexes 1966, 2 Enlarged ed. by
               Marsoobian, Wallace & Corrington (S.U.N.Y. Press
               1990)

               "Ontological Parity," in J.P.Anton ed. *Naturalism and
               Historical Understanding: Essays on the Philos. of
               J.H.Randall* (S.U.N.Y. Press 1967)

               "On a Strain of Arbitrariness in Whitehead's System," *The
               J. of Philos.* Oct. 2, 1969)

               The Main of Light (N.Y. Oxford U.P. 1974)

               Replies to His Critics *The Southern Journal of Philosophy*,
               XIV.1 (Special Issue. by B.Singer & J.Grassi, Spring
               1972.

               "On the Concept of the World," *Review of Metaphysics*, June
               1978.

               "Probing the Idea of Nature," *Process Studies*, Fall 1978.

A.Edel   *Ethical Judgment* (Glencoe: Free Press 1955)

               Science and the Structure of Ethics (University of Chicago
               1961)

               Aristotle and His Philosophy (U. of N.Carolina Press 1982)

A.Marsoobian   K. Wallace, R. Corrington *Nature's Perspectives* (S.U.N.Y Press 1990)

B.J.Singer   *Ordinal Naturalism: The Philosophy of Justus Buchler* (Lewisberg: Bucknell U.P. 1983)

B.J.Singer   and J. Grassi eds. *The Southern Journal of Philosophy XIV.1*, Spring 1976; Special Buchler Issue.

V. Tejera   La Filosofía y el Arte Poético, *Revista Nacional de Cultura* (julio-octubre 1956)

¿Qué es la Estética? *Revista Nacional de Cultura* (julio-agosto 1958)

"Pluralism and Method in Recent Aesthetics," *Proceedings of the Fourth International Congress of Aesthetics* Athens, Greece Sept.1960.

"Professor Sheffer's Question," *Philosophy and Phenomenological Research* Summer 1961.

"The Nature of Aesthetics," *The British Journal of Aesthetics* Vol.I No.4 (1961)

"Art & Intelligence in Human Society," *VI Intl.Congress of Aesth.*, Stockholm 1968.

"Contemporary Trends in Aesthetics," *Journ. of Value Inquiry* 1974;

Reprinted: M.Lipman ed. *Contemporary Aesthetics* (Allyn & Bacon 1974)

Art and Human Intelligence (N.Y. Appleton-Century 1965)

Modes of Greek Thought (Appleton-Century 1971)

"The Human Sciences in Dewey, Foucault, & Buchler," *The Southern Journal of Philosophy*, No. 18, 2 (1980)

"Cultural Analysis & Interpretation in the Human Sciences," *Man and World*, 12.2 (1979)

Plato's Dialogues One By One (New York: Irvington 1984)

"On the Nature of Reflective Discourse in Politics," *Philosophy and Rhetoric*, Vol.17, No.2

History as a Human Science: The Conception of History in Some Classic American Philosophers (Lanham: U.P.A. 1984)

Nietzsche and Greek Thought (Dordrecht: Nijhoff 1987)

Semiotics From Peirce To Barthes (Leiden: Brill 1988)

History & Anti-History in Philosophy (Dordrecht: Kluwer 1989)

V. Tejera   *Literature, Criticism, and the Theory of Signs* (Amsterdam: Benjamins 1995)

"Community, Communication, and Meaning in the Theories of Buchler and Habermas," *J.of the Soc. for Symbolic Interaction* 1985.

"Derrida's Poetics: a Report to the Muses," *The Southern Journal of Philosophy* XXVI, 4 (1988)

Bakhtin, Dialogism, and Plato's Dialogues *Ellenike Philosophike Epitheorese*, 6,(1989)

"On the Form and Authenticity of the *Lysis*," *Ancient Philosophy* X.2 (1990)

"Eco, Peirce, & Interpretationism," *The Amer.Journ.of Semiotics*, 8, 2-3 (1991): Review-Essay of Eco's *The Limits of Interpretation*.

"Peirce's Semeiotic, and the Aesthetics of Literature," *Trans. of the C.S. Peirce Society* XXIX, (1993)

"Listening to Herakleitos," *The Monist* Special Issue on Heraclitus, 1991 1992.

Review of G. Deledalle *Charles S.Peirce: and Intellectual Biography, Journal of Speculative Philosophy* VI.2 (1992), 166-169.

"Strauss's Socrates: the Composite," *Skepsis* Athens, Greece Vol.1, No.4 (1992-3).

"The Primacy of the Aesthetic in Peirce, & Classic American Philosophy," in H. Parret, **PVT**.

Abbreviations

TGT	=	Toward a General Theory of Human Judgment
NJ	=	Nature and Judgment
CM	=	The Concept of Method
MNC	=	Metaphysics of Natural Complexes
ML	=	The Main of Light
NHE	=	Nature and Historical Experience
NP	=	Nature's Perspectives
ON	=	Ordinal Naturalism
PVT	=	Peirce's Value Theory

CHAPTER V

American Philosophic
Historiography

(i) *Rereading Western Socio-Intellectual History*
as Active & Exhibitive Judgment

In this chapter, our theorizing about history, literature, and science
will continue to be Peircean, Deweyan, Santayanian, and Buchlerian.
The practitioners to whose texts we will be referring are first of all
Josiah Royce in both his history of California and his remarks on
interpretation, Herbert Schneider and John Herman Randall Jr.; but
we will not be above remembering Santayana's practice of history or
inspiring thoughts about it as the natural history of mankind. Nor
will we scant Peirce's semiotic discoveries, in order to clarify our
subject-matter. We will also consider the practice and reflection of
G.H. Mead in his writings about the past, about French thought, and
about community—the last a topic of importance to the other thinkers
mentioned.[1] In this way, both the theorizing invoked and the practices
analyzed will be those of some classic American thinkers.

Philosophic historiography in the United States is autochthonous
in the respect that it takes its rise from William James's rich
interactional reconception of the notion of experience, and from C.S.

Peirce's idea of the ongoing community of inventive, corrigibilist investigators out of whose work and agreement the truth emerges, ever ready to be rectified and retested. While this turns the idea of truth into a limiting, but critical conception—into a critical *ideal*—the associated idea itself of the community of investigators was, like his formalizations of logic (Critic, as he called it), a product of his close *observation of the discourse*, history, and practice, of the nomological sciences.[2] The addition of Santayana's *The Life of Reason* (1905-1906) to the canon of American works attempting to socialize and naturalize our view of the human process, gives actual historico-intellectual form and narrative substance to Dewey's idea that "the history of human experience is a history of the development of the arts" (**EN** 388).[3] As we noted in Chapter III, Santayana contextualizes "human experience," into the wider background of cosmographic nature and social history where Dewey is content with an anchoring of human conduct in biology and social responsiveness. This doesn't mean, however, that Dewey is less sensitive than Royce or James, Henry Adams or Santayana to the individual's spiritual and expressive needs.

We have reviewed with Buchler the deficits in Dewey's conception of human experience. Armed with this critique, we are free to employ the term "experience" again, but as reconstituted by reference to the concept of proception, when it is not replaced or swallowed up by the less precise notion. Buchler's fundamental co-ordinative distinction among the three modes of judgment also honors, while incorporating and superseding, Dewey's distinctions between expression and statement,[4] between the animistic logic of poetry (**EN** 181) and the causal basis and deductive logic of propositional discourse. Dewey's insistence that expression is *transformative* and that, as reflection, it is *medium-bound thinking* (**AE** 60-78) is likewise honored and not neglected by the distinctions in Buchler's metaphysics of utterance, as we will see in connection with poetry and history. Dewey's insight, shared with Santayana, that the principle of culture is not different from that of art, and that the basis of civilization itself is inventive *communication*, will be deepened and extended in the clarifications afforded by Buchler's probing of the nature of communication as presupposing distinguishable species of community.

Any natural impact on the individual is a potential sign-situation, namely, could be a communicative impact more than a mere impact—difficult as it is to pin down the limits of a sign-situation (**TGT** 30f.). In general, procepts which are appropriated communicatively, not merely assimilated, are those which give rise to "reflexive communication."

> The ocean communicates its vastness; history and the history of one's time communicate in the sense that they transmit symbols for proceptive assimilation. To the historian the past not only communicates but communicates directly; it . . . affects [and] dominates his proceptive direction. The historian, the scientist generally speaking, interrogates nature . . . for what it can communicate.

There is no "transmission of intent" in this kind of communication. Buchler calls it *asymmetrical* communication. What is called "mass-communication" is *non-symmetrical*: the impact that generates signs in this case may or may not be reciprocal.

"Anything," says Buchler, "communicates to an individual if, in consequence of its impact, he directly begins to communicate with himself about it" (**TGT** 30). This species of communication in which the individual uses and interprets signs to himself, this cross-section of his proceptive domain, Buchler calls *reflexive* communication. The term "reflexive communication" grasps better than "reflection" the continuity between social processes and proceptive processes, and is less purely dilemmatic or problem-solving. Symbolic interactionists will no doubt recognize in the concept, a development of G.H. Mead's view of the self as dialogical.

The creative artist, notes Buchler, communicates asymmetrically with the spectator by contributing new elements for proceptive manipulation and assimilation (**TGT** 31). Response to the work will be more or less critical "depending on the extent to which the work, as subject, dominates reflexive communication." It is in art, for both Dewey and Buchler, that we see communication to be, basically, a process of *sharing*—rather than of the plain transmission of a "message" or discrete bits of information.

Buchler insists, moreover, on the plurivalence or pregnancy of both the verbal texture of works of literary art, and the plurivalence of (or challenge to) the determinative context itself of the meanings of the work (**TGT** 32). But what a work communicates does depend on cultural conditions and human receptivity; so, "the function of criticism in science, philosophy, or art is to serve as both medium and catalyst for this process [of influence on subsequent communication]. For criticism is articulation; articulation extends meaning" (**TGT** 33).

Notice, when we take the ocean to be communicating something, that we are being animistic about it; namely, we are in a state of imputed community with it. It is easier to see that communication necessarily presupposes community in the case of *symmetrical* communication. But of what is community itself the result?

> in order that community should obtain, it is necessary that some natural complex be a dominant procept for more than one individual in the same respect.

And this is facilitated by the fact that individuals' proceptive directions may show a parallelism in a given respect. For example, "one man's striving . . . is not the same as another's; but it may be the same kind of striving."

> If we can suppose that objects may resemble one another, or that symbolic systems may be isomorphic, we can suppose that proceptive directions may be parallel.

In symmetrical communication each individual must be a procept for the other, and there is joint manipulation and assimilation of signs relating to the dominant procept. There are implicit mutual demands in social or symmetrical communication; the demand is for overt manifestations of proception, for utterances which have been given form, "to act in this or that way, to adopt [such and such] a policy" (**TGT** 35). Here, Buchler throws in a great little peroration on the philosophy of inquiry:

The most highly refined form of communicatory demand is mutual interrogation. It is in the depth and power of interrogation that the depth and power of thought consists, whether it be individual or inter-proceptive. Misology, aversion to ideas, is aversion to self-interrogation. The Socratic method was both an exhortation to become free of this fear and an attempt to exhibit the value of the liberation. It sought to formalize interrogation, and by this means to remove the natural mist from symmetrical communication.

The relata of communication are, of course, proceivers. But by this is meant "individual histories," specifically, "individual histories cumulatively represented" (**TGT** 37). Communication must presuppose "the presence in the individual of communal traditions—communities cumulatively reflected." While, on the one hand, "social and reflexive continuity are conditions of individuality," on the other, alteration of his proceptive domain occurs because the individual can abstract himself from complete identification with it. The individual cannot reject all community, because "community and history are ingredients of the of the self" (**TGT** 38).

Some community is, naturally, accidental; other forms of community, such as language-community, are inescapable. Given the latter kind of antecedent mutuality, contingent mutualities become the proximate conditon for a communicative situation to arise; namely, they "determine the conditions for proceptive parallelism in some respect, when each agent has become a procept for the other." The sufficient condition for a *community*, then, is that it be a class of proceivers "for whom a given natural complex functions as a dominant procept" (**TGT** 39). Communication will occur, i.e. community will be actualized, when members become procepts for each other, and jointly manipulate the same set of signs.

The minimal requirement for community is a quantum of proceptive parallelism, not loyalty or even group awareness. And communities don't *necessarily* have histories as Royce thought, even though their members must have (**TGT** 42).[5] Buchler's way of categorizing it, allows us to see that the strength of community lies, not in a more and less evident sense of union, nor in the existence of external symbols of unanimity, but in the strength of each of the parallel proceptive directions. Allegiances are, of course, procepts; though no procept is fully visible in all its relations. Many communities intersect in the reflexive community which is the self, and allegiance doesn't depend on the proximity or tangibility of the object.

> The community and its members are "in" one another, but with varying efficacy. We stand in more communities than we know, and often with a firmness that is greater or less than we suspect (**TGT** 45).

This is all relevant to philosophic historiography because it is groups and individuals and the relations between them that are the subjects of histories, and because society is both a product of man's condition and an overwhelming factor shaping that condition. Structural historians are right in the endeavor to make visible the initially less patent, more enduring or "underlying" communities in a society for the purpose of explicating both sociohistorical development and changes of a less secular sort. The intellectual historian has also to be aware that easily identifiable changes in some more visible communities may not be the best indexes of intellectual changes in society as a whole. In any case, the historian's useful predisposition to see individuals and groups as responsive, or re-active, to objective conditions finds its 'explicitation' and explication in the classic American thinkers, from William James's slogan "All action is thus *re*-action upon the outer world" (**EFM** 114), to Buchler's recommendation that "activity . . . ascribed to a positive impulse is . . . better interpreted as a response than as a drive . . . . For the most part 'activity' is best regarded as drawn from the individual rather than as contributed by him" (**TGT** 61).[6]

Of course, "in reacting *to* his environment, man reacts *on* his environment. . . . and thus creates a new environment to which [he] must again adjust."[7] Human history is, for Buchler, the cumulative progression of the judgments by which he makes himself as he transforms the world by the force of his sayings, his doings, and his makings. These, says Buchler, "are equal as forces of history. But," he adds tychistically, the irony of history, consisting in the chance intersections of judgment, looms large in determining the magnitude of effects. Much has been wrought by the unintended results of an *act*, by the adventitious responses to a work of *art*, and by the sheer deductive expansion of a *sentence* (**NJ** 65, my emphases).

As for written history, the interrogative process that takes the career of a society or group for its subject-matter, that is also the communicative or rhetorical process wanting to share its findings, a moment's reflection tells us that history is *query*, and that this species of query is an active, constructive or exhibitive effort as well as an assertive special-science inquiry. So, while histories are assertive insofar as their inquiries are archival, socio-economic or archaeological, the judgments reached in this phase of their composition are held together by means of the presentational (exhibitive) devices which unify them into an interpretive narrative or exposition.

It isn't difficult to see how Buchler had to coin the term 'active judgment' in order to characterize adequately *The Communist Manifesto* as the political *act* or *gesture* which it primarily is, hortatory or eloquent prose as it may also be. The problem is much the same with Machiavelli's *The Prince*, if we don't take it in isolation from the republican political philosophy of his *Discourses* on Titus Livius. *The Prince* is not accurately categorized if it isn't seen to be the '*exhibitive* contrivance' which it is, and which puts under observation all the devices that a Renaissance prince might resort to in order either to found a state, or to take one over in times of crisis. How, again, to characterize the communicative effect of the Eiffel Tower (once it was completed) and the new determinacies it gave rise to, except as a tacit *adjudication* of new priorities and a promissory *exhibit* of structural and industrial possibilities?

Teachers of history, of intellectual history especially, must be grateful to Buchler for the metadiscursive coinages provided by his theory of judgment. Not content simply to rehearse the development of the Western heritage and consider the practical lessons it might yield, Buchler's philosophic self-reflection about it also happens to have advanced our understanding of the human process as such. We already referred in Chapter III to the deep interest in history of all the classic American philosophers;[8] here we see both the value to philosophers of historiography, and the advantages of philosophic discipline to intellectual historians, when this discipline is not rigidified by logicism and literalism.

(ii) *Royce on Interpretation, Community, and History*

Under the influence of Peirce, Josiah Royce found the simplest illustration of interpretation in the act of comparison. He found that comparisons cannot be performed in the absence of a mediating third, this third being the provider of the *interpretant*. Sensing that the problem of interpretation "takes us at once to the very heart of philosophy" (**PC II**, 110) Royce's description of interpretation unabashedly adapts sign-theory to his own religious idealism and ethical interests. Interpretation, he finds, is needed not only to understand other persons, but to understand ourselves as well (**PC II**, Lectures xi-xiii). The self turns out to be nothing less than a series of interpretations. More, "were there no interpretations in the world, there would be neither selves nor communities"; for, community is a matter of holding life-interpretations that are alike (**PC II**, 111-112).

The present self interprets certain past *signs*—in one's diary, for instance—as a commitment (*object* of the sign) to perform certain deeds. According to Royce, one is in fact interpreting them *to* the future self which is the behavioral or teleological *interpretant* of the entry in the diary. Royce also takes up Peirce's ideal of the community of investigators as a good illustration of what he means by a community of interpretation, and as a confirmation of his own views about the social nature of knowledge. He notes, however, that philosophers have nothing like the kind of community found among scientists. "The charity of mutual interpretation is ill-developed amongst them. . . . They . . . do not edify . . . they are especially disposed to contend. . . . We cannot expect them . . . to agree [on] any one philosophical opinion" (**PC II**, 254). Nevertheless, he concludes, they do have in common the feature that their principal task is one of interpretation.

A present-day parallel to this is the paradox presented by instances of Critical Theorists, so named, who are verbally anti-dominationist in their philosophy but thoroughly dominationist in their academic practice. The case is worth citing because the gap between theory and practice, here, has to be a reflection of misconceptions about the relation between the two—in spite of the fact that Critical Theory has sought to be innovative in its categorizations of human practices. Critical Theory, in the respect mentioned, misses the Buchlerian point that to practice dominationism is to think domination; a dominationist action is a dominationist judgment. Insofar as an action is the (teleo)logical interpretant of one's thought, such *allothentic* interpretants, within the reflexive community of the theorist, are a negation in the active mode of judgment of the thought-signs which s/he preaches in the assertive mode, and claims to believe. In terms of Critical Theory itself, such practice degrades the theory into another ideology and makes it irrelevant both to human practice and to the human interest, while also delegitmating the cognitive interest of which it claims to be a component.

However this may be, that "the philosophers are neither the only interpreters, nor the chiefs among those who interpret, we now well know," says Royce.

> The artists, the leaders of men . . . the students of the humanities, make interpretation their business; and the triadic cognitive function . . . has its application in all the realms of knowledge. But in any case the philosopher's ideals are those of an interpreter. He addresses one mind and interprets another. The unity which he seeks is that which is characteristic of a community of interpretation (**PC** 255-256).

Interpretation, for Royce, is the foundation of community; and just as "the world is the [Great] Community" and "contains its own interpreter, so *the* interpreter is

> the spirit of this universal community [which]—never absorbing varieties or permitting them to blend—compares and, through a real life, interprets them all" (**CP** II, 324).

The Absolute in Royce has, thus, become the world-community of mutually interpreting persons. As both the matrix and object of moral consciousness, however, it is something *ideal*, namely, also an object of aspiration. It is the true object of human love and loyalty. And loyalty in Royce's system is, as we know, the supreme value, and, therefore, the expression of love and respect for the *whole* community. Royce is talking, here, out of his boyhood contact with the traces of new but disappeared communities in early California, out of his hearsay about them, and out of his adolescent experience of socialization. But, unlike most of us, who do not articulate our need for community except in fragmentary actions, Royce developed the topic explicitly. His message, in the end, is not different from that which Aeschylus tacitly teaches in the *Oresteia*, and which the classicist L.A. Post reverbalized in the slogan "salvation is identical with civilization."[9]

Now, Royce's notion of mind as an activity of comparing and interpreting might seem to offer, at first, an anticipation or reinforcement of Santayana's posited realm of essence. Earlier in **PC** he had said, characteristically jumping from a phase or part of a process to a whole of his own positing,

> any one who compares distinct ideas, and discovers the third or mediating idea which interprets the meaning of the one in the light of the other, thereby discovers, or invents, a realm of conscious unity which constitutes the very essence of the life of reason (II, 188).

But, as an argument based only on a possible implication of Royce's thinking rather than on the ways in which wholes and parts can be found to be related or on the nature of different kinds of wholes or wholenesses, it fails to convince. The whole *may* be implicit in the parts; but it also may not. And, while it is true that meanings emerge in contexts of interpretation, what Royce has posited is not a collateral context of actually relevant information but a hypostatization of possible meanings.[10] And, contrary to what some semiotic neopositivists suggest, a dictionary of these possible infinite— and infinitely ramified—meanings is simply imposssible to construct. Royce was right that the reality of the concrete communicative individual is social. But he did not avail himself of the visible fact that the *matrix* of human communication is, precisely, human society and its conventions.

So we come to Royce's actual practice of political and intellectual history. As could be expected Royce's history of California is interpretive, and bent on drawing general lessons from experience about human nature and about the nature of community. Clendenning goes right to this point when he says,

> Royce saw the upheavals of early California as parables that might teach philosophic truth—the history of the conquest, the Downieville lynching, the Vigilance Committees, and the squatter revolts—are precisely those which dramatize the issues which Royce would later raise in *The Philosophy of Loyalty* and *The Problem of Christianity* (**LJR** 26).

The problem which the latter work undertakes to solve by means of its theory of interpretation is, of course, that of community. In **PL**, Royce finds human solidarity or unification to be achievable through attachment to ethical principles, unlike Henry Adams who thought of it as a historical or cultural achievement. And the central ethical principle by which the world can be unified and redeemed is that of loyalty.

As it turns out, the overall philosophic moral that Royce draws from the history is that of social idealism, and is similar to that of other works of his,[11] namely,

> After all . . . our lesson is an old and simple one. It is the State, the Social Order, that is divine. We are all but dust, save as this social order gives us life. When we think it our instrument . . . and make our private fortunes the one object, then this order rapidly becomes vile to us; we call it sordid, degraded, corrupt, unspiritual, and ask how we may escape from it forever. But if we turn again and serve the social order . . . not merely ourselves, we soon find that what we are serving is simply our own highest spiritual destiny in bodily form. It is never truly sordid or corrupt or unspiritual; it is only we that are so when we neglect our duty (*California* p.501).

As a claim which isn't inductively warranted by the facts narrated in the history, and which calls for the insertion of further premises before it can be validated, it does seem to reinforce the hypothesis offered in my *History as a Human Science* about the tendency built into idealism, when thinking holistically and in terms of social wholes, to come to endings that open the door to totalitarianism (**HHS**, p.5). But it also shows how, when we are confronted vividly enough with the reality of anarchy and violent disorder, we tend to over-value *unqualified* law and order for its own sake.

The book is nonetheless historiographically sound, enthusiastically researched, carefully documented and very reflective. About it Royce himself says that it was composed "to serve the true patriot's interest in a clear self-knowledge and in the formation of sensible ideals of national greatness" (ibid. 40). Later historians and critics have confirmed its judgment that the American consul Larkin's approach to Spanish California would have been preferable to Frémont's uninformed, glory-seeking response to the political vacuum there and the danger of a British or French coup on the West Coast, particularly since it was in the self-interest of the Californians to favor the connection with the United States rather than that with the even more remote and neglectful government in Mexico. Royce naturally condemns "the fearful blindness of the . . . behavior of the Americans" towards foreigners as "something almost unintelligible" (*Cal.* 281). Actually, it is explainable as reinforced by greed. In connection with the land which they were so quick to seize, which the Californians held under Mexican grants, Royce is acidulous about the rationalizations of the invaders.

> Providence . . . and manifest destiny were understood in those days to be on our side, and absolutely opposed to the base Mexican. Providence, again, is known to be opposed to every form of oppression; and . . . eleven leagues of land is a great oppression. And so the worthlessness of Mexican land-titles is evident. (*Cal.* 472).

Yet, as Royce points out,[12] from the crimes, follies and misfortunes of the conquest there did come a viable social order. But, insofar as from this a positive lesson can be drawn, Royce does it nationalistically rather than Hegelianly or in terms of human nature and circumstance. Namely, he attributes the ability to create political order out of *the chaos they themselves* created to some kind of "greatness" in these same people. He has not noticed that the same kind of "greatness" would be equally attributable to the original Spanish conquerors of the native civilizations of central Mexico and Peru.

> The lesson of the whole matter is as . . . plain as it is . . . denied by a romantic pioneer vanity; and our true pride, as we look back to those days of sturdy and sinful life, must be, not that the pioneers could . . . show by their popular justice their . . . instinctive skill in self-government . . . but that the moral elasticity of our people is so great, their social vitality so marvelous, that a community of Americans could sin as fearfully as . . . the mining community did sin, and could yet live to purify itself within so short a time, not by a revolution, but by a simple progress from social foolishness to social steadfastness. Even thus a great river for an hour defiled by some corrupting disturbance purifies itself merely through its own flow over its sandy bed, beneath the wide and sunny heavens (*Cal.* 375).

That Royce could be so optimistic in the face of his own testimony, when in our time this testimony forces us to opposite conclusions about America and about community, is proof of the power of the prevailing climate of opinion and its changing assumptions. Royce's conscientious doubts about the conquest and our negative conclusions from his evidence allow us to refocus his masterful history as a symbolic anticipation, not a caricature, of the United States in its subsequent confrontations with other peoples in a world which is not yet an "international community."[13]

"Faithfulness to history," says Royce in *The Spirit of Modern Philosophy*, "is the beginning of creative wisdom" (p.viii). As an interpretationist, however, Royce should have added, "as long as we are completely honest in our interpretation of history"; while we, his critics, are bound to add that all historical interpretations—from the moment of their formulation—are subject to revision because the past they interpret is ever incomplete in the consequences and ramifications that remain to emerge or to be seen. What we can say, therefore, about Royce's practice of intellectual history in *The Spirit of Modern Philosophy* is that it is faithful to the history and context of the German idealism which was his own great interest and inspiration. Among the consequences of this fidelity is Royce's loyalty to the historicist dimension of idealism, which he explains as an interest in growth and development, as an interest in *process* as *subsuming mechanism*.[14]

One can see here an important antecedent of Dewey's later arbitration between mechanicism and teleologism in *Experience and Nature*, and of the interest in "the world in its wholeness" (**SMP** 292) which is distinctive of the classic American philosophers. Royce's stimulating account of the emergence of the historical conception of the world in modern times leads him to the conclusion both that "history is worth studying for its own sake," and that "there is still no knowledge so profound as the knowledge of the history of things" (**SMP** 290F.). While this true love of history bonds Royce to the other classic American philosophers, there is an idiosyncratic consequence which he draws from historicism that separates him from them, because it sets the seal of his idealism upon his view of nature. This is that the historical approach to nature proves "that therefore ideals are responsible for nature's mechanism" (ibid.).

(iii) *Herbert Schneider on the History of Philosophy*

Like Buchler, Herbert Schneider believed that "[any] philosophy as a whole must be characterized by other predicates, not by true and false." He points out that, if we call "science" the cooperative and systematic search for experimental evidence," then "philosophy as it is being carried on today shows traits which distinguish it from science" (**PCA** 467). Unlike science, "no philosophical system is wholly impersonal either in form or content . . . . Like poetry and the other arts, philosophy is a personal creation and expression even in its aim at universality" (**PCA** 469f.).[15] But philosophers make poor historians, in Schneider's view, because "each conceives of his ideas as the logical outcome of all previous thought."

Nietzsche put it more strongly when he said "lack of historical sense is the congenital defect of all philosophers" (HATH #.2). At the same time, from another perspective, the history of philosophy is not cumulative—unlike science whose history can be seen as the successive correction of previous errors. But there is a message in this for our monological, alienated, polemicists:

> philosophers of all ages must take each other seriously, as though all were engaged in a common dialogue and shared a single pursuit. Such study is more then [than] the study of history; it is a human fellowship of experience and reflection, a communion among lovers—and not without jealousy (PCA 470).

If the question is whether philosophy will become, on Schneider's suggestion and on the example of the state of literary criticism since Bakhtin,[16] more *dialogical*, we can only speculate that it is unlikely to do so as long as it persists in the *limited logicalism* that doesn't admit Peirce's expansion of logic into a discipline that applies 'speculative grammar' and methodeutic (transuasional analysis, i.e., 'speculative rhetoric'), to the subject-matters that come into its ken. Not to realize that the great works of philosophy from which we live today, are themselves *in dialogue with each other* is, more than an evasion of their historical dimension, a failure to respond to a constitutive ground of their full meaning. And by ground I mean that to which the thinker, as sign-maker, is responding in his abstracting, constructing and inferring. For, there is also a sense in which the great thinkers' works "live out of time," as Nietzsche said, "contemporaneously with each other" like "that republic of geniuses of which Schopenhauer speaks. One giant calls to the other across the waste space of time . . . in noble dialogue" (ADH #.9).

When Schneider speaks of a philosophy as having a "life-span" (PCA 471), he is not acquiescing in Woodbridge's or Randall's model for treating historical subject-matters as having "careers."[17] Randall himself concluded that, as a temporal entity, philosophy has enjoyed a history but not a career. He titled his work *The Career of Philosophy* only because, he says,

> modern philosophy has been sufficiently integrated by its . . . recurrent problems in a single culture to . . . have enjoyed a unified 'career' from its outset in the thirteenth century (**CP** xi).

This situation however has changed since Randall wrote, not because of the nominally anti-metaphysical stance of neopositivist and formalist logicism, but because the anti-pluralism and *intolerance* to other approaches *built into* the new mode of so-called linguistic analysis, has destroyed the broad unity of the philosophic quest in the West.

What makes the unity impossible to recover is *the change* decreed by logical linguisticism *in the subject-matter* of philosophic query itself. Philosophy may now *only* uncover and interrogate the formal-logical structure of the language in which we theorize art or politics or nature, not art itself or politics-in-practice or nature-in-process. Such first-order inquiries must be left to the special sciences: nature to the physicists, politics to the political scientists, and art . . . to whom: to the makers of art, to the critics of art, or to its historians? But who will mediate between the historians and the critics of art, or between the politician and the political scientist, or among the physicists and the historians of ideas and sociologists of knowledge? Certainly not somebody restricted to analyzing *only* the concepts of political science; for such a mediator must at once become, for example, a *rhetorical* analyst of the public discourse about citizenship, representation, foreign policy, and so on. And the philosophy of science in our day has shown that reflection on the concepts of physics, in relation to the other knowledges of the culture, cannot be done well without reference to the history of the science and the culture.

Further to this problem, we have to note that there are those who think that any activity rightly called "analysis" necessarily has language for its subjet-matter, as if only verbal complexes were analyzable and *primary* subject-matter was not. Nor is mere distinction-making more than a necessary condition of analyzing; it is not a sufficient condition.

Distinctions will have to be *in the subject matter*, will have to be economic, aesthetic, political—namely, material—not just verbal, if they are to be about their subject matter rather than the way in which it is spoken of.

In other words, language may always become the *proximate* subject of an investigator's analyses, as it often does in Aristotle's dialectical introductions to his substantive analyses of problems. But, just as it is not fully reflective to fail of being historical about historical documents or subject matter, so it is a failure of reflection to make *only* linguistic distinctions in connection with non-linguistic subject matter. That would be reflection about a *mediating* factor of the inquiry rather than substantive interrogation of the natural or social factors which have brought about the phenomenon under investigation. Analysis in this fuller sense is, in Buchler's terms,

> the process whereby a given natural complex is explored with respect to its integrity as a complex rather than with respect to its possible bearing upon the integrity of another complex (**ML** 169).

The emphasis in an extended analysis, then, is on what is relevant to the given complex rather than on what *it* is relevant *to*. In this case, query is properly said to be *analytic* of a complex's integrity; but query and the categorizing that goes with it, may also be *coordinative* when it brings out the relevance of a given complex to other complexes.

Another reason that Schneider rejected the analogical application of the concept of "a career" to human histories is that the human past, what he called "historical being" (**WB** 54ff.), is too complex a process, with too many kinds of historical prevalences and alescences, too many kinds of determining factors and self-determining agents, to be narratable as a single story in the form of the career of humanity or even of a nation. It would always have to be a history of the career of the United States, let us say, *as* a maritime power or *as* a nation with an exceptional constitutional development. In his own *A History of American Philosophy*, Schneider takes both single individuals and differentiable traditions of thought as the subjects of his history. As producers and products of their culture, what he calls the "life-spans" of these subjects is not incompatible with the idea of their having had a career. What Schneider avoided and disapproved of in standard accounts of thinkers and traditions, was the treatment of them in terms of their "rise and fall." Such tendentious terms conflate the account of the worldly emergence, or *publicist* success, of a philosophy with analyses of its validity as a form of thought, a serviceable methodology, or expressive construction.

More precisely Schneider saw that it is the way in which a philosophy succeeds in communicating its sense of what is important,[18] that seems to determine its readability at a given time, its viability for an audience. And this is a contingent circumstantiality. There is irony, therefore, in the fact that unhistorical but fashionable philosophers fail to perceive that the succession of schools which have preceded them were once as credible as they conceive themselves to be at the moment. Conversely and correspondingly, as I have said elsewhere **(HHS** 64), the impact which a knowledge of the sociohistorical context of a philosophy (or succession of philosophies) has upon our understanding of that philosophy (or that succession), is so great as to be undeniable as an experience.

Schneider's attention to the "life-span" of philosophies avoids depersonalizing them or diminishing their recoverable vitality; it does not begin by reducing them to abstractional units in a bodiless history of mere ideas **(PCA** 470). By treasuring "the philosophical life" in them *as a* measurable *function of* their cultural relevance to a particular moral environment and its urgencies Schneider succeeds in recapturing that life. So it is the responsibility of the historian to trace out the role of particular philosophies in the "cultural fields of operation" in which they were meaningful. We see, however, that this variable, namely, their attractiveness to a generational or geographic audience, is independent of their validity. An example of this, among many that could be cited, is the important use that Analytic epistemologists make of the distinction, original to Santayana, between the *reasons for* and the *causes of* an action, while refusing to read him or, else, not knowing that it is his distinction.

The task of history is to build, maintain and use the past intelligently **(WB** 57), not ideologically. And the "intelligent funding of human experience" calls for both imagination and tolerance, because "unless you understand and respect things foreign, you will never perceive the special character of things at home or of your own mind," says Schneider quoting Santayana (**MHW** 35). For Schneider, moreover, it is not possible to possess a meaningful future unless we have appropriated our past maturely.

> Consciousness . . . having a full present is precisely the interplay of past and future, the bringing together of the learned and to-be-lived. . . . 'Having a mind' and 'being historical' are therefore two ways of describing the same fact (**WB** 58).

Schneider is very aware that "natural happenings continually intrude on the course of human operations (which are the immediate subject of history)." But admitting this (**WB** 54), he does not admit "that human history is a chapter in natural history" or "that historical explanation is the same as physical explanation." And with this we have to agree, I myself for the reasons given in my chapter on 'explanations in histories,' in *History as a Human Science*: histories are simply not nomothetic-deductive or predictive. But it reminds us that when Santayana calls historical query the 'natural history of mankind' he is using the term metaphorically; he means—more exactly, and in the Peircean sense of the term—the 'speculative' natural history of mankind.

Schneider on the other hand is thinking of 'natural history' in the regular special science sense, because *his* point is that "historical being" is a fundamental dimension of "cultural being," not of "natural being." His explication of historical being as the culture's "funding" of its experience can be given a more detailed analysis, should we wish it, in terms of Buchler's account of proceptive parallelism and community.

Where nature does not admit such divisions as past, present, and future, history (i.e., cultural being) is divided into just these different "times." Of these the present is, indeed, the only one "in operation" (**WB** 56). But in human experience or culture, the present "is dependent on having a past. . . . It must carry its historical past with it into the future, and this 'living' past in the present is . . . what has been funded for reference and recall when needed." And this is the deeper reason why "historical composition must be up-to-date, continually reshaping its perspectives to a changing present." We all need, says Schneider,

> a bigger and better past as our present. Or . . . as a French existentialist warns us, we are being robbed of our future because so much of our past is meaningless for the narrow present. . . .

Of course, even the most carefully funded past is only an approximate guide to the future (**WB** 58); but, intelligently used, it does provide clues toward judging the quality or tendency of the present. In any case, if the future were subject to prediction instead of imagination, the "becoming present of the future would have no excitement in it."

> The disparity between what comes to be and what was supposed to become keeps the mind alive and incites interest. This gamble in historical existence . . . is known among metaphysicians [as] . . . contingency, [it] is the essence of the present and its meanings, the union of what [is] . . . call[ed] *Dasein* and *Sosein*.

Schneider had said, in *The Puritan Mind* (1930 p.3f.) "past and present are . . . alike mysterious, but . . . they nevertheless make each other intelligible."[19] In that book he had been concerned that "a world of thought [which] is slowly created . . . [like] the mental world of New England . . . may perish overnight," because of the great rift between the assumptions of our great-grandparents and our own. At the same time he felt that such rifts "make a history of the mental life of a people almost as impossible as unprofitable." Here Schneider has simultaneously pinpointed both the need for and the difficulty of intellectual history.

His solution to this difficulty of intellectual history recognizes, first of all, that "the arts are not surplus products of life; they are rather life's very essence" (**PM** 5). Secondly, if we are "to understand why these flights [of religion and philosophy] appeared to afford wider perspectives and fresh points of vantage for the lives out of which they arose," the difficulty must be undertaken in a "spirit of imaginative adventure." Thirdly, because philosophies are such that men live and die within them; and because they are not disembodied contributions to knowledge (**PM** 6),[20] the intellectual historian must be concerned with the biographical facts of "the lives and deaths of famous ideas." Fourthly, because no living thing can feed only on itself, "nor do ideas grow out of the mind," to be able to understand the origin and import of an idea "one must examine the teeming world by which it was generated and into which it falls."

By their *import* Schneider meant, not their dialectical correlation to some desocialized abstractions ensconced in somebody's anatomical museum of skeletal forms, but their *temporal* meanings to those who held them "and in whose lives they played a living part." For Schneider "a living ideal is understood when seen in terms of its environment." In contrast, the anatomical dissection of it can be no more than instrumental to the study of the living functions it served.

Looking back at Schneider's philosophic and historical achievement, we can now see that his success in characterizing basic themes of American thought,[21] from puritanism and transcendentalism to evolutionism and pragmatism, has depended not only on his creative doubts and philosophic ability but also, and basically, on the methodological insistence that to neglect the circumstantial background and social habitat of ideas is to put the living functions and working natures of ideas beyond the reach of good understanding.

2
(iv) *Randall on the Philosophic Use of Intellectual History*

In his collaboration with the young Buchler on their *Philosophy: An Introduction*, Randall conceived of philosophy rather too broadly as "the intellectual phase of cultural change" (**PAI** 2, 22, 35f.). Philosophy, as I've said elsewhere, is not all of the intellectuality of a time, unless we stipulate that it will mean just that, including the spirituality of that time and all the incompatible assumptions that, as a culture, it acts upon and does not doubt.[22] Randall seems to have been thinking, rather, of what he calls the cultural *function* of philosophy: as "the process by which conflicts within a culture are analyzed and clarified, resolved and composed," and "as the method of criticizing and reorganizing beliefs." And, like Plato's Socrates, he thinks of this process as, most basically, search: as "searching thinking" driven by the most "basic conflicts within a culture" (**PAI** 35).

Philosophic problems, for Randall, can only be defined operationally, "as those questions in which philosophic minds have become interested. . . . They emerge, the record reveals, whenever the strife of ideas and experiences forces men back to the fundamental assumptions in any field; when it compels men to analyze them, to clarify, criticize, and reconstruct them" (**HPUP** 18). Randall does not deny that philosophy can be many other things, personal or individual, expressive, therapeutic, as technical or as popular as you please. But in *How Philosophy Uses Its Past* he is focusing, not on philosophy as a way of salvation but on what it has also always been, on the record and from its beginnings, "a social and cultural function." And this is what, in turn, allows it to be taken by intellectual historians, as "the expression in thinking of cultural change" (**PAI** 19). That philosophy is a critique of the fundamental assumptions of any of man's enterprises, of his art, his politics, his sciences, his practices and his religions, is also the view of the other classic American philosophers and of this book.

Here, and because times have changed, we have to differ from Randall's observation that "for any man with a genuine philosophic impulse this is a glorious age in which to be alive." It has become, rather, an age of "deconstruction," where iconoclasm is enjoyed for its own sake and in which, philosophy having been redefined as applied logic, logic is wielded as a '*philonikean*' (victory-seeking) weapon. Winning the argument is not the same as the Socratic following of the argument wherever it may lead. Nor, as we have seen, is arguing all that philosophy does. It would seem to follow from this that the urgent cultural problem which philosophic thinking must face today, before it can turn to face the problems of post-industrial society and international relations,[23] is that of (i) retrieving and revalidating the non-logicist equipment discarded or neglected by the applied logicians, and (ii) mediating between the philosophic interests which have successfully yielded to the application of formal logic and the philosophic interests which will yield only to the rest of the Aristotelian *organon* and Peirce's additions to it, namely, to rhetoric, poetics, and semiotics—with all that the latter includes.

When philosophies have been abandoned or neglected it is, as Randall notes, (**HPUP** 21f.), not because they have been "disproved;" but because they have become irrelevant to what the readership thinks are its needs. The oddity, in connection with the fashion for Analytic philosophy, is that it does not claim to make (or admit that it makes) any substantive contribution to knowledge or to meet any need of its followers—except for the need to show that philosophy, as practiced in the past, is a quite unnecessary sort of interrogative exercise. The Carnapian variant of this tenet believes that a logical proof of this can be provided, even though Carnap's own life-long search for such a proof was in vain.[24] And this suggests that its claim to abstain from first-order inquiries is, in fact, a screen-dogma of neopositivist thinking, a defensive polemical device rather than a valid methodological recommendation which restricts inquiry to the logical aspect of linguistic material.

Analytic thinkers, like all of us, are interested in knowledge; but not *as philosophers*. As 'analysts' they are concerned only to uncover (only) the logical conditions under which a predicate is true or false as applied to a given subject. Two conclusions would seem to follow from this, one about the relation of analytic methodologists to philosophic query, and one about the fashionable neglect of classic American philosophy—in spite of its possession of insights and approaches that would be of great help in the clarification of questions that analysts say they are interested in.

The first is that such thinkers—such readers of philosophic material—no longer *need* 'philosophy' in any substantive traditional or creative sense, because they are not the kind of thinkers capable of what Aristotle called wonder. An authentic desire for knowledge, or response to wonder, would have led them into the interrogative arts or sciences themselves, had they *needed* to find answers to their questions for themselves, or into interrogative scrutinies (synoptic or piecemeal) of the *material* claims of the special sciences and the experimental arts. But like others who call themselves philosophers, they are interested in certain kinds of question related to knowledge: from the possibility of *what* knowledge *is of*, namely, of what-there-is to the possibility of knowledge-in-itself.

And this is a special grade of wonder, if it can be called wonder at all: to wonder 'epistemologically' about 'knowledge-itself' after the fact of knowing and in abstraction from the knowing process is to ask about an *intransitive* relation-without-a-relatum, that is distinct from the *transitive* process-with-a-cognate object that is knowing. As a secondary elaboration, *this* inquiry takes up a false trail *away from* the quarry: the knowing activity in pursuit of its objects. Plato's *Theaetetus* provided us long ago with an exhibitive demonstration in practice of the futility of trying to answer the question "What is knowledge?" when it is formulated in this *essentialist* way.[25]

Discursive illations such as these are lent some countenance in the philosophical tradition by the pseudo-Kantian legacy that lets one wonder whether something is possible after it has occurred and *even though* it has occurred. But: if *x* happened, *x* was possible. Whether it *had* to happen is, as we know, another question. The only operational answer which the question "How was it possible?" can have, is a genetic inquiry into the antecedent conditions under which it *did* happen. As an existence, the event can in no way be derived from a purely logical analysis of the discourse relevant to it.

Thus, the non-cirumstantial *purely discursive* question "How is it possible?" is an expression of pseudo-wonder. It acts as if what has happened has not; and then asks how *could* it, *against the surface-probabiliies*, have happened? In other words, the wonder involved in the inquiry into the so-called 'conditions of possibility' of a thing or process, is driven by a word-caused dilemma. Now there can surely be wonder about the tricks that discourse is capable of; but it is a secondary kind of wonder, not of itself continuous with philosophic wonder at phenomena.

The question that remains, however, is how the focus on language that Analysis has made its specialty could have failed to notice that, here, it too is in the very condition that Analysis accuses other philosophies of being, namely, of resting on a mistake due to a linguistic confusion. Is it because 'analytic' wonder about language is *not* about 'language' as a natural phenomenon subject to examination in its operation, and is able to be understood both as speech (*parole*), the human practice, and as language (*langage*), the grammarians' construct? Could this have been due to the calculator's habit of seeing language and speech under the form of 'logic' whatever logic may have been at a given time. The old dream of a universal, artificial or mathematical, language with which to encompass phenomena no doubt played some role in this development. Yet, unless duly contextualized, this artificial-intelligence or mathematicist sort of interest in 'language' is not a philosophic concern.

The conclusion that emerges about the neglect of classic American philosophy is that, as a non-epistemologizing movement of thought, it was proof against the claims to legitimacy and inclusiveness of this secondary, or special, interest in language and its misbehaviors. In line with Randall's suggestion, we have to say that classic American philosophy simply does not serve the interest of a readership that comes to philosophy with mostly logical training, with no interest in poetics, rhetoric, semiotics or the humanities, and with an interest in the sciences that restricts its concern to the discourse of the exact sciences, and the approximations to this exactness of the social sciences.[26]

The problems which have generated the response constituted by classic American philosophy were both intellectual and social. They were, on one hand, the challenge of the new ideas coming from Newtonian and nineteenth-century physics as well as from Darwinism and the biological sciences, and, on the other hand, ideas arising from new social experience, from new forms of social and industrial organization. Thus, Peirce was in dialogue with (and contributing to) contemporary advances in the natural sciences, and answering the methodological questions which these advances provoked, while

Dewey's effort was to respond to the new demands both of social inquiry upon philosophy and of the new biology upon the psychology and philosophy of mind.

In this respect Peirce and Dewey represent *the present* reconstituting its intellectual life on the basis of questions that had to be asked of *the* intellectual *past*. This is the respect in which their philosophies are cumulative, continuous with past intellectual achievement, and progressive, namely, looking to the advances in understanding possible to the culture. And we see that the *innovativeness* of these two philosophers is not different from their interrogative and dialogical embedment in the *traditions* of the arts and sciences.

Now, it is whole *traditions* of thought that are, properly, *the real units* in the history of philosophy or the history of culture—as Randall has shown in theory and in practice. If we're speaking of history of philosophy itself rather than of the relation of intellectual history to philosophy, then we must say that to be history the history of ideas has to be sociohistorically contextual and contextually adjudicative of the values involved in past ideas. If it is to deal with intellectual realities rather than artifacts, it must analyze idea-complexes in the contexts of their effectiveness as parts of (as meaning-structures in) a social world, and as developments in what we call an intellectual tradition. For it is these traditions that allow us to grasp a particular philosophy or proposal both in its originative or home context, and to compare it fairly with a corresponding philosophic proposal in another line of intellectual development—made, namely, on the basis of different starting-points or premises.

But a reminder that many philosophers, in neglecting context, are actually assuming a great deal of history when they think they are being only philosophical, will not serve unless it is also shown that intellectual history brings *philosophic* understanding. And this is the question that Randall considers in his chapter on "How History Brings Philosophical Understanding"; there he says,

> It has recently been claimed that the sole function of philosophy is to clear up the muddles [of] past philosophers, by means of a careful analysis of the misuse of language that generated them. But a far more

convincing method of clearing up past muddles is historical analysis, which can . . . reveal the inconsistent and unfruitful assumptions that originally provoked them. This is the liberating and emancipating function of historical knowledge. . . Such historical and genetic analysis can eliminate problems that have become . . . "academic," because . . . taken over from the past dealing with issues [no longer] at the focal point of intellectual tensions . . .[and]. . . because it can reveal the inconsistent assumptions . . . made only because men then accepted . . . ideas . . . long since abandoned (**HPUP** 96).

An instance of this is the historical understanding we now have of why religious beliefs which in the seventeenth century were a challenge to the procedures and working assumptions of the sciences, no longer are, and the consequent disappearance of the "epistemological" problem that this created. Another example that Randall cites—too briefly, to be sure—is that of the equally "epistemological" problems that appeared to exist when the purely mathematico-mechanical view of process dominated the climate of opinion in which scientists and savants lived, but which disappeared when the emergence of molecular biology, statistical methods, and functionalism in psychology[27] began to minimize the gap beween matter and motion on the one hand and life and mind on the other. For such historical examples prove that,

> It is not only the analysis of language that can prove emancipating and therapeutic. Historical knowledge is the greatest of all liberators from the mistakes and muddles, from the tyranny of the past (**HPUP** 77).

It is a matter of observation—neglected as the observation is—that what makes the standard unhistorical histories of philosophy look distinctive, in contrast to general intellectual history or history of ideas, is not so much their total focus on philosophic texts or texts upon which philosophers have rationalized,[28] as the procedure that assumes that ideas or idea-clusters derive *only* from each other, in a kind of abstract parthenogenic though temporal, dialectic in which successor-ideas develop or correct previous ideas. But ideas do not change *only* because of further inspection by intellectual professionals.

So, in accepting Randall's claim that the best definition of philosophy comes from studying what philosophy has been and has done in the past, we have to qualify it in two ways. First, we should not take, as our models of written *history of* philosophy, the purely 'dialectical' histories which have become standard but which fail to document the socio-intellectual, psychological or existential circumstances which gave rise to the questions which past philosophies seek to answer. And on Randall's own recommendation in **TPHS**,[29] we should also reject as models those histories that do not make explicit what their principles of selection are, with respect to the material they have decided to treat. We should also reject those that, in addition, do not make clear what the interpretive bases are of their judgments of previous philosophies; for, all history is interpretive, and all historians select their material on the basis of what is important to them, or what they think is important to their readers.

Secondly, like other historians except the historians of sophistry, Randall misses the opportunity of developing, or illustrating, the theme of the continuing lapses of so much past philosophy into paraphilosophic sophistics. Of course, what is deemed sophistic is as much a matter of interpetation as what is deemed philosophic, except that in the case of the former the characterization that a given line of thought is sophistic has *necessarily* to be accompanied by explicit statements of the premises on the basis of which it appears sophistic. And this is not the same as tracing out, in the history of past thought-systems, what emerges as genuine philosophy because it is not incompatible with the historian's own philosophy.

In looking at past epochs of thought, what the historian looks for is not individual philosophies, but rather "the dominant problem that these philosophies were designed to solve," as J. Barzun says in *Romanticism and the Modern Ego* (p. 21f.). This means that, having identified the matrix presuppositions of the epoch, the historian can judge what argumentation (in attacking the central problems of the age) is 'deviant' in the positive sense of 'original,' and what is 'sophistic' in the sense of serving interests that the argumentation or discourse fails to rethink or in the sense, not that it is mistakenly paralogical or ex post facto, but in the sense that it is deliberately paralogical *because* it is casuistic or ex post facto. What will also emerge from this inquiry is the non-sophistic nature of some philosophies that appear non-forward-looking because they turn out not to have addressed the central, propulsive problems of the age.

A well-known example of this is the work of Robert Filmer,[30] so acceptable in its time and so marginal in the somewhat longer run. That Locke, arguing on different non-biblical grounds, was so soon able to refute Filmer, reminds us of the incompatibilities that can exist in the most basic assumptions of a culture.[31] The case would also seem to show that to address central problems from starting-points about to become obsolete or irrelevant, is not really to have grasped the central problems in their full intellectual bearings or circumstantial ramifications.

Yet, that Randall the intellectual historian and historian of philosophy found it necessary, in his lifetime and in practice, to write *both* what we call a general intellectual history, *The Making of the Modern Mind*, and a specialized history of philosophy in two or three volumes, *The Career of Philosophy*, provides us with much to ponder as well as with some leading questions about the relation of intellectual history to philosophic history. We can distinguish cases in which intellectual history helps provide history of philosophy with greater sharpness about or better understanding of intellectual subject matter, and the case in which intellectual history and philosophy come completely together because there the need is to uncover the 'indubitables' of a society. The indubitables are the deeply held, mostly unquestioned usually unnoticed, suppositions upon which a society or group acts, builds, and speaks.

This kind of intellectual history or philosophy is sometimes called 'foundational analysis,' in the sense that it is an uncovering or critiquing of the buried dianoetic starting-points of action, assertion, and construction in the society.[32] And it is needed because very often, unless we recover the unstated missing premises of past arguments, they will seem defective. We may also miss their cogency if we are unable to capture the originative design and spirit of many a past work. As stated in the essay just cited,

> The test of a successful recovery of missing steps or premisses, [or] of the generative design in past philosophies, is that their presence [restores] both the cogency which the . . . argument had for its author and the integrity, tendency and shape which was built into the ancient philosophic expression by its maker(s).

The aim of *The Making of the Modern Mind*, says Randall, was

> by entering sympathetically into the spirit of the past, to make the thought of the present more intelligible. . . . [the book] does rest, so far as possible, upon a first-hand acquaintance with the words of those who have expressed the intellectual currents of their times. This explains the abundance of quotation . . .; for it has seemed best to try to look at the development of thought with the eyes of those who participated in it (p.iv).

He adds that, in revising the book, "it is the history men have lived rather than the history scholars have discovered that has dictated the thoroughgoing revision of the chapters . . . dealing with the last hundred years." This statement implements two well-known theses of Randall's, namely, that the meaning of a given past (as well as the account of it) changes with time as more of its consequences and aftereffects unfold, and that as the needs and self-understanding of *the present* change, what seems relevant to it in the past also changes. On the assumption that it is men who make history, not history men, and that civilization is a precarious *achievement*, **MMM** is an in-depth survey of how we arrived (since the Middle Ages) at "the complex of beliefs and ideals by which the modern world lives and with which it works . . . as . . . an achievement of a long succession of generations" **(MMM** 9). **MMM**, then, is a book primarily oriented to understanding the modern civilized world. It is guided by what is sometimes called a *presentist* interest.

The Career of Philosophy, on the other hand, is "an attempt to write a history of modern philosophy from a perspective of American philosophizing in midcentury." And this is not the perspective of nineteenth-century idealism from which previous large-scale or unified histories of Western philosophy have been written. **CP** also wants to fill the gap between the thirteenth and the seventeenth century "when modern philosophy is conveniently supposed to have begun" (**CP** viii). Research had increasingly brought out the essential continuity between medieval and modern philosophy, so that "seventeenth-century philosophy, in Descartes, Spinoza . . . Hobbes . . . Leibniz, can be understood only as the bringing to bear of some one of the medieval philosophic traditions on the interpetation and generalization of the basic ideas of the new science of nature." Hence the need for a knowledge of these medieval philosophies of science and what happened to them during the Renaissance, as well as for a knowledge of how that science itself emerged since the twelfth century. The story that **CP** tells will be that of the fruitful encounter (and its conseqences) between philosophy and science since that time, and of the successive stages of individualist protest against, and liberation from, medieval institutions that find expression in the social and political thought of the seventeenth century and the Enlightenment. These protests were as much a stimulus to intellectual change as the new science, even though they often used language or view-points suggested by the concurrent development of science.

The subject matter of **MMM** and **CP**, the development of Western thought from the Middle Ages to modern times, is, then, nominally the same. But the emphasis is different. The student of **MMM** gets from it what **CP**, and this chapter, say is needed to understand past traditions and their ideas accurately and fully, namely, a grasp of their wider cultural *background* and circumstantial *matrix* in the climate of opinion and communicative practices of their time. **MMM** is, indeed, accurately subtitled "A Survey of the Intellectual Background of the Present Age."

And we see that "intellectual" here includes the eschatologies, the political reflection, the expressive or medium-bound thinking of the arts, and the reflective quality of the practices of a time, not just its theories or explicitly stated beliefs. The different emphasis of **MMM** is also reflected in its greater readibility since it can take the form of a narrative of events and a report of beliefs, rather than a close analysis of them—as **CP** has to be. **MMM** has to be sociohistorical in the existential or circumstantial sense, where **CP** has to be sociohistorical in the dialectical, or dialogical, sense of uncovering and taking the point of view of the systems of thought it is analyzing (in dialogue with), and so being able to provide endogenic criticism of them as well temporal perspective about them.

Finally, we must attend to a possible response to Randall's claim that the place in which to look for the best definitions of philosophy is in the history of what it has done and been in the past. This is that it might preclude philosophy's doing anything different from what philosophy has done in the past. The rejoinder does not work because the history itself illustrates how many different things philosophy has been and done. But a rejoinder to the rejoinder would also be, that if what self-named philosophers claim philosophy should be is not just *different*, but is actually *not philosophy* at all—pure computability research, say, or, as the definition now runs, simply "applied logic," then philosophy is indeed as dead as these philosophers[33] say. But it becomes clear who has killed it and, who, by abandoning it is no longer interested in its recovery or practice.

(v) *G.H. Mead's Experimentalist View of the Past*

Mead's insightful *Movements of Thought in the Nineteenth Century* is not fully served, from the philosophic point of view, by Merritt Moore's Introduction to it. Conscientious as the introduction is, it misses one of the book's generative concerns. For, **MTNC** emerges as practicing intellectual history under what we can anachronistically call Randall's prescription for writing it, namely, it is the result of Mead's "attempt to teach the history of [nineteenth-century] philosophy from a perspective of American philosophizing." And I say teach instead of "write" because the book is a transcription of (mostly) stenographic notes from lectures which, in being repeated, were always subject to refinement and expansion. Moore does perceive that Mead's genius was that of "the research thinker" (**MTNC** xi), but his paraphrastic anticipation of the book's contents is not up to the mark set by Mead himself.

Merritt's Moore's simplifications tend toward a scientism of which Mead, the research scientist, cannot be accused, and fails to appreciate how widely and existentially Mead casts his nets to capture *the meaning* of new ideas *for the society* in which they arise. Nor does the work only "demonstrate the organic continuity of ideas" (xxv), it also shows how they fail to apply or be taken up, as in the case for example of De Maistre's ideas about community. Moore, however, does perceive both the consistency of Mead's conception of history with his practice of it, and the *social* nature, in Mead, of the actors and thinkers whose ideas he is surveying.

Philosophy as it existed in France, Mead tells us in an appendix, "had sunk," during the time of the Ideologues, "to a very low ebb." There "the empirical philosophy," as imported by Voltaire and appropriated by political thinkers, was known as "sensualism" instead of as the philosophy of sensation (**MTNC** 434). Even though it appeared to make knowledge impossible, and "reduced man to a simple congeries of separate sensations," it replaced the more coherent but politically inappropriate ideas of De Maistre and De Bonald. The sensationist analysis of the older ideas, Mead points out, was *successful* in breaking down their dominance; but the hoped-for reconstruction of society, based on truths derived from the simple thought-elements revealed by sensationist analysis, was a *failure*. This part of the story ends with Royer-Collard emphasizing the active nature of knowledge, and importing the common sense and intuitionism of the Scottish school, in order to remedy the deficiencies in Condillac and the Ideologues. A point that Mead wants to make explicit in all of this is "that all French philosophy of the period had a political bias" (**MTNC** 441), and that "every philosophy and every philosopher in France during this period has a political status" (445).

But another point worth noting is the precedent and pattern according to which the importation of British empiricism into France had such destructive consequences for philosophy as to make it "almost disappear from the universities" (**MTNC** 434), as it entirely did, in later decades and under the added influence of Comtean positivism, in some South American universities which imitated French educational models. A related socio-intellectual point that Mead makes is that, because at this time "the stream of French life" was flowing not through Paris but through the country-side, which was now farmed by owners rather than serfs or tenants, the thought of the period was superficial in the respect that it didn't express French consciousness as a whole. And this, too, anticipates what has become a chronic attribute of French intellectual life, Paris-centered as it is. It would seem that the publicist modes it has gotten into both reflect this unrootedness, and are an attempt to compensate for it. A last negative point that Mead notes about English empiricism as opposed to French, is that in it "introspection" never means an examination of the spiritual life of the soul but only and always "a process of locating certain cognitive experiences" in consciousness (**MTNC** 445).

Interest in the activity of the ego is a characteristic of French thought in Mead's conspectus of it, from Montaigne through Romanticism. A dramatic interest in history is also characteristic of it in the latter period: "it was the essence of the Romantic movement to return to the past from the point of view of the self-consciousness of the . . . period, to become aware of itself in terms of the past" (**MTNC** 447f.). When Mead notes the effect of Kantianism in France "by way of" the eclectic idealist Cousin, he could—startlingly—be describing the idealism of Josiah Royce: French philosophy, he was saying, takes over the problems raised by "the doctrine of common consciousness in which are given the forms of mind which are also the forms of matter." Then, he notes (**MTNC** 447),

> By this method men could turn . . . to study themselves with a feeling that the study of the self was also a study of the world; that the same drama was present in the mind as in nature; that nature was free, an odyssey of spirit. One could study nature, its reality, its structure, in some sense, in our own minds.[34]

Finally, as an American interested in history, Mead faults Cousin's superficial approach to the subject. He "never had a real interest in the study of earlier philosophy and in the presentation of it on the basis of actual documents and their interpretation in terms of historical criticism" (448).[35]

Having shown that the interest of French philosophers in the early part of the century was not in epistemology but in refuting established political and clerical doctrines, Mead brings out how appeal to Reid's philosophy of common sense left "the field of the experience of the individual as a field which may have interest in itself" (**MTNC** 469). And this, at a time when philosophy was being re-established "on more . . . philosophical bases" than the previous political interest. An important concomitant of this promising turn was concern with the problem of mechanism versus determinism in matters psychological and, consequently, in matters cosmological. But this is not a theme that we will pursue here; we take note instead of Mead's critique of Comte.

Comte, who must be credited with insisting that society should be an object of scientific inquiry, inherited this emphasis on the dependence of the individual on society. "He conceived," says Mead (p.465), "of the individual as determined by society as an organism." But, wishing to apply the scientific method to whatever he studied, Comte's conception of it—in Mead's analysis—was deficient. He tried, for instance, to *reduce* psychology to biology. In doing this, he also turned away from the confident common sense view of our ability to know (thus opening the door again to the pseudo-problems of epistemology). Nonetheless "he was the first to . . . attempt to build . . . philosophy along the lines of the scientific method" (p.452).

As a research scientist Mead's interest in method is what Peirce would call "heuretic," namely, interested in inquiry not only as hypothetical but in hypothesizing *as a response* to obstruction or difficulty, and in observation as what occurs not in mere recognition but when our context is such that to look is to focus on something *not* anticipated. And this is *observation as discovery*. The "logical weakness of positivism" for Mead, then, is that it didn't distinguish between analytic or abstractive observation, between recognition of characteristics and scrutiny of them. "In other words, science is really research science. Research always implies a problem. Where there is nothing of this sort, we are not engaged in research" (p.460). Comte, moreover, was unresponsive to evolutionary doctrine or method, even though he was taking *events* instead of substances for his objects of inquiry.

Not recognizing the element of novelty in the practice of observation, neither were Comte's views of development adequate to the evolutionary subject matter of biology. In short, and in Mead's summary, though Comte assumed that science was the most efficient method of knowing, he did not give a competent account of the scientific method. Mead's wider and more creative view emerges in his sketch of Bergson's antecedents and critique of his views (507f.). For Bergson's attack on science, like Comte's advocacy of it, also "represents a misconception of its method and ideal" 510).

> [Science] is always presenting hypotheses of the world as it is, but [it] is a research affair and goes forward on the basis of the fact not only that the world will be intellig[ible] but that it will always be different from any statement that science can give of it. That is, we are looking for an opportunity to restate any statement which we can give of the world. That is the implication of our research science.

The above incomplete sampling must suffice as a demonstration of Mead's skill in intellectual history, and of his skill in applying it to past philosophies. Hopefully, it also clues us into some of Mead's particular philosophic concerns. Mead's philosophical project was at least twofold: philosophy must recategorize nature so that a human nature which is social can be reincorporated in it, and made continuous with it. It will also be up to philosophy to reconcile the knowledge-based determinism of the sciences with the facts of change both in a world constituted by *events* and in the self-conditioning individual (**PA** 108f.).

Mead came to success in this endeavor by developing (in contrast to Bergson) a more adequate theory of time. It is therefore not surprising, in retrospect, that Mead's theory of time is not only the middle term between the natural sciences and the human sciences, but is also the basis of the deep-seated continuity between his philosophy of history and his philosophy of science. In respect to the unity of Mead's philosophy of history with his theory of time, we also find, if we turn to F.J.E. Woodbridge his contemporary, that it presents a parallel with, perhaps a model for, the oneness of the theory of time and the theory of history in the latter's work on history, nature, and metaphysics. Woodbridge, like Mead, perceived that the picture of nature which sees it as an unheeding congeries of relentless processes without appeal, is a falsification of nature because it leaves out mankind (**EON** 149). The positive point retrievable from the picture, for Woodbridge, was its dramatization of an aspect of time, namely, its irreversible order or connectedness.[36]

But this irreversibility is characteristic only of time, not of the past. For, one of the tenets which most distinguishes this generation of American philosophers and the next is, notoriously, the common insistence on the necessary revisability and hypothetical nature of the past. "Real" or experienced time, efficacious or productive time is always present time, as opposed to lapsed or future time. These are recoverable or made available by being posited in thought as abstractions.

Just as in Aristotle change is the substrate of time, so for Mead, time is a function of change (**PP** 28-31; **PA** 638).[37] It is duration, not time, that is a function of consciousness. For Mead "[the] reality [of a past] is in its interpretation of the present" (**PA** 616). "What we have," Mead says, "is a passing present, compounded of the past which is determined by the interpretation of the present and the future which comes to us as alternative possibilities" (**ibid.**). Mead's view that new pasts continuously emerge, and that there is no part of the now accepted past which is irrevocable, rests on assumptions derived from his observation of the process of research science and, no doubt, from his own pursuit of scientific knowledge. Mead saw that the function of research is not merely to gather information or even, as the epistemologists were beginning to claim, to "explain" phenomena nomothetically-deductively, namely, by subsuming them under appropriate "laws."

Mead saw science not as referring new phenomena to old laws, but as working to devise and test new hypotheses that would "account for" problematic data and anomalous phenomena in the sense of allowing some blocked advance or inhibited action to resume. New or problematic data become intelligible or manageable, not by resorting to old ways of interpreting or doing things but by means of a reconceived past or a newly constructed history. Thus, a past is as hypothetical as any future; and the validity of hypotheses about the past can only be tested in the present or by future experience: "the past is a working hypothesis that has validity in the present within which it works but has no other validity" (**PA** 96).

Mead is not lapsing, here, into the rigidities or anachronisms of "presentism" since, for him, what "the significant content which historical research reveals" is not "the past object as implied in the present." It is rather "a newly discovered present which can only be known and interpreted in the past which it involves" (**PA** 94). This newly discovered present includes a "pictured extension which each generation . . . spread[s] behind itself [as its past]. One past displaces and abrogates another as inexorably as the rising generation buries the old" (**PA** p. 95).

The effective past is that which allows us to understand or "interpret" the present. "No scientist secure in his experimental method would base that security upon the agreement of its results with the structure of any changeless past . . . within his ken" (**PA** 96). Mead speaks of the present as something that is "interpreted" because our knowledge of it, too, is hypothetical. The question of the validity of a [hypothetical] past only arises in the presence of some problem. The verification of the hypothetical solution to the problem constitutes the solution *as knowledge*. For, that is knowledge, according to Mead, which solves problems (**PA** 95). And, as knowledge it "fits into the world that is there, so that we act with reference to it as we do with reference to the world that is there."

Furthermore, "so far as experience is concerned [it] is there also, until in conduct we find that it is not there; and then we have a problem on our hands and have to find out what is there—a problem of inference of implication, of knowledge." And just as it is (our understanding of) the present that tests the past, so it is the future that will test the present which we are (hypothetically) defining to ourselves. Recapitulating: the past interprets the present, it does not fully determine it, though it is the present that makes the past selectively determinate. The sense in which "the past . . . is in the present" is that in which "the past is there conditioning the present and its passage into the future."

The future is chosen by the present as alternatives are realized among potentialities; but the actual future will test and reconstruct the present. The future, we can be sure, will not see us as we see ourselves. It follows that those who know no history or have no sense of it, simply live in an impoverished and barely intelligible present. The reality of the historical past is, thus, not ontologically secondary. It is indispensable "to our present undertaking of interpreting our world . . . for [the sake of] present conduct and estimation" (**PA** 97). We can now recognize frankly "that the only reason for research into the past is the present problem of understanding a problematic world, and the only test of the truth of what we have discovered is our ability to so state the past that we can continue the conduct whose inhibition has set the problem to us."

Thus the function of the philosophy of history is not to predict the future, for it is not predictable in the sense required by the nomological view of historical studies. The latter view is true to its formalist understanding of the deductive sciences, but it is demonstrably not true to either the nature of the human past or the nature of historical query and the ways in which it presents its results. It is not scientific to assimilate new problems to pre-structured types of solution if the problems are really novel. It emerges that the deep contrary-to-fact implication of the nomological philosophy of history is its unstated inference that change in human affairs can be assumed to be always orderly, as it would have to be to be systematically explainable in a nomothetic-deductive way.

Because we now know that values will always change with time, Mead says, and because we know what sort of conditions favor or explain eventful changes we in fact do have "a philosophy of history" in the traditional sense. And this philosophy of history is different from the other-worldly philosophy of history of the West before the Renaissance (**PA** 503). In "the philosophy of history of church doctrine

... all values were authoritatively defined and fixed." But as a matter of fact, for Mead, "A philosophy of history arose as soon as men conceived that society was moving toward the realization of triumphant ends in some great far-off event" (**PA** 504).

The historical fact, unfortunately, has been that "The histories that have most fastened upon men's minds have been political and cultural propaganda, and every great social movement has flashed back its light to discover a new past" (**PA** 94). It would follow, for Mead and his reader, that the present cannot be coped with in a problem-solving way if the histories available to it are not scientifically sound, whatever the way in which they may be presented. This is why historical query must include a scientific dimension, and why philosophy of history must recognize that, variegated as the tasks of history are, the severest test of the adequacy of written histories is their contribution to an intelligent coping with present problems.

Trenchant "factual" monographs and eloquent popular histories which affect the sensibilities of an epoch will only complicate its predicament if they lead into misinterpretations of the present. It will therefore be the task of the philosophy of history to uncover such slippages wherever and however they occur in constructed histories, and in the uses that are made of them. This insight is fundamental to Mead's conception of the philosophy of history:

> it is just this reinterpretation of values in the face of the problems of society that constitutes the subject-matter of the philosophy of history, and it is the theory of this reinterpretation that is that philosophy" (**PA** 511).

In his observation of the methods of historical research, Mead found two distinguishable ideas about the past to be operating. There is a kind of plastic past with which we interrogate the problematic domain we have entered as historians. This past is working "when we are at grips with a problem and are seeking its solution. . . . it takes on now one sense and now another; we are seeking its meaning, endeavoring to find in it the course we should follow" (**PA** 507). Then, once we have been able to formulate a solution to the problem "the whole falls into a single story that we read in terms of a [hypothetical] causal series. . . . we build up a hypothesis which we test and perhaps act successfully upon, and then the problem takes the interpretation which our hypothesis places upon it." The outcome is a reconstruction of the meaning of the past for what we confront at present. Hypothetical as it is, this meaning is "always subject to conceivable reformulations, on the discovery of later evidence," as Mead had said in *The Philosophy of the Present* (29).

The past is also conceived by Mead as the meaning of what happened in a present. So, if the analysis of meaning is the peculiarly philosophic activity that it is thought to be today, it follows that historical investigation is necessarily a philosophic activity in one of its phases. In this sense, historical studies that wish to be as fully reflective as possible cannot do without philosophy of history. On the other hand, philosophic analysis that wishes to be fully informed about the meanings it is analyzing, cannot ignore the social histories which have conditioned those meanings.

About community, finally, Mead is both social-psychological and normative. His critique of Royce's religious conception of community is sociohistorical and very focused. Just as people do feel that the advantages they happen to enjoy are adventitious, so, says Mead, "do we feel that the intelligence which makes society possible carries within itself the demand for further development in order that the implications of life may be realized" (**SW** 404). In difference with the kingdoms of Europe, the historical process in America was not one of reformation and social reconstruction, but one of construction and development of its institutions. While "culture," in its European form naturally, was sought and celebrated in the colleges, lyceums and clubs, that culture "did not reflect the political and economic activities that were fundamental in American life" (**SW** 381). Romantic idealism did carry a sense of the individual in the community and the social reality expressed in the individual. But in its European form, German or British, it could not possibly interpret the relation of the American individual to his society.

Royce, consequently, did not present the problem in terms of the European philosophy in which American thinkers had then, perforce, to train themselves. He was, nonetheless, an absolute idealist. So, "it was the passionate struggle of his great mind to fashion, in his philosophy of Loyalty, an expression of this idealism that would fit the problem of American thought" (**ibid.**). Now Royce calls on the individual "to realize himself in an intellectual organization of conflicting ends" [the community] "that is already attained in the absolute self." But, Mead points out, "there is nothing in the relation of the American to his society that provides any mechanism that even by sublimation can accomplish such a realization. Not even in the Blessed Community, with Royce's social analysis of the self," does Royce get to "an American social attitude that will express his undertaking" (**SW** 382).

Nor does Royce's analysis of the self-representation of the individual reflect the self-consciousness of the American individual. Again, "the American even in his religious moments did not make use of . . . his self-consciousness to discover the texture of reality." Causes, and the groups to which Americans were loyal, were particular and aimed at specific ends, and not such as to be seeking "resolution in an attained harmony of disparate causes at infinity." And "he did not think of himself as arising out of a society, so that by [looking] into himself he could seize the nature of that society." On the contrary,

> the pioneer was creating communities and ceaselessly legislating changes within them. The communities came from him, not he from the community. And it followed that he did not hold the community in reverent respect.

The religious principles of the pioneer, like his political doctrines, had to be portable, "part of the limited baggage with which he could trek into the unpeopled West." No American in the sectarian meeting-houses of a western community, even in his philosophical moments, says Mead, "would have felt at home in the spiritual landscape of Royce's Blessed Community" (**SW** 383).

In Mead's historical judgment, Royce's moral sense, his love of community, and his philosophy "belonged to a culture which did not spring from the controlling habits and attitudes of American society." Here is Mead's personal judgment:

I can remember very vividly the fascination of the idealisms in Royce's luminous presentation. They were part of that great world of *outremer* and exalted my imagination as did its cathedrals, its castles, and all its romantic history. It was part of the escape from the crudity of American life, not an interpretation of it.

We see that Mead was more experiential and historical than Royce in his reflection upon the adjustive experience of the earlier Americans, as they let go of Europe and settled the wilderness. But, in criticizing his teacher and predecessor, Mead only seeks, not to abandon, but to develop the themes of experience and community, themes which— like that of the relation between imported doctrine and actual experience—are, as we have seen, central to the classic American tradition of philosophy.[38] Mead is no less historical than either Royce or Santayana in his appreciation and analysis of the American experience, but he is closer to it than either the passionate Californian or the detached Bostonian.

Notes

1. "The nature of community is one of the most serious problems of philosophy" (Dewey, **AE** 334). For Santayana, see **RS** Ch.II, "History"; and **HHS**, Ch.3.

2. It is probable that the motivation for Peirce's renaming of what is called 'formal logic', Critic, derives from his habit of closely reading whatever he read in the arts and sciences *methodeutically*, namely, with an eye to both the logic of the inferences being made, and the validity, appropriateness, and contextualization of the investigative techniques and strategies applied (**1.3-1.4**). Most relevant to this is Peirce's remark that "in my own feeling, whatever I did in any other science than logic was only an exercise in methodeutic and as soon as I had the *method* of investigation thoroughly shown, my interest dropped off (Fisch PSP 392f., and Brent PL 75).

3. Significantly, Dewey adds: "The history of science in its . . . emergence from religious ceremonial and poetic arts is the record of a *differentiation of* arts, *not* . . . of separation from art" (my emphases).

4. See AE 85ff., EN 117-179, 390-391, LTI 134-136, e.g.; and AHI 34-35, 60-61.

5. Here we see that Buchler takes community to mean a set of shared presuppositions, *not a material institution*. More simply, while everything can in one sense be said to have history, the coming-into-operation or emergence of the fact that a belief, an interest, a value, etc. is shared need not have a history.

6. As he says in *Nature and Jugment*: "Man is born in a state of natural debt, being antecedently committed to the execution or furtherance of acts that will largely determine his individual existence" (p. 3).

7. In the cooperative volume *Man in Contemporary Society* (Columbia U.P. 1962), p.4. Besides his work as editor of the earlier collections of historical source material listed in the bibliography, Buchler's contributed a valuable monographic essay on "Reconstruction in the Liberal Arts" to the Bicentennial volume *A History of Columbia College on Morningside*.

8. Chapter III, page 5 and footnote 7. The reader must consult the essay referred to in note 5 on the problem of the educational transmission of the sources of contemporary Western thought, for his philosophy of liberal education, "Reconstruction in the Liberal Arts." It is in *Columbia College on Morningside* (Columbia U.P. 1954); pp.48-135.

9. In *From Homer to Menander* (University of California Press 1951).

10. And this is like the deconstructionists' misleading claim that a given word in a literary work is operatively related to *all the other* words in the language, rather than to those in the work itself, in the company of which it is helping to create the integrity and effectiveness of the work.

11. As social history, however, it tacitly works to negate the claim of *The Religious Aspect of Philosophy* that "this world is the home of a Spiritual Life" (**RAP** 480).

12. On this point see also, V. Buranelli, *Josiah Royce* (N.Y. Twayne 1964); p.40f.

13. In spite of our use of the latter term, when it suits our propagandistic purposes.

14. See especially Lecture IX, "The Rise of the Doctrine of Evolution."

15. This is worth comparing with Royce's remark in **SMP**: "Artists are often unconscious philosophers, but great philosophers, from th[e] romantic point of view, are never more than consummate artists" (p.175). Because Kant was Royce's paradigmatic 'great philosopher' who however fails to deal adequately with art, we have to admit that it is possible to be philistine in one's theories about creativity while remaining on the whole creative in one's practice; for, there is no denying the monumentality of Kant's philosophical construction. In connection with *the form* of constructed

philosophies Royce says: "*Die Welt als Wille und Vorstellung* is in form the most artistic philosophical treatise in existence, if one excepts the best of Plato's dialogues" (**SMP** 250). The difference between Plato and systems such as Schopenhauer's or Santayana's is that, in Plato's dialogues, their dialogue-form is an *indispensable* constitutive condition of their reflectiveness and integrity, where in works that are both expository and exhibitive it is not.

16. M.M. Bakhtin *The Dialogic Imagination* 1975, Ed. & Tr. Holquist & Eemerson (U. of Texas Press 1981); and *Problems of Dostoyevsky's Poetics* 1929, Ed. & Tr. by C. Emerson (U. of Texas Press 1984).

17. *The Purpose of History*, p.23ff.; and *The Career of Philosophy*, p.x-xi.

18. This touches on the other reason why predicates other than "true" or "false" must be applied to philosophies, namely, that they are *transmitters of values*. Historians of philosophy do, in fact, habitually apply other predicates to the philosophies they pass in review.

19. The following paragraphs repeat quite closely the last words of the section on Schneider in Chapter IV of my *History as a Human Science*, "Philosophic Practitioners of History."

20. That men live and die *within* "a philosophy," both gives more meaning to and is echoed by the literary theorists' notion that we cannot help living "within a discourse," be it a personal, a professional or a national "narrative."

21. In, especially, his *A History of American Philosophy* 1946, 2 ed. (Columbia U.P. 1963).

22. *History and Anti-History in Philosophy*, Ed. with T.Z. Lavine (Dordrecht: Kluwer 1989); 216f. As that essay deals with "The Philosophic Historiography of J.H. Randall," I here focus on Randall's conception of the relations between intellectual history and philosophy.

23. Those which Dewey called the problems of men, rather than the problems of philosophy: "philosophy recovers itself when it ceases to . . . deal . . . with the problems of philosophers and becomes a method, cultivated by philosophers, for dealing with the problems of men" "The Need for a Recovery in Philosophy," (**MW** Vol.10, p.46).

24. For a pointed afterview of the ironies in the career of this logical constructionist and reductionist, see J. Agassi, *The Gentle Art of Philosophical Polemics* (Open Court 1988), "The Secret of Carnap."

25. Cf. PDOBO, Ch. 12, "The *Theaetetus* and the Birth of Epistemology," for a reading that validates this interpretation.

26. See, e.g., M. Simon, *Understanding Human Action* (Albany: S.U.N.Y. Press 1982) in which it is claimed that because the discourse of the natural

sciences is inadequate to describe human action or nature, *therefore* (!) that of the social sciences must be even less adequate to the task.

27. Along with other changes in the climate of opinion.

28. Such as Newton's *Principia*, Dante's *Divina Commedia*, or Aristotle's *De Anima*.

29. "Controlling Assumptions in the Practice of American Historians," with G. Haines IV; pp. 17-52.

30. Author of *Observations on Hobbes' Leviathan* 1652, and *Patriarcha* 1680.

31. *Two Treatise on Government* 1688, Ed. with Introduction, P. Laslett (Cambridge U.P. 1967).

32. Cf. "Intellectual History as a Tool of Philosophy," in **HAH** pp.122-134, expands briefly on this topic, and gives a few examples of aid to philosophic analysis from intellectual history—aid without which there can only be misconceptions about the nature and structure of the work under scrutiny, as there are in the case, for example, of a work such as the Aristotelian *Metaphysics* that was edited into existence centuries after Aristotle's lifetime.

33. As they call themselves, in spite of the fact that the claim refutes the name. Ironically, the claim about the death of philosophy, if they are to retain the name, leaves self-named philosophers no alternative but to become philosophic historians of philosophy-when-it-was-alive.

34. Another place where Mead's comments on French philosophy seem to anticipate the case of Royce is his remark on Comte who "would put up the good of the community itself through an emotional expression which should be essentially religious in character. That is, men should actually worship the Supreme Being in the form of society. Society as . . . that which is responsible for the individual, should be worshipped; and on this basis Comte . . . set up a positivistic religion (**MTNC** 464f.). Royce's proposal in the same direction is, of course, not positivist but idealist.

35. As a student of Greek philosophy and the classic American approach to it, the present author has to note that when Cousin undertook to translate the *Laws*, a work of the platonic Academy, he was so unhistorical as to follow Ficino's Latin translation from a Greek manuscript, now lost, and the earlier French translator Grou who also followed Ficino. It appears that Cousin also relied on the work of assistants in this labor. Would these have known more Greek or more history than Cousin their supervisor? See, e.g., A. Boeckh, *In Minoem* (1806); F. Ast, *Platon's Leben und Schriften* (1816); E. Zeller, *Platonische Studien* (1839); G. Müller, *Studien zu den Platonischen Nomoi* (Munich: Beck, 1951); and Burges's preface to his translation in vol. 5 of the Bohn Library edition of *The Works of Plato*.

36. There is a brief discussion of Woodbridge's philosophic historiography in Chapter III of my *History as a Human Science*. The next few pages of the present chapter rehearse some of the material in the section on G.H. Mead. Chapter IV of *Semiotics From Peirce To Barthes* covers "The Theory of Meaning of G.H. Mead."

37. Cf. *J. of the History of Philosophy*, Vol.XI, No.1 (1973): Review of L. Ruggiu *Tempo, Coscienza e Essere nella Filosofia di Aristotele*; p.111-115.

38. The latter theme finds extensive development in John McDermott's *The Culture of Experience*, and *Streams of Experience* (N.Y.U Press 1976, and U. Mass Press 1986, respectively).

References & Bibliography

Aristotle *De Anima* Ed. & Tr. R.D. Hicks, Intro. & Notes (Cambridge U.P. 1907)

J.Barzun *Romanticism and the Modern Ego* (Boston: Little, Brown 1943)

J.Buchler Editor, *Introduction to Contemporary Civilization in the West A Source Book*, 2 vol. (Columbia U.P. 1946-1961)
"Reconstruction in the Liberal Arts," in *A History of Columbia College on Morningside* Edman, Trilling, Buchler et al. (Columbia U.P. 1954)
Man in Contemporary Society (Columbia U.P. 1962).
Toward A General Theory of Human Judgment 2 rev. ed. (N.Y. Dover 1979)

J.Clendenning, Editor *The Letters of Josiah Royce* (Chicago U.P. 1970)
The Life and Thought of Josiah Royce (U. of Wisconsin Press 1985)

H.T.Costello *Josiah Royce's Seminar, 1913-1914* Ed. by Grover Smith (Rutgers U.P. 1963)

Dante *Inferno, Purgatorio, Paradiso* Text & Tr. 3 vol. Ed. Oelsner, Carlyle, Okey, & Wicksteed (London: Dent repr. 1962)

J.Dewey "Search for the Great Community," Ch. V of *The Public and Its Problems* (N.Y. Holt 1927)
Art as Experience (N.Y. Minton, Balch 1934)

R.Filmer *Patriarcha*, Ed. P. Laslett (Oxford U.P. 1949)

W.James *Essays on Faith and Morals* (N.Y. Longmans 1943)

B.Kuklick   *Josiah Royce: An Intellectual Biography* (Hackett Publ. 1985)

J.McDermott *The Culture of Experience: Philosophical Essays in the American Grain* (New York University Press 1976)
Streams of Experience: Reflections on the History and Philosophy of American Culture (University of Massachusetts Press 1986)

G.H.Mead   "The Nature of the Past," *Essays in Honor of John Dewey* (N.Y. Holt 1929)
The Philosophy of the Present (La Salle: Open Court 1932)
Movements of Thought in the Nineteenth Century (Chicago U. P. 1936)
The Philosophy of the Act Ed. C.Morris (U. of Chicago 1938): "History & the Experimental Method," and "Experimentalism as a Philosophy of History."

M.Minnigerode *The Fabulous Forties 1840-1850* (N.Y. Garden City Publ. 1924)

I.Newton   *Principia Mathematica Philosophiae Naturalis* (London: Royal Society 1686; Florian-Motte Transl. ed. Cajori: U. Calif. Press 1962)

F.Nietzsche *Human All Too Human* Tr. Faber & Lehmann (U. of Nebraska 1984)
On the Advantage and Disadvantage of History for Life Tr. P. Preuss (Indianapolis: Hackett 1980)

L.Pitt   *The Decline of the Californios 1846-1890* (U. of Calif. 1970)

J.H.Randall Jr. *The Problem of Group Responsibility in Society: An Interpretation of the History of American Labor* (Dissertation: Columbia U. 1922)
The Making of the Modern Mind (Boston: Houghton 1940)
"Epilogue: The Nature of Naturalism," *Naturalism and the Human Spirit* Ed. Y.H. Krikorian (Coumbia U.P. 1944)
"Controlling Assumptions in the Practice of American Historians," in *Theory & Practice in Historical Study*," (Soc.Sci.Research Council 1946)
Nature and Historical Experience (Columbia U.P. 1958)
The Role of Knowledge in Western Religion (Boston: Starr King 1958)

J.H.Randall Jr.   *The School of Padua and the Emergence of Modern Science* (Padua: Antenore 1961)

How Philosophy Uses Its Past (Columbias U.P. 1963)

The Career of Philosophy I: Middle Ages to the Enlightenment (Columbia U.P. 1963)

The Career of Philosophy II: German Enlightenment to Darwin (Columbia U.P. 1965)

"Josiah Royce and American Idealism," *J.of Philos.* LXIII, No.3 (1966)

Hellenistic Ways of Deliverance and the Making of the Christian Synthesis (Columbia U.P. 1970)

Philosophy After Darwin. Chapters for *The Career of Philosophy III*, and Other Essays Ed. by B. Singer (Columbia U.P. 1977)

J.H.Randall Jr.   "The Department of Philosophy," in *A History of the Faculty*
& J. Buchler   *of Philosophy* Randall, Hadas, Torrey *et al.* (Columbia U.P. 1957)

Philosophy: An Introduction (N.Y. Barnes & Noble 1942)

J.Royce   *California: A Study of American Character* (N.Y. Houghton 1886)

The Spirit of Modern Philosophy (Boston: Houghton 1892)

The Problem of Christianity Vol.II: xi-xiii (N.Y. Macmillan 1913);

The Hope of the Great Community (N.Y. Macmillan 1916)

Basic Writings 2 vol. Ed. J. McDermott (Chicago U.P. 1969)

Letters Ed. by J. Clendenning (Chicago U.P. 1970)

H.Schneider   *Science and Social Progress: A Philosophical Introduction to Moral Science* (Lancaster: Arch. of Philos. No. 12, 1920)

Three Dimensions of Public Morality (Indiana U.P. 1956)

The Puritan Mind, 1930 (Ann Arbor 1958)

A History of American Philosophy 1946; 2 ed. (Columbia U.P. 1963)

Ways of Being: Elements of Analytic Ontology (Columbia U.P. 1962)

Sources of Contemporary Philosophical Realism in America (N.Y. Bobbs-Merrill 1964)

H.Schneider   "Philosophy Will Never be a Science," *Philosophy and the Civilizing Arts* Ed. by C. Walton & J. Anton (Athens: Ohio U.P. 1974)

A.Schopenhauer *Parerga und Paralipomena* in *Sämmtlich Werke in Fünf Bänden*
Ed. by H. Henning (Leipzig: Inselverlag 1910)

V. Tejera   *Art and Human Intelligence* (N.Y. Appleton-Century 1965)
Modes of Greek Thought (N.Y. Appleton-Century 1971)
Plato's Dialogues One By One (N.Y. Irvington 1984)
History as a Human Science: The Conception of History in Some Classic American Philosophers (Lanham U.P.A. 1984)
The City-State Foundations of Western Political Thought 1984, 2 rev. ed. (Lanham: U.P.A 1993)
Nietzsche and Greek Thought (Dordrecht: Nijhoff 1987)
Semiotics From Peirce to Barthes (Leiden: Brill 1987) and T. Lavine, Editors *History and Anti-History in Philosophy* (Dordrecht: Kluwer 1989)
"Santayana and the Western Tradition," *Papers of the Santayana Conference*, Avila, Spain 1992.
"Santayana's Whitman Revisited," *Bullet.of the Santayana Soc.* 10 (1992).
Literature, Criticism, and the Theory of Signs (Amsterdam: Benjamins 1995)

F.J.E.Woodbridge *The Purpose of History* (Columbia U.P. 1916)
The Realm of Mind (Columbia U.P. 1926)
Nature and Mind (Columbia U.P. 1937)
An Essay on Nature (Columbia U.P. 1940)

Abbreviations

ADH	=	On the Advantage & Disadvantage of History	Nietzsche
CP	=	The Career of Philosophy	Randall
EFM	=	Essays on Faith & Morals	James
EON	=	An Essay on Nature	Woodbridge
EN	=	Experience & Nature	Dewey
HATH	=	Human All Too Human	Nietzsche
HHS	=	History as a Human Science	Tejera
HPUP	=	How Philosophy Uses Its Past	Randall
LJR	=	Letters of Josiah Royce	Clendenning
MHW	=	My Host the World	Santayana

ML	=	The Main of Light	Buchler
MMM	=	The Making of the Modern Mind	Randall
MTNC	=	Movements of Thought in the Nineteenth Century	Mead
PA	=	Philosophy of the Act	"
PAI	=	Philosophy: An Introduction	Randall & Buchler
PC	=	The Problem of Christianity	Royce
PCA	=	Philosophy & the Civilizing Arts	Schneider
PL	=	Peirce A Life	Brent
PM	=	The Puritan Mind	Schneider
PP	=	The Philosophy of the Present	Mead
PSP	=	Peirce, Semeiotic, and Pragmatism	Fisch
SMP	=	The Spirit of Modern Philosophy	Royce
SW	=	Selected Writings	Mead
TGT	=	Toward a General Theory of Human Judgment	Buchler
TPHS	=	Theory & Practice in Historical Study	Randall
WB	=	Ways of Being	Schneider

Index

About the Author

V. Tejera (Ph.D. Columbia University) is Stony Brook University Professor of Humanities Emeritus. Other books by him are *Art and Human Intelligence* (1965); *Aristotle's Organon in Epitome: The Poetics, the Rhetoric, the Analytics* (1966–96); *Modes of Greek Thought* (1971); *Plato's Dialogues One by One* (1984); *History as a Human Science* (1984); *The City-State Foundations of Western Political Thought* (1984, 2 ed. 1993); *Semiotics from Peirce to Barthes* (1987); *Nietzsche and Greek Thought* (1988); *History and Anti-History in Philosophy* (with Thelma Lavine, 1989); *Literature, Criticism, and the Theory of Signs* (1995). He is the editor, with Richard Hart, of *Plato's Dialogues: The Dialogical Approach* (in press). His journal essays have been in the field of Greek philosophy, classic American thought, and literary theory.